D0777179

Fridays With Art

ii

Fridays With Art

INSIDERS' ACCOUNTS
OF THE EARLY DAYS OF
THE TV BIZ BY SOME OF THE
GUYS WHO MADE IT WORK

Edited by Dick Woollen

Parrot Communications International, Inc.
Burbank, CA

Parrot Communications International, Inc.
Publishers Since 1981

Parrot Communications International, Inc.
2917 N. Ontario Street
Burbank, CA 91504
Phone: (818) 567-4700
Fax: (818) 567-4600
Email: *info@parrotmedia.com*

ISBN 1-882438-01-9
Printed in the United States of America
Published simultaneously in Canada

10 9 8 7 6 5 4 3 2 1

Cover photo courtesy of vintage TV collector, Kevin Walsh.

First Edition, October, 2003

Dedication

Art Greenfield was a catalyst and a mentor to many of us. Art was all the things we love about this business...independent, helpful, intelligent, articulate, friendly, knowledgeable, and never a hard-boiled sales guy. When we toast Art at these Friday luncheons, we're glad to have been in the business with him. Even though Art Greenfield is no longer among us, these pages are lovingly dedicated to his memory. May *Fridays with Art* go on forever!

...The Authors

TABLE OF CONTENTS

(Continued on Page 2)

1

TABLE OF CONTENTS (Continued)

Edited by Dick Woollen *
*(Except for Lew Blumberg's chapter, which he preferred be unedited.)

FRIDAYS WITH ART
FOREWORD
by Dick Woollen

Art Greenfield and I started having lunch together every Friday about thirty years ago...at least every Friday when business did not call one of us away from our operating base in Los Angeles. I was a buyer of programming for a major group of TV stations and Art was a program distributor for a modest list of movies and programs. When he first offered me his product, I explained that my stations didn't need it. And that was the last time we discussed the matter.

Effective Fridays at 12:30, we were no longer buyer and seller. We were just friends. It became a time to relax at the end of the week and to swap gossip about our industry and the fascinating people who work in it. I suppose I shouldn't refer to it as "our" industry because I believe the entire American public has a possessive feeling about movies and about TV.

It's THEIR industry.

The fare served up on screens both big and small becomes the basis of debates, of fads, of adorations and of social attitudes, ranging from clothing to sexual practices.

Gradually over the years the cast of *The Friday Lunch* expanded. Sometimes there would be four of us and sometimes as many as ten. All were members of *The Biz*. Several of the men had spent their careers calling on TV stations for the purpose of getting them to buy the programs they were representing. Some of us had worked for TV stations as program buyers. A few were veterans of selling movies to theaters for first run exhibition.

Everybody had stories to tell. Horror stories about bad hotels

3

and scary airplane rides and blizzards and tornadoes. And joyous stories about discovering an excellent restaurant in an unlikely city, or latching onto a hit series which all of their customers wanted to buy. But the best stories of all were about people. About the buyers they called upon and about their competitors on the sales side. Mostly funny, sometimes sad, but always very human.

One day somebody said, "You know, some of these stories are really interesting. Do you suppose people other than us would enjoy them?"

Then somebody else said, "Why don't each of us write a chapter about our adventures and we'll put them all together in a book."

So we did. And here it is.

Even though Art Greenfield is no longer among us, these pages are dedicated to his memory.

*"Our business is like sex. Even when it's
lousy it's still pretty damn good!"*
...Art Greenfield

Ah Cain't Find Words to Say!
by Jim Stern

Honest reporting requires verbatim quotes, or at least as close as one can come to them in a public journal, so here's what the man said to me in his rich southern drawl:

"This guy (*a vulgarity for "defecates"*) cream puffs!"

The drawler was the General Sales Manager at one of Norfolk, Virginia's two TV stations to which I had been trying to sell a new show starring the talented but extravagantly flamboyant piano player, Liberace.

The way he lisped slightly as he cooed the lyrics of love songs did nothing to dispel the image of homosexuality, nor did his penchant for glittery jackets with lacy cuffs and candelabra poised prettily on his piano. Liberace's show first aired on a local Los Angeles station in 1952, and by 1954 had exploded onto TV stations in 217 cities. But it wasn't easy getting him there.

It took a lot of hard selling to convince any of my customers, either businessmen-advertisers or TV station managers in the south-eastern part of the nation that this odd entertainer who today in our era of political correctness would be referred to as a "gay" entertainer, but was then more bluntly referred to as a "fag," could attract viewers week after week. They said "No" to me in Norfolk and Richmond and Roanoke, and in Greenville and Charleston. But finally I struck pay dirt in Columbia, South Carolina.

After dozens of futile audition screenings I had discovered that the louder I turned up the sound volume the better the schmaltzy piano music sounded...and also, the more it attracted the avid attention of any women who were within earshot. So before screening for a major appliance dealer in Columbia I corralled as many secretaries as I could to join us in the company's conference room, turned the volume up full, and let it roll.

When the film ended, the appliance guy seemed uncertain and unhappy. I asked him what percentage of his customers were women. He said, "About 90%." I then asked one of the girls how she liked the show, and with a tone bordering on reverence, she said, "Ah cain't find words to say!"

So I made my first sale.

I then revisited Richmond and Roanoke and Charleston and Greenville and Charlotte, and sold those markets too. But my success didn't bring any gratitude from my boss, Reub Kaufman. He hired a new sales manager who hired another salesperson to supervise my territory. I was upset by these changes so I left the company, secure with the knowledge that I knew how to sell TV programs.

I'm sure it was my experience in the Army during World War II which imbued me with the need to prove myself under dire circumstances. I was an infantryman in the 78th Division when we were dispatched to Europe to help the bogged-down First Army fight it's way out of the Heurtgen Forest in the Ardennes. I was a private in *I Company*, the assault company, and my job was to be the Captain's runner. I didn't know there was such a job as runner, but I quickly learned it involved a high degree of hazardous action.

It almost seemed as if my real name got lost in the shuffle somewhere and was replaced with "Goddamit, soldier"...do this or...do that.

My job as runner found me living in snow and slush and with wet socks and leaky shoes. And although I survived the shells and bullets, I eventually came down with trench foot, an early stage of gangrene. So only a day before the start of the infamous *Battle of the Bulge* I was sent back to England and hospitalized. The doctors managed to save my feet but I suffered from the feeling that I had abandoned my buddies, so many of whom were killed during the action which followed.

From those early days forward I have been driven to fulfill and complete whatever task I have been faced with. And my next employer proved to be a worthy challenge to my resolve.

It was the giant TV production and distribution company called Ziv. Ziv introduced a new half hour syndicated TV series into the marketplace every three or four months. A remarkable feat of production. To sell these shows they had at least one salesman in every state and if he failed to sell a show he usually got fired. But only after he had worked his way through every prospect in his territory.

Armed with a 16mm film projector, cans of film, samples of promotional material and a bulky flipcard presentation, all comprising a physical load of over 40 pounds. Clearly, the job of the syndicated TV salesman required both strength and courage.

When I first applied for the job, filled with my 27 year old optimism, I asssured Ziv's Sales Manager Bud Rifkin, "I'll sell the hell out of your programs!" Rifkin's only response was "I should hope

7

so," then turned me over to Al Goustin, Sales Manager for the eastern division

Goustin's high-pitched voice wheezed out of the corner of his mouth as he spoke. "We've carved out a new territory for you, Jim. West Virginia!"

I think I managed something like, "Thanks a lot," as I mentally gulped and felt a brief sharp stab in my stomach.

"I know," he said. "They're down to earth people who spit on the floor. But look at it this way...we've never sold anything out there, so it's wide open for you."

First I was put through what I privately referred to as "basic training." For a full week I absorbed and memorized a preamble which described the history of the Ziv Company and its success. Then I had to memorize every detail of a 12 page flipcard presentation of that new show, *Mr. District Attorney*, starring David Brian. And then, in my new Chevy coupe, I headed off to Charleston, West Virginia and the *Daniel Boone Hotel*, where I was delighted to find they had indoor plumbing. This was where I was to meet Jack Gainey, Assistant Sales Manager and the man who would train me in the field.

Having been invalided out of World War II before I could demonstrate my bravery, I viewed my new career as my personal World War III. This was going to be a battle, and I would win it!

The meeting with Jack Gainey began promptly at 9 a.m. Monday. Jack was a nice looking, dapper gent from Charlotte, North Carolina. He wore a homberg hat and sort of cocked one eye as he spoke to you with great sincerity. He had been a radio announcer at one time and had a good speaking voice with a little whiskey rumble for character. The training was all business, although I did learn later on that day that the real lesson was how you can sell effectively without allowing work to interfere with your drinking and girl-chasing.

What looked like an insurmountable job at hand was how to sell

8

Mr. District Attorney in Charleston, West Virginia. Unlike other areas where account executives (for that's what we called ourselves) would arrive with their golf clubs and make a holiday out of their sales calls to the TV stations, the stations in this town (there were only two) wanted nothing to do with us or with our show.

This called for "Plan B."

"Plan B" was to take the phone book and check out the local businesses. There were department stores, jewelry stores, car dealers, dairies, bakeries, gas and oil companies, etc. We also scanned the newspaper ads and charted TV advertisers, knowing all were fair game. Then we got on the phone and made a few appointments with some of the obvious high rollers.

At our first appointment Jack pulled out all the stops and showed me how to give a full Ziv presentation. He parked the projector on the boss's desk after first removing any distracting material. He requested there be no phone calls, closed all doors, set up a screen and a 12 page flip chart, and after as much small talk as necessary to build a trusting rapport, began his pitch.

He started with an oration about the merits of the company. He named sponsors, especially all of the well known regional ones like breweries, etc. He extolled all the previous hit shows our company had produced and the name stars who appeared in them. Then, as he felt he had sufficiently impressed the merchants, he started introducing the new show. He set up the flip chart and recited its well-written contents with sincerity and drama. He finished up with a description of the massive promotional backup provided for the show.

It would be nice to be able to say we sold the show that day, but, as in many instances, it didn't happen that easily. We spent the whole day pitching the department store and the two TV stations, and then Jack proceeded to educate me as to how to relax after all those hours of intensive pitching.

When the hour of 5 p.m. arrived, Jack declared that he never talked about or thought about business until the start of the next day. This was really foreign to me because I usually ruminated or cerebrated constantly about deals lost or which were in the making.

But I soon realized that Jack had no such burden as I heard the familiar music of ice clinking in a glass, followed by the "glub, glub, glub" of Early Times bourbon being splashed onto the ice. Now I was no puritan, being one who enjoyed a bottle of beer with my dinner or maybe a couple of drinks if my bachelor self was lucky enough to snag a date or get invited to a party. But being a good student, I poured myself a water glass of ice and bourbon and discovered I had a rather substantial capacity for such stuff.

Then, allegedly to complete my education, Jack insisted I accompany him as he headed to the local department store again. He headed for the necktie department where an attractive young blonde whom he had never seen before waited on him. As she displayed the neckwear to Jack he gave her a wink. He then uttered a few words to her about the color of her eyes or something and within a few minutes it was obvious he had made his sale for the day. And the night!

Later, when I did try to emulate Jack's technique it did sometimes make my life more interesting, but my batting average with the babes never came close to my first official "trainer."

And while I'm sure the "necktie lassie" had nothing to do with it, the next day we closed a deal with the department store to buy *Mr. District Attorney* and Jack was on his way home. Before he left he let me know that he thought I would "knock 'em dead," and as a reward I was to head up to Parkersburg and sell '*Mr. D. A.*' on my own.

Have you ever been to a town so small that it only had one hooker...and she was retarded? Welcome to Parkersburg, West Virginia. The only hotel in town was called *The Blennerhasset*. The state was dry...no liquor allowed. But at least *The Blennerhasset's* desk clerk was decent enough to direct me to the town's only speakeasy, and after being inspected through the peephole in the door, I was finally allowed to enter.

I managed to find a seat next to a female who could not exactly be described as being pretty, but who became less ugly by the time I had my third drink, and who managed to match me drink for drink while I played the role of "big spender."

By the time we were served our seventh round I was surprised to see that she still seemed sober, so when she left to go to the ladies room I sipped a sample of what she was drinking and found it was plain ginger ale. Before I complained about paying bourbon prices for soda pop, I asked a couple of my new drinking buddies to also take a sip and they confirmed my suspicions.

I had fallen victim to one of the oldest scams in the bar business. The B-girl who cons drunks into buying her drinks, then splits the profits with the house. With all the indignant courage of a bourbon-soaked barfly I demanded to speak to the management. Well, the manager turned out to be the same hillbilly giant who functioned as the bouncer and doorman. Undismayed, even though I had to bend my head back to look into his bloated face, I proceeded to tell him what a lousy impression this incident made on me, a New York television executive, one who was visiting Parkersburg for the first time.

As I paused for breath a question arose. Was I about to get a punch in the mouth?

But for reasons I will never completely understand, this burly West Virginian grinned, shook my hand and said, "Y'all come back and see us, ya hear?" And believe it or not, the next time I did show up I was treated to free drinks!

Being accepted as a regular at the speakeasy was a lot easier than selling *Mr. District Attorney* in Parkersburg. I pitched my heart out to the town's only TV station but they turned me down flat. After a couple of dozen calls on various merchants I came upon one who at least had some experience at advertising on TV. He was a sponsor in the late night movie where he sold his house trailers. He also lived in one of his trailers, so while his wife watched and their infant gurgled in his high chair, I set up my projector and all my propaganda and went into my song and dance for the whole family. It turned out he was a fan of *Mr. District Attorney* and told me right after the screening that he would buy it...but he could only afford half sponsorship. Great!

But also, "Ouch!" I knew the TV station would never come up with the money for the other half.

I had decided I was doing my best thinking while huddled over the bar at the speakeasy so I headed back there. One of my new drinking buddies turned out to be in the storm window business and by 2 o'clock in the morning I had convinced him to buy one quarter sponsorship in the show. Then, by 3 o'clock the next afternoon I finally convinced the TV station to pick up the remaining one quarter of *Mr. District Attorney* and the siege of Parkersburg was finally over.

I had spent six weeks to achieve an order with a total value of $7,500!

And Ziv rewarded me by assigning me to cover Knoxville, Tennessee.

At this particular time, Ziv employed somewhat more than sixty salesmen, but no one in the company had ever previously been sent to Knoxville. That's how hot a prospect it was.

But ignorance is bliss and so I felt quite confident as I called upon the only TV station in town. I was given a very friendly greeting and four members of the management team sat through my verbal presentation of *Mr. District Attorney* and then it was time to turn down the lights and roll the film.

But while the film was running, the two salesmen, the Program

Director and the General Manager all, one by one left the room, saying they had to take a leak. So when the film was over and the lights came back on I was the only one in the room. When they came back in they apologized for their incontinence and then broke into raucous Tennessee-style laughter, slapping each other and me on the back while watching to see if I would be man enough to join in their hilarity. I figured it was sort of an initiation and they were testing me to see if this foreigner from New York could be accepted as a good ol' boy, and fortunately I seemed to have passed the test.

But did I make a sale here at the city's only TV station? Nope. They agreed the show was a good one but that they could get along without it. They agreed that if I could bring in the show fully sponsored, they'd work out a time period for it, but selling the show was up to me.

And so began the siege of Knoxville.

Having experienced first hand the "anything for a laugh" unpredictable country boy attitudes of the station's management team, I decided I had to worm my way into their confidence. I volunteered to become a member of their sales team and at no charge. I told them I would notify them of every client pitch I made. And while I was deliberately rather vague on some of the details of what I was offering them, it did create between us a cooperative atmosphere rather than an antagonistic one.

And it worked beautifully! I wound up selling *Mr. District Attorney* to a flour company, but only after hoisting myself up a rope to reach the boss's office at the top of a grain elevator. I sold *The Eddie Cantor Theatre* to a car dealer who had to leave in the middle of the screening in order to sell a car, thus never seeing most of the film. But the strangest circumstances surrounded the sale of *The Cisco Kid* to the owner of a supermarket chain.

The only time he could see me was during the actual live broad-

13

cast of a radio show which he hosted. His practice was to introduce a given act and then, during their performance, come backstage to negotiate deals. He wasn't totally sure about '*Cisco*' so he had his secretary call folks at random from the phone book and ask them if he should buy the show. Fortunately the good citizens of Knoxville liked the idea of '*Cisco*' and we made the deal after his show ended.

But then I hit a bump in the road. I had managed to sell half sponsorship of our newest series, *Science Fiction Theatre,* to the Johnson Electric Company but the sale was contingent upon my being able to sell the other half to a group of electrical contractors. This would require selling six separate Knoxville electricians a portion of the show. I did sign up five of them, but had been unable to nail down the necessary sixth. So Jack Gainey, my old trainer, came to town to help out.

To celebrate our reunion we indulged in a little debauchery that night but still managed to have clear heads the next morning as we faced our big day. It was an appointment to make our presentation to our sixth and final prospective sponsor.

We were invited to make our presentation in the company's garage. A table was set up for the projector and the screen was set up across the room. I tacked up a half dozen posters on the walls. The chief electrician was the father who was in his seventies. The other members of the audience were his three burly sons, also electricians.

Jack Gainey was in his glory.

With a full head of steam he not only gave the full Ziv presentation, flip board and all, but embellished it considerably. He promised that the stars of the show (Broderick Crawford, Dana Andrews, Rock Hudson or others whom Jack could think of from the top of his head) would come to Knoxville and give testimonials for Krueger Electric Company. He said that I would come every week and change the posters in front of their building and on their trucks; that we would create their commercials which would appear every single week before, during and after *Science Fiction Theatre*. In actuality, their sponsorship would have engendered about 13 seconds worth of airtime, plus having their company name listed along with the five other sponsors, but this was no time for reality.

When the screening ended there was tension in the garage as the jury of four left the garage and went to their office to deliberate the fate of the show. After about 25 minutes, heavy footsteps resounded, the door handle creaked, then flew open to admit Charlie who weighed about 285 pounds and stood six feet four. He smiled and bellowed, "Put the show on the road!"

The Krueger men agreed to meet us at the offices of the primary sponsor, the Johnson Company, for the signing of the contract. But as they were leaning over the desk, pen in hand, the phone rang. It was Pop Krueger, the old man. "I have a weak heart and I'm canceling the show!" he cried out frantically. Embarrassed but obedient, his sons left the office with the contract unsigned. Fortunately, the Johnson Company stepped into the breach and agreed to pick up the paltry (by today's standards) $16 a week which the defection represented.

Jack Gainey left town knowing he would get half of my commissions but at least he had the decency to leave me, as a parting gift, the phone number of the half-Jewish, half-Cherokee girl he had picked up at the Johnson Electric Company.

But the Ziv saga for me was winding down. After two years, considering the turnover in Ziv personnel, I was considered a veteran and an old-timer. But the commute between my New York home and Tennessee and West Virginia was wearying and the territory became a bore. It was time for me to move on.

Years later, when I was Sales Manager for Allied Artists Pictures, I encountered an old acquaintance, Ty McCloud, who had been Sales Manager at the Knoxville station when I was calling on them. Noticing my new title, he drawled in slow Tennessee, "It's good to see that one of our boys made good."

It was only then that I realized the degree to which I had been accepted.

I guess you could say I was indulging in a fair amount of hype when I stated to Herman Rush, President of Official Films, "I've got a *million dollars* worth of experience!" But he was even greener than I was, so he hired me anyway. The owners of 'Official' were some wealthy executives of RCA and they gave the job of running 'Official' to some of their nephews and they ran the company more or less by the seat of their pants. I think Herman was all of 22 years old at the time. Certainly a far cry from the highly structured Ziv operation.

So they hired me, but assigned me to a territory where they had never yet sold anything: the prosperous but hard-nosed area of southern Ohio which included Cincinnati, Dayton, Columbus and Zanesville. My job was to sell two off-network rerun series. One of them was *Trouble with Father,* a forgettable sitcom starring Stu Erwin (a.k.a *The Stu Erwin Show*) and the other was the better-known *My Little Margie*, which starred Gale Storm.

Foolishly, I made the nonstop drive all the way to Zanesville from my home on Long Island, which then required an urgent visit to a chiropractor as soon as I arrived so as to relieve the painful knots in my back acquired during the long hours in the car's bucket seats.

The doctor's treatment made me feel better, but I felt even better yet when the General Manager of the town's only TV station, Alan Land of WHIZ-TV, expressed interest in the two shows and started negotiating with me. We finally settled at a license fee of only $30 per episode, but as he took all 260 episodes, that meant we had a deal worth $7,800 out of Zanesville and my bosses in New York were delighted when they heard the news.

Flush with this success I headed off to Cincinnati, which even though it had three TV stations, was known as a very difficult market for film salesmen. I was not too optimistic about my chances at the third and final one, WKRC-TV. I knew it was owned by the Taft empire which had been a power in the state of Ohio for generations. The Taft family had been sending its men to Washington, D.C. for many years, including President William Howard Taft, his son, known as 'Mr. Republican,' Robert A. Taft, who became Senate Majority Leader just before his death in 1953, and then *his* son, Robert Taft, Jr., who was in the Senate from 1971 to 1977.

So you can imagine my surprise and trepidation when I was granted an appointment with WKRC's General Manager who was David Taft, son of Robert Jr. I figured he would be an aloof and imperious type, but instead he turned out to be a friendly, gregarious fellow who called his Sales Manager to join us in his office and then insisted we all join him in sipping some bourbon-on-the-rocks.

It was 10 o'clock in the morning!

But by the end of the second round of drinks I had sold them both *My Little Margie* and the *Trouble With Father* series. I then went back to my hotel to stretch out and sober up before lunch.

Fridays With Art

My name is Dick Woollen. I've worked both sides of the street.
I was a sales executive for such TV distribution companies as Desilu,
Columbia Pictures Television and MTM (Mary Tyler Moore's company).
But most of my years were spent as a program executive for TV stations.
I spent 11 years at KTTV, an independent station in Los Angeles, and later
14 years at Metromedia Television, which owned stations in seven major
markets. The bulk of "Working Both Sides of the Street" relates to incidents
recalled from my years at KTTV, which I joined in 1952.

Working Both Sides of the Street
by Dick Woollen

The female voice on the telephone said, "How would you like to have the former Vice President of the United States do Tom's show tonight?"

The caller was Ann Duggan, wife of television talk show host, Tom Duggan. The former Vice President she was referring to was Richard Nixon.

In the world of Los Angeles television in 1962, Duggan was a phenomenon. For a full hour, five nights a week, this articulate, outrageous, brilliant, opinionated Irishman kept a packed studio audience and several hundred thousand home viewers fascinated with his extemporaneous shenanigans.

But Tom Duggan was also an alcoholic. And on the evening Ann telephoned me at my home with her question, he had disappeared and a substitute host was needed.

19

My response to her question might well have changed the course of history. I say this because when she put Nixon on the phone, during our conversation I could tell he was drunk.

For weeks, as Program Director of KTTV in Los Angeles, I had been embroiled in a nasty election. It was the gubernatorial contest between Richard Nixon, who had served as President Eisenhower's Vice President for eight years, and his opponent, Pat Brown, who was running for reelection as Governor of California. One of the leaders of Brown's Democrat Party campaign was a feisty, abrasive woman named Rosalind Weiner Wyman, whose greatest claim to fame (and deservedly so) was her successful effort to clear the way for the Brooklyn Dodgers to move to Los Angeles when she was a member of the Los Angeles City Council.

During the gubernatorial campaign, Duggan never missed an opportunity to take verbal pokes at Brown and to praise Nixon during his hour-long nightly broadcast on KTTV. Naturally, the Democrats were incensed.

Rosalind Weiner Wyman arranged for members of the Democratic campaign staff to hold a stopwatch on Duggan each night and total up the time spent blasting Brown. Because of an FCC rule called *The Fairness Doctrine*, we were obliged to make available to the Democrats an amount of broadcast time equal to that used by Duggan for his tirades. Naturally we did so, giving the Democrats their time immediately following the Duggan show. And of course this only served to further annoy Duggan, and as a result he would sharpen his verbal knives even more.

The FCC's concern became so great that each morning I would receive a telex from them, some of them more than a yard in length, outlining the gist of Duggan's comments from the night before and underscoring our responsibility to allow the Democrats a forum to reply. Rosalind also somehow managed to obtain my home telephone

number and would frequently call me late at night to complain bitter-
ly about Duggan's antics.

Well, despite the efforts of Duggan and many others, Nixon lost
the election. You may remember, or have read about, his famous press
conference the next morning where he conceded defeat and then bit-
terly added, "This is my last press conference, so you (members of
the media) won't have Dick Nixon to kick around anymore."

But Nixon wasn't the only one who was bitter. Duggan took the
defeat personally. I envisioned him grabbing a large bottle of vodka
and heading off for one of his secret alcoholic benders. He left word
he wouldn't be doing his show that night and that I should arrange for
a substitute, so I recruited staff announcer Don Lamond to fill in for
him.

After the tensions of the previous weeks I was slumped
exhaustedly in my den about 8 p.m. when Ann Duggan, Tom's wife,
called me with her startling question: Would I like to have Nixon fill
in for Tom that night? Airtime was 11 p.m.

I mumbled something inconclusive and she said, "Well, Dick
Nixon is right here. I'll put him on."

I was dumbfounded. In his (at the time) darkest hour, Nixon
hadn't gone home to his loyal wife, Pat. He hadn't even stayed with
any of his closest confidants such as Bob Haldeman or Herb Klein.
Instead, he had somehow wended his way to Duggan's home where
he found Ann home alone.

When Nixon came on the phone it was obvious he was drunk.

I was scrambling for reasons to tell him why I didn't think it
would be a good idea for him to do a live one hour telecast "after such
an exhausting day," and one of his slurred responses was so memorable that it has become a staple of our family repartee ever since.

I could almost envision him drawing himself erect as he chided
my resistance by saying to me, "Well, I'm not eshackly wifout intel-

ligence, ya know!"

I finally told him I'd think about it and get back to him.

As soon as I hung up I called KTTV and spoke to the guard at the security gate, giving him firm orders that if Nixon showed up, not to admit him on the lot.

Then, knowing that my colleague, Rev Winckler, was a close friend of Nixon's Communications Director, Herb Klein, I called Rev with the urgent suggestion that he find Herb or somebody else close to Nixon and send them out to put a butterfly net over him. Rev reached Herb with the news, Herb tracked down Haldeman who then dashed over to Duggan's house and carted Nixon back to where he belonged.

I've often mused over the incident. Call it the "what if" syndrome.

What if I had let Nixon do Duggan's show that night?

What if a drunken Richard Nixon had babbled on for an hour on live TV?

Would he ever have later been elected President of the United States?

Or would the press reports have been so devastating that it would have finished him politically?

These are interesting things to ponder.

But now let's slide back to a few years earlier...to 1952 to be precise.

I was then working in Chicago as the Program Manager for the Central Division of the ABC Radio Network. For the prior six years I had been a staff writer-director-producer based in Hollywood. But after a year the "promotion" to Chicago, with its frigid winter, had inflicted severe strains on my family so I resigned...determined to return to Los Angeles. Fortunately, a former ABC.executive had just become General Manager of Channel 11, KTTV in Los Angeles, and when he heard I was available he hired me via a phone call.

KTTV occupied a red brick building at the corner of Sunset Boulevard and Van Ness Avenue, a structure which had originally been built as a motion picture studio by the long-forgotten Nasser Brothers. The lot was blessed with three huge sound stages plus two small studios so there was plenty of physical space to do production. And upon my arrival my new boss, Dick Moore, advised me my title would be "Director of Program Development" which, to me, carried the implication that I was expected to fill those stages with vibrant, exciting creations which would merit the loyalty of every viewer in L.A. But after a tour of the lot I was relieved to find that I wouldn't really have to fill those stages.

The studio was doing a healthy business by renting out most of the space to producers who were shooting films for this infant industry called television. One stage was completely occupied by the set for the *Lassie* series, another for the *Eddie Cantor* series, and a third by the producers of a memorable series starring movie actor Jon Hall, titled *Ramar of the Jungle*. 'Ramar' was memorable, not for its quality, but because of the ingenuity of its producers.

It supposedly related to the adventures of a white hunter in darkest Africa. The producers had cleverly found and purchased what seemed like miles and miles of black and white film footage of animals, all filmed in Africa. To augment this they rented about 10 shrubs and three small trees, put Jon Hall in a pith helmet, hired four local black actors and dressed them in loin cloths and handed each of them a spear.

Hall would be filmed peering anxiously through the bushes, the "natives" would mumble "Bwana, Bwana," and then the scene would cut to some of the stock footage showing a lion eating an antelope. In order to make the visual quality of the stock footage match better with the studio-shot footage, the producers put both segments through a sepia-tone process which then made the whole thing appear as a single piece when run through a projector. The show was a tremendous hit, especially with the kids.

On KTTV, 'Ramar' was sponsored by *Planter's Peanuts* and our on-air host, Bill Leyden, took evil delight in identifying the sponsor as "*Planter's Penis*." Nobody ever called to complain so I guess they thought he had a speech impediment.

As Director of Program Development my door was open to anyone and everyone who thought they had an idea worthy of TV.

By far the most bizarre candidate who called upon me was a small, elderly man who entered my office carrying a huge suitcase. He laid his case on a chair, opened it and removed a large round brass gong which he held aloft with his left hand. Then with his right hand he extracted from his case, one at a time, various items which he would use to strike the gong. The oddest object I can recall was a raw potato. He was so enthused about what he perceived as being the different types of sounds he could make by striking the gong with different items that I felt almost guilty when I gently told him we weren't interested. But he just quietly packed up his potato, his bar of soap, his light bulb and other tools of his art, and left.

By 1956 I had been promoted to Film Director and Assistant Program Director.

KTTV had no network to provide it with programming, so everything we aired we had to acquire ourselves, including the feature films which were such an important staple. Most of the movies then available for use on TV were relatively small productions gleaned from independent producers. The major movie studios were reluctant to release their product to TV because they feared a backlash from the nation's theatre owners who were loudly complaining that TV was threatening to kill their box-office.

And one of the most reluctant of the majors was MGM. For

24

years and years, MGM was the outstanding movie studio in the industry. And my shrewd boss, Dick Moore, was determined to be the first in line if MGM ever gave any hint that their golden vaults would be opened for TV. So when he got word from a friend of his, Bud Barry, who was in a high corporate position at MGM, that they were considering an offer from CBS, Moore hopped a plane to New York to meet with the financial executives who ran the studio from their Manhattan offices. Unable to get a conclusive answer from them, he hired a limousine and on a Sunday afternoon had himself delivered to the Long Island estate of Arthur Loew, then Chairman of MGM.

The story of his success was chronicled in banner headlines in the trade papers. On Tuesday, August 14, 1956, The *Hollywood Reporter* had screamed:

"CBS NEAR DEAL ON MGM FILMS. Long term lease is being negotiated for 750 titles by network owned stations." But the very next day, the banner headline told a different story:

"MGM-KTTV IN FILM & OWNERSHIP DEAL.

$5,000,000 for pix: 25% of stock bought by MGM."

Before leaving Los Angeles, Moore had obtained approval from the '*L.A. Times*' (which owned the station) to offer MGM a minority ownership in KTTV as a lure to sealing the deal, and his ploy had worked.

And when he called us at the station to gleefully announce what had happened he surprised me by saying, "And Dick, I want you to get on the next plane and come to New York. I need your help in working out the details of the contract."

I spent eleven days in New York and we met with the MGM lawyers for long hours on each of those days. MGM had never previously licensed movies to a TV station so they were nervous and cautious about the language in the contract.

Some of the sticking points were ludicrous. For example, in

renting films to theatres, MGM had always granted a theatre a certain geographical area of exclusivity so that no competing theatre could siphon off potential customers. And they were willing to grant us exclusivity for TV in Los Angeles, but wanted to withhold from us the right to air the films in San Bernardino. And they were stubborn about it. So I drew them a sketch of Mount Wilson, topping it off with a sketch of our transmitter at the peak. Then I explained that the only way to keep our TV signal out of San Bernardino would be to build a wall around the city...and a very high wall, indeed. MGM finally conceded the point.

One of the all time greatest hits in the history of Broadway theatre had just recently opened, and one night during my stay in New York, MGM managed to get me a ticket to see the musical masterpiece, *My Fair Lady*. I was so thrilled by the show that as I walked back to my hotel afterwards, I stopped in an all-night record store and bought two copies of the cast album.

And another thrill awaited us when Moore and I stepped off the plane when we returned to Los Angeles, signed contracts in hand. As we climbed down the steps after our nine hour flight on the DC-7, we saw a KTTV remote truck, cameras, lights, and announcer Bill Welsh with microphone in hand. Around him were about 40 employees from the station, many of them waving large placards proclaiming our triumph. We heard Welsh announce, "We interrupt our regular programming in order to bring you this special report," and then he proceeded to interview Moore and me while the group applauded and cheered. The other puzzled passengers must have thought they had debarked into a nest of lunatics. It was several minutes before we realized the "telecast" was just a hoax. We were not really on the air. It was just the staff's way of paying homage. The celebration carried over into a party room at the airport, stocked with lavish food and lots of booze. It was a memorable night indeed.

So suddenly KTTV owned telecast rights to 714 pre-1948 features and it was my job to select which of those we would air first. The best of the crop were reserved for 8 p.m. Fridays, where the broadcast was fully sponsored by Colgate. I had lobbied hard to launch *The Colgate Theatre* with the epic war film, *Thirty Seconds Over Tokyo,* and was gratified when the ratings showed that over half the TV sets in Los Angeles tuned in that night to watch. We got a 30 rating and a 54 share of the audience!

But we had many other time slots to fill with the Metro library, and I didn't want to schedule those time periods blindly. MGM hadn't yet made the 16mm prints used by TV stations, so in order to screen the product I had to go out to the MGM studio where they could run the 35mm theatrical prints for me. I decided that by looking at the first and last reels of a movie I could get a sense of how well a picture would play on TV. If the first 20 minutes of a film were slow or dull, I'd relegate it to one of our less critical time periods.

By giving the studio a list of my desired titles in advance, they'd pull the prints out of their vaults and have them stacked up for me when I arrived. Once there, I'd sit in my own private screening room in the *Thalberg Building* (which room was as large as some of today's multiplex auditoriums) while my own personal projectionist previewed for me as many as 10 to 12 different films each day. This went on for over a month, with me arriving at the *Thalberg Building* about 9 a.m. and staggering out about 6 p.m., eyes glazed and clutching a handful of notes scribbled in the dark.

In addition to big ratings and big profits, a couple of amusing incidents arose from the airing of those films.

The *Thalberg Building* was named in honor of a young genius who was the head of production for the studio until his untimely death in 1936. He was survived by his wife, Norma Shearer, an actress who had starred in 42 major films between 1923 and 1942, most of them for MGM.

One of those films was *Romeo and Juliet*, with the role of Romeo portrayed by that fine British actor, Leslie Howard.

But that film was released in 1936, so twenty years later, in 1956, I was a little surprised to get a call from one of MGM's lawyers. He was passing along a complaint he had received that morning from Norma Shearer. It seems she was watching KTTV when we aired a promotional slide calling attention to our upcoming telecast of that film. Her complaint stemmed from the fact that our promotion slide read *Leslie Howard and Norma Shearer in Romeo and Juliet*. She had apparently reminded the MGM lawyer in no uncertain terms that SHE and NOT Mr. Howard was to receive top billing!

I could sense the Metro lawyer's embarrassment and was sympathetic to his awkward position. The widow of the studio's legendary production boss was screaming at him, demanding her contractual rights, even though the movie in question was 20 years old and Norma Shearer herself had not appeared in a film for the previous 14 years!

In my mind's eye I had the image of a wrinkled old lady, alone and pouting in a Beverly Hills mansion, with nothing better to do than monitor her TV set and fiercely protect her once-famous name. If you've ever seen the film, *Sunset Boulevard*, you'll know what I envisioned.

So we changed the slide.

I guess it's understandable that the performers were watching TV a lot in those days because it was their first opportunity to look at some of their earlier work.

However, when *Daily Variety* published a complaint voiced by Barbara Stanwyck to the effect that KTTV was guilty of butchering her films by editing them, I fired off a letter of protest to Dave

Kaufman of that publication, which he dutifully printed as follows:

"Righteous indignation Dep't: KTTV's Dick Woollen reply-
ing to Barbara Stanwyck's beef here that the oldie pix on TV
are being slashed on Channel 11 (KTTV), 13 and 2. 'We are
very proud of the fact that we do not cut even one frame from
any MGM feature we play. We have too much respect for the
writers, directors, producers and editors who created those great
films for MGM to think we can improve these great movies by
further editing. I can understand how a star, seeing a picture
which he or she made some 15 years ago, might honestly
believe something had been cut out when it hadn't at all. The
star may recall working in a particular scene which was actually edited out by the producers before the picture was released
theatrically, but with the passage of years, TV gets the blame.
Clark Gable accused KTTV of cutting scenes out of
Boomtown, yet MGM later proved that we presented the picture exactly as it was released theatricaly. Miss Stanwyck is
such a fine performer I only wish she had made more movies
for MGM. Then she would be able to watch herself in a full,
uncut presentation of her talent ' "

And a few days later, *Daily Variety* followed up with this:

"The next voice you hear is producer Alex Gordon who says,
'Regarding the dispute between Barbara Stanwyck and KTTV's
Dick Woollen, I keep a complete record of all motion pictures
back to 1900, with their original running times. While Woollen
is right in saying Channel 11 does not cut its MGM pictures,
Miss Stanwyck is also correct in her findings, except she must
have mistaken Channel 11 with Channel 5. Channels 5 and 13
are the worst offenders with cut and mutilated features.' "

So much for vindication. I simply found it great fun to have my

29

name linked in the trade press with such luminaries as Clark Gable and Barbara Stanwyck.

My oldest son, Bruce, got linked with Clark Gable in another way. One of our staff announcers at the station was the brother of Gable's wife at the time of Gable's death. He brought in one of Gable's suits as a gift for me but I was too tall to wear it, and much too narrow in the shoulders. So we had it cut down a bit and Bruce wore it on his "heavy date," thus achieving a degree of bragging rights in his social circle. Strange thing: Gable's custom tailored suit had buttons in the fly. No zippers for him. I guess when you're that handsome you don't have to be in a hurry.

It was about this time that my wife Marilyn and I met and spent a social evening with Walt Disney.

The original Disneyland in Anaheim had been open for several years and was doing outstanding business during the daytime hours, but the park always closed its doors as the sun set. Finally someone in their management group realized they were missing a potentially huge crowd of ticket buyers by shutting down at sunset.

So when they decided to stay open at night they realized they needed a publicity boost to let everyone in Southern California know about the delights of the nighttime entertainment which would be available to them at *The Magic Kingdom*.

Because KTTV was the station airing *The Mickey Mouse Club*, the Disney people came to us first with their ideas and we quickly struck a deal to televise a series of one-hour live telecasts to originate from the park on Saturday nights, and to be titled *Date Night At Disneyland*. The deal called for the Disney people to have complete creative control of the elements of the show, and we would provide all the technical equipment and personnel, plus a TV director and the free airtime.

Tommy Walker was their designated producer and I had many

planning meetings with him, most of them at Disneyland. One day he gave me a fascinating tour of the behind the scenes areas of the park...places which the public never sees. The maintenance and repair shops and all the secret passages which connect one area of the park with another so that workers can scurry around doing their jobs without being seen by the customers.

His plans for the premier telecast were awesome. If you've ever been to Disneyland you know what a huge area it occupies, and Tommy's format called for locations to be scattered far and wide. It took a little gentle persuasion to convince him to scale down his concept. Our director, Buck Pennington, and I pointed out that we simply didn't have enough cameras or miles of cable to cover all that he envisioned. So compromises were arrived at and the first telecast of *Date Night At Disneyland* was a smashing success.

The show ran for 13 weeks during the summer and achieved its purpose of drawing crowds of people to enjoy the new experience of Disneyland after dark. And in celebration of that success, Marilyn and I were invited to a dinner at the *Disneyland Hotel*.

But it was the after-dinner portion of the evening which was the most memorable.

We were invited to join Mr. and Mrs. Walt Disney in their private apartment in Disneyland. I had no idea where such an apartment could be located but we soon found out.

As you enter Disneyland, immediately on your left is a building labeled *City Hall* and just past that is a replica of an old-fashioned fire station. Clinging to the far side of the fire station is a deliberately obscured stairway which led us up to a small but beautifully decorated two bedroom apartment with a fully equipped kitchen, all inconspicuously tucked away above the fire station.

"This is where I entertain V.I.P. visitors," Walt explained. "We've had U.S. presidents up here and various heads of state from all over the world." Then, with a conspiratorial grin, he added, "And this is the only place in the park where you can get a real drink. What'll it be? I've got scotch, bourbon, vodka, gin or beer."

While Walt was in the kitchen acting as bartender, we sat with Mrs. Disney, looking through the window which overlooked the little circular green park which sits just inside the main gate.

"Let me tell you a story about Walt," she said. "When the park first opened, he and I were sitting up here watching the people stream in. I noticed that many people were taking shortcuts across the park and I was concerned they would ruin the lawn. So I pointed this out to Walt and suggested that fences should be put up for protection. But he disagreed. 'No, dear,' he said. 'If people want to walk through there then we should put in sidewalks for them, not fences.'"

This simple little anecdote tells reams and reams about the reasons for Walt Disney's legendary success. He knew his audience; appreciated his audience. He knew *they* were *his* boss, and he always gave them what they wanted.

Years previous, my bosses at KTTV had given me the full authority to do the negotiating with program distributors for all of our film shows, be they half-hours, hours, feature films or cartoons. As a result I became acquainted with a fraternity of fascinating characters...the so-called "film peddlers." But, if that sounds like a derogatory label, I assure you it is not so intended.

David Wolper, the multi-award winning producer, called on me when he was a film peddler. Charles Wick, head of the U.S. Information Service during the eight years of the Ronald Reagan administration, was first known to me as a film peddler. As was Tom Moore, later President of the ABC Television Network. I truly enjoyed the verbal and mental skills of people like Danny Goodman, Bob Greenberg, Lou Friedland, Pierre Weiss, Dalton Danon, Cliff Ogden, Ed Hewitt, Alan Gleitsman, Charles McGregor, and others too numerous to mention.

Negotiating with these men can best be described as a combination of chess and poker. Bluffing was intrinsic, augmented by moves and countermoves from both sides of the desk. It was a combination of a duel and a ballet, spiced with a degree of espionage. Did the distributor know how important it was for me to successfully acquire what he was offering? And did I know whether the distributor really had one of my competitors ready to buy the show if I passed?

Acquiring programming is a lot different from buying a lawnmower at Sears.

At Sears, you look at the price tag and either agree to pay the stated price or not. No haggling, no application of charm or wit or personality. No pleading of economic hardship or expression of doubt about whether you really need the item. No verbalizing about the relative quality or potential durability of the product. Just pay the price and get the lawnmower...or don't, and leave.

But with film there is no price. The distributor always has an "asking price," but both sides recognize that this is an inflated figure which simply serves as a starting point for maneuvers which can continue for several hours or several weeks before a deal is struck.

Came the day when the *Los Angeles Times* made a deal to sell KTTV to a New York company called Metromedia, and shortly thereafter I decided to resign. The new structure would have meant some of my autonomy and authority would be transferred to a corporate office in New York, and I wanted no part of that, so I quit.

My friend, Dick Dinsmore, had recently resigned from Screen Gems to accept a position as President of a newly formed TV distribution division at Desilu, the company owned by Lucille Ball, Desi Arnaz having been bought out following their divorce. I remembered that several times over the years Dinsmore had expressed his admiration for me and stated that someday we should work together.

So late in August of 1963 he welcomed me to Desilu with enthusiasm.

Even though I had dabbled somewhat in selling programs during my KTTV days, I felt over my head when Dinsmore told me he wanted me to function as sales manager of Desilu's U.S. operations so he could concentrate on the foreign markets. *"Director of Sales* will be your title," he said. Being always the negotiator, I said that I was reluctant to lose my identity as a programmer. I said, "Instead of that, how about *Director of Sales and Programs*?"

"O.K.," he shrugged.

His response was typical of how casual he was. While he was one of the most effective salesmen I had ever encountered, it soon became obvious to me that he was not a good administrator. I think this is true of many people who are imaginative and highly verbal. They can weave a magic carpet of words which can seduce the most reluctant buyer, but the details of running an organization bore them to death. So, being a dullard and a drudge, I became the perfect compliment to Dinsmore. And he gave me the ball and let me run with it.

The first and finest show Desilu ever produced was *I Love Lucy*, but we didn't have the distribution rights. Lucy and Desi had sold all current and future rights of that series to CBS so they could get enough money to buy the old RKO Studios at Melrose and Gower in Hollywood. Renamed Desilu Studios, it was where my office was located, in one of those typically crummy old buildings built by all the studios in the late 1930's when the movie business was first booming. I had a small ground floor suite with windows that looked across to the studio barber shop where performers like Fred MacMurray, Bing Crosby, and occasionally Lucy herself could be seen passing by on their way to the commissary.

Our first major sales effort was focused on syndicating the off-network reruns of *The Untouchables*, an excellent show. However it was the first to be tarred with the label of "too violent" by the do-gooders, including a few vocal U.S. Senators, so it was a tough sell. Broadcasters were often afraid to buy it because of all the righteous articles in the press, especially the protests of Italian-Americans who resented the fact that most of the bad guys portrayed in the series had names which ended in a vowel. This, despite the fact that among the most prominent indicted criminals of the era being portrayed, history records their actual names as being Capone, Nitti, and Costello. Frequently protesters do not let facts stand in the way of their shouts. They prefer not to be burdened with the truth.

We also had a few feature films but most of them were foreign made so they weren't too exciting to the buyers.

Then through Dinsmore's friendship with a wacky genius named Jay Ward (creator of the seminal cartoon classic *Rocky and Bullwinkle*), we acquired a series of half hours composed of footage from old silent movies, hilariously hosted and narrated by Hans Conried. The series was titled *Fractured Flickers*, and because it was both fresh and funny we had good success with it. But then we inherited a batch of 39 one hour dramas starring Jack Palance based on the adventures of a circus troupe and titled *The Greatest Show On Earth*...which it certainly was not.

Believe me, it was not! But we managed to sell it.

My only contacts with Lucille Ball would occur when I would attend the weekly staff meeting of department heads whenever Dinsmore was traveling in foreign lands. I found Lucy to be very human, very smart and sometimes very funny. Our meeting group consisted of only about eight people, with Lucy usually the last to arrive. At my first meeting, when she entered I was shocked at her appearance. She was wearing a bandana over her hair and no make-up. I couldn't believe how old she looked, and marveled at the magic of what theatrical makeup did for her when she went before the cameras.

Clearly she knew she didn't look so hot either because her opening remark as she took her seat at the head of the table was, "All right fellas, so I look like hell. But I can act!" And with that topic laid out on the table and out of the way, she proceeded to chair the meeting.

It was during one of those meetings that I got called out of the room to take a phone call from Dinsmore. I had no idea where he was so I asked the natural question, "Where are you calling from?"

"I'm in Africa. In Zaire," he said.

"Zaire? I didn't know they had TV stations in Zaire!"

"They don't," he said. "But they might someday."

That was Dinsmore. He loved to travel, especially on the company's expense account, and he always managed to include his wife, Betty, on the trips because, as he explained, "The way business is conducted in foreign lands involves a lot of social entertaining, and wives are a big asset in that endeavor."

But in countries which did have television stations he did his usual effective job of getting our product sold, and as far as I knew, the company never complained about his expense accounts.

During one of the staff meetings, Herb Solo, head of production, was outlining the concept for a new series they were planning which would be called *Star Trek*. The discussion turned to the matter of casting the lead role and eventually I meekly piped up and said, "How about John Glenn?"

Lucy almost jumped out of her chair.

"Who said that?" she asked.

I raised my hand.

"That's a sensational idea! Herb, I want you to jump on a plane and go down to Houston and see if you can get him!"

36

For those too young to remember, John Glenn was the first of the nation's astronauts to orbit the earth in a space capsule and his name had been in the headlines every day for weeks. Houston was where he and the headquarters of NASA were located.

But Herb and the other production types around the table were wiser in knowing the demands of the role of Captain Kirk, and finally managed to calm Lucy down by pointing out that they really needed a genuine actor for the role, not an astronaut. So instead they cast some little-known Canadian actor named William Shatner in the part. I guess you'd have to say their judgment was correct, but at least I had the fun of getting Lucy's full attention. John Glenn's career didn't suffer either, becoming, as he later did, a U.S. Senator from Ohio.

A few weeks later Lucy hosted a reception and cocktail party for the Desilu Sales group at her Beverly Hills home and I was pleased when she seemed to remember my name. Well, my first name at least. But maybe she had me confused with Dick Dinsmore. I dunno.

In those days the broadcasting industry's annual convention was organized by the *National Association of Broadcasters* (NAB) and was held, three years out of four, at the *Conrad Hilton Hotel* in Chicago. On each fourth year it was staged in Washington, D.C. so as to cuddle up to government regulators.

While working at KTTV I had attended this affair annually in my role as a program buyer, and always thought of it as more of a chaotic mess than a convention. Even the massive *Conrad Hilton Hotel* could barely handle the horde of TV and radio station personnel from all corners of the nation. The sellers of technical equipment, such as transmitters and cameras, would take over the entire block long exhibition hall in the hotel's basement to hawk their newest designs to the Chief Engineers of stations ranging from big city TV powerhouses down to "mom and pop" FM operators.

37

But the TV program suppliers took a much more gaudy approach. Their exhibition suites scattered throughout the hotel made liberal use of food, booze and broads to lure potential customers into their space so they could screen their newest programs for "the visiting firemen."

In the years when I was a buyer of programs for KTTV I would walk through those halls and be regularly greeted loudly and enthusiastically, and yanked into room after room to listen to the various sales pitches. But now I was on the other side and things were different. Now I was one of the guys who had to stand in the Desilu doorway all day, trying to spot TV Station Managers and Program Directors and yank them into our hospitality suite.

And I didn't like the duty at all.

Standing all day made my feet hurt. And my back. And acting the role of jovial greeter all day was a bore. The dialogue at each encounter was always the same:

"Hi! Great to see ya! Lemme buy you a drink!"

"When did you get in town?"

"How long are you staying?"

"Seen any new shows you like?"

"Well, we've got one you're gonna love!"

And on, and on, and on...day after day. But my first Desilu convention was not at the *Conrad Hilton*. The year prior, the NAB had become so outraged at the antics of some of the program suppliers that they had banished the whole fraternity from the convention. One of the reasons was because many of the girls hired as "hostesses" by some of the companies were dressed in extremely scanty costumes and ordered to patrol the halls and lure prospects back to the suites by flashing bulging cleavage and undulating thighs. The many delegates' wives didn't appreciate this at all.

But it was the Bible salesman who got all the program sellers thrown out.

Some scum-bag produced a single half-hour show designed to convince the viewers to purchase some "new" edition of the *Holy Bible*. Word flashed through the convention that each broadcaster who agreed to air the show was being treated, in the bathroom of the exhibitor's suite, to a quick "sexual favor" by one of the exhibit's hostesses.

That did it.

The NAB decreed there be no more program exhibitors at the *Conrad Hilton*.

So my first Desilu convention, in 1964, found all of us distributors occupying newly established headquarters at the *Pick Congress Hotel*, a block away from the '*Hilton*.' And while the Bible salesman's lip service girls were absent, there were still plenty of lightly clad hostesses standing outside most of the exhibition suites. But at least they were limited to smiling and greeting. No more hanky-panky.

However, I can't describe the atmosphere as dignified.

Too many animals for that. Real animals.

The distributor of the *Lassie* show had that Collie dog in his suite. The distributor of *Animal World* had a boa constrictor.

But we were the worst. As distributors of the aforementioned circus show, *The Greatest Show On Earth*, we had a baby elephant on display in the lobby and a chimpanzee in our suite! Now, even a small elephant can commit a rather large indiscretion on the carpet, and the '*Pick Congress*' evicted the fat little beast for that reason during the very first afternoon, but the chimp stayed with us for the whole tour of duty.

Whatever dignity I thought I had acquired during my years as a broadcaster was being severely eroded while sharing the Desilu suite with a monkey. He was a horny little bastard too, with a tendency to grab at the crotches of males and females alike. We were thankful that his trainer arranged to dress him in diapers and trousers before his arrival each day.

The following year, 1965, the convention was in Washington, D.C. By then the program suppliers had organized themselves under the banner of *Television Program Executives* and we took over the *Sheraton Park Hotel*, hoping to lure broadcasters to make the five minute trek from their convention headquarters across the street. But nature conspired to dump a massive blizzard upon our nation's capital, and we spent most of the days and nights staring down the empty hallways, swapping lies with other lonely distributors, and playing gin rummy with each other.

"He's the only one I know who can walk into a
revolving door behind you and come out ahead of you."
...Art Greenfield (refering to Sandy Frank)

Legend of the Pink Shirt and Peter McGregor
by Norman Horowitz

So there I was on January 20th, 1952, the first day of my Air
Force basic training, standing in several feet of snow at about twenty
degrees below zero, the wind blowing about thirty miles an hour, convinced that I would freeze to death within the next hour and that my
life would be over at the age of nineteen. But I did make it through
the world's easiest non-military training and my major battle for survival did not involve guns and mortars, etc., but only the challenge of
not getting pneumonia or dying from some other respiratory infection.

While in the service, I studied radio maintenance for about a
year and ultimately taught in the same school (Scott Air Force Base,
Bellville, IL) for three years. At the same time, I played golf, went to
college, chased women, and drank...all while polishing my skills at
being irreverent and significantly insubordinate to officers, particu-

larly second lieutenants.

I especially enjoyed being on the base and "throwing" a snappy salute to a second lieutenant with my left hand. Or being on the base without my hat (big-time frowned upon) and "throwing" a salute with my right hand. I expect that this was the laying of a groundwork for my attitude and my career hostility to corporate management. I never did meet a finance executive who did not remind me of a second lieutenant.

I was discharged near the end of 1955 and studied electrical engineering at a school which no longer exists, called *The RCA Institute*. It was during that period that I "broke into show business" when I became a part-time, minimum wage shipping clerk and messenger (20 hours per week) at the editorial department of Screen Gems, the television subsidiary of Columbia Pictures.

When I graduated in 1960 from RCA, I obtained a full-time job in the international sales department of Screen Gems. It was then that I realized that engineering was not for me, and that the international sales of movies and television programming sounded significantly more interesting.

I worked for extremely difficult people who treated most of their staff, but particularly me, poorly. It was, however, an incredible learning experience. I traveled regularly to Toronto and also went to California where I stayed at the famous *Beverly Hills Hotel* (a scary experience for me) while I worked out some details with the production people at the *Dean Martin Show* which we were distributing. I got to travel extensively in South America where no one else wanted to go, so they sent me. I was thrilled to have the opportunity to go to Mexico, Puerto Rico, Argentina, Venezuela and Brazil. Unfortunately, no matter how well I did, my boss always wanted to know why I hadn't done better.

It was during these periods that I made a firm personal commitment that if I were ever in charge of an organization, I would not treat the people who worked with me the way I was treated by my bosses at Screen Gems. An exception was Larry Hilford, with whom I had developed a relationship that lasted until his death ten years ago. He was one of the brightest and nicest people I have ever known. Larry had left Screen Gems in the early sixties to join CBS Enterprises as Director of International Sales. When he was promoted to run another division of CBS, I was rescued by Ralph Baruch and Willard Block who invited me to replace Larry at CBS.

The transition from Screen Gems to CBS was like moving from *Motel 6* to the *Four Seasons*. CBS "reeked" of style, class, dignity and tradition, all things missing at Screen Gems. I was treated as a grown-up by every segment of CBS management and I was proud to be a CBS executive.

Unfortunately, that came to an end when the FCC forced CBS to spin-off or divest itself of its syndication activities and cable holdings into a new company...Viacom. I remain convinced that this action by the FCC was precipitated by the Nixon administration's desire to warn ABC, NBC, and particularly CBS, that criticism of the war in Vietnam was not to be tolerated. To demonstrate how smart I was, I concluded that Viacom could not be successful if disassociated from the flow of product from CBS and would soon run dry, so I returned to Screen Gems, this time to run the international sales division. (Today it sometimes seems that Viacom owns about half the media world, including, ironically, CBS!)

I began the most interesting part of my career at Columbia/Screen Gems, joined by crazies like myself: principally Herb Lazarus, Ken Page, Mark Kaner and Brian Pike. (Think *Monty Python* in the TV business!)

Our corporate management was in New York, led by President Alan Hirschfield, who was obviously interested in things like movies,

43

records and flirtations, but didn't seem to care very much about television. I was at a meeting with him once when he looked at me and said, "Norman, I'm not sure...do we do television in this company?" He was of course joking, but from his perspective (and one shared by most of the Board), television did not in fact matter. Movies mattered.

But Hirschfield, however, was enamored with the deal we made to distribute *Barney Miller*. He loved the notion that we had advanced its producer, Danny Arnold, only a couple hundred thousand dollars and were going to generate over one hundred million dollars. We would get to keep almost half of the money! He was so impressed with this that he said to me, "Many of the people in the corporate group will tell you that they want to help you (the second lieutenants) and if they begin to get in your way (which they tried to do), call me and I'll get them out of the way."

People in the industry who knew Herb, Ken, and I, knew of our friendship, compatibility and respect for one another. Most knew that we were crazy as well, and would do crazy things.

In the early seventies the three of us made a trip which took us, among other places, to London, Paris, Munich, Frankfurt, Rome, and Milan. One of the problems which everyone had while taking a trip like this was laundry, in that we did not stay in any city long enough to have laundry done. We finally arranged to have it done one morning in Frankfurt.

When Herb's shirts came back from the laundry he took them out of the box and hurriedly put them all in his suitcase. Late that night we went to our next destination. When we arrived, Herb unpacked his bag and found that the laundry had sent him an additional shirt that did not belong to him. It was both ugly and a shocking pink.

The next morning Ken Page came into our suite and was greeted by Herb in the living room where Herb said, "I have something for you, but there's a condition attached. If you accept what I'm giving you, you may not give it back to me." Ken accepted this condition and Herb proceeded to give him the pink shirt. Ken, whom we all loved, but had the worst taste in clothing of any person in western civilization, *loved* the shirt, but was chagrined to find that the shirt did not nearly fit his very large frame. They refolded the shirt, returned it to its wrappings, and a few minutes later I arrived and was offered the same deal by Ken that Herb had offered him. When given the shirt, I was appalled at how ugly it was and did not want it, but I could not give it back.

What followed for the next five or six years was the "Legend of the Pink Shirt" which involved members of our staff, as well as our customers. The shirt would be delivered to people all over the world, in hotels, restaurants, bars, and even brothels. You never knew where it was going to show up next, and people would even change hotel reservations to avoid the shirt. No one knows, to this day, what became of it, but we were all convinced that if our management knew what we were up to, they would have been very upset. We enjoyed the thought.

In the late seventies Columbia suspended David Begelman from his position as Head of Motion Pictures and Television because he committed a felony. It was proven that he had forged a company check for his personal account and had stolen other moneys from the company as well. Then the company fired, not suspended, but fired Alan Hirschfield who had been foolish enough to believe that check forgery and larceny were not minor transgressions and thus had resisted the reinstatement of Begelman.

Hirschfield's position was replaced by an "army of second lieutenants." They made everyone crazy with foolish rules and regulations to make sure no one "saluted with their left hand."

Ken Page and I decided to have a sales meeting in Cannes, to be attended by all of the salesmen in our organization and their wives. This meeting was planned, in part, to annoy our management. It required special handling to obtain a budget variance from the "second lieutenants" in order to have this meeting. Because we were careful to play by all the rules, the budget variance that we needed was, in fact, approved.

Ken and I, along with a variety of co-conspirators, decided to have our opening night dinner for our sales meeting in Cannes at a restaurant called *The Pizza Milanese*. We notified one of our senior executives in London, George Blaug, of the decision. We asked him to make the necessary arrangements. This should have been easy for George, the only problem being that the restaurant did not exist!

Part of our roles in life was to, from time to time, attempt to make George crazy, as we were doing in this case. To that end, we had made cocktail napkins, matches, and cocktail stirrers all with the name '*Pizza Milanese*' and had compounded George's misery by making sure he saw this stuff. We even placed an ad in a European trade magazine stating that the nonexistent owner of this nonexistent restaurant welcomed all his friends and clients who were coming to Cannes! There was, of course, no address and no telephone number in the ad. It was difficult for George to admit that he could not make the reservation that we needed because he couldn't determine the location of the restaurant. We ultimately told him the truth, which possibly saved his sanity.

I left Columbia a couple of months before the sales meeting, after a major fight with senior corporate management. I had been in New York trying to sell a show when I received word that the Chairman, the President, and the Chief Operating Officer of Columbia required my presence. I walked into the meeting and faced three very pissed-off executives. I was told that the company wanted me to renew my employment agreement and they wanted to have it

46

done in the next few days even though I still had nine months remaining on my contract. Not knowing exactly what to say, I looked at the three of them, each with their arms folded, until the President said to me, "Norman, what is it that you want?" I thought furiously for what seemed like an eternity until I said, "I want someone to say please." Of course, that made them nuts.

It's probably not fair to say that all "second lieutenants" are primarily interested in "snappy salutes," but my guys and I were making a gazillion dollars for the company and, unfortunately, that was not enough for these "second lieutenants." What they really wanted was total compliance and conformity. I realized early in my career as a manager that successful executives, at least to a certain extent, were most effective when allowed the freedom to be creative, to be aggressive, and I realized that blind adherence and conformity "SUCKS" and does not get the job done as it needs to be done.

Years later, Ken was running the distribution company for Lorimar, Herb was running the distribution company for Metromedia, and I was running Polygram Television with two of my Columbia associates, Mark Kaner and Brian Pike. Because we trusted one another and felt it would be good for our business, we formed a joint-venture distribution company called Amicus. We opened offices in Australia, Canada and South America.

We were attending the MIP Television market in Cannes and decided that Amicus needed a sales manager, but unfortunately we had no budget for the position. So we decided to create a fictional sales manager. We announced that we had hired Peter McGregor, recently of NBC Spot Sales and previously an advertising executive at Coca-Cola. He was married to the former Rachel Schwartz, he had two children, and his family lived in Darien, CT. We sent this release to the trades and it was picked up by all of them. Countless people came to me to tell me how pleased they were that we had hired Peter and told me that they knew him very well from NBC or Coca-Cola and that he was a "great guy." I was questioned by the "second lieutenants" at Polygram who had scoured our operating budget and could not find any approval to hire McGregor. I somehow satisfied them without coming clean that McGregor did not exist.

A year later, we were all back in Cannes and we decided that we could no longer afford the luxury of a sales manager and that McGregor had to go. It would be too simple to fire him, and too embarrassing to have him resign, so we decided the only honorable thing to do was to have him killed. It was too ordinary to have him die in a car accident or of a heart attack, so instead, we issued a press release that said McGregor was an unannounced passenger of a recent space shuttle launch and while he was fine-tuning the Amicus satellite, designed to deliver entertainment programming to space travelers, the satellite was accidentally launched from the cargo bay, along with McGregor, and it was impossible to retrieve him. It also said how NASA had announced a few days later that all life support signals had stopped and that McGregor had indeed died in space. Among other things, the release stated that because of the very generous Amicus insurance policy, McGregor's widow (the former Rachel Schwartz) had enough money to buy a large condominium in Ft. Lauderdale, FL, with enough left over to buy a large telescope so that the McGregor children could see their father for eight minutes every morning, orbiting over the Eastern horizon.

The trades picked up the release and once again, people came up to me to express their condolences concerning the death of our beloved Amicus Sales Manager, Peter McGregor. I also recall that the MIP organization requested a minute of silence in honor of McGregor the following afternoon at the Cannes 'Palais.'

It's not only fair to attribute most of the craziness in this to Ken Page because he's not alive and therefore cannot defend himself, but

I expect we could all take credit...Herb, Ken, Brian, Mark and I, for acting like fifteen year olds and participating in a scam of this magnitude. No "second lieutenant" that I've ever known could ever understand the boyishness and the joyousness that is had by grown-ups doing this kind of stuff.

Ken died a couple of years ago, Herb is at Carsey-Werner, Mark is at 20th Century Fox, Brian at CAA, and I am a consultant still saluting "second lieutenants" with my left hand.

We certainly did a significant amount of business, but at the same time we were dedicated to having fun whenever possible and to making the process enjoyable for our clients as well. Little did I realize while freezing my ass off in January of 1952, that I would end up at NATPE (*National Association of Television Program Executives*) in Las Vegas fifty years later, having had a fun career in television. Those of us who have been in television during "the joyous years" can look back on the pleasures of our chosen profession...the travel to other cities and countries; dealing with other cultures; hanging out with interesting and intelligent people. And all of this certainly does beat working in a steel mill or doing what the vast majority of people do throughout the world in order to earn a living.

While I've never been big on expressing gratitude, I expect it would be appropriate for me to work on that.

49

Fridays With Art

*"When a potential employer in our business says
you're overqualified, it means you're too damn old."*
...Art Greenfield

Playing The Numbers
by Ave Butensky

The world of advertising via television has been at the cross-roads of American commerce for over fifty years. And it seemed to come upon us with a rush. First there was Guglielmo Marconi, sitting on the big porch of the *Grand Hotel Miramare* in Santa Margherita, Italy, telling the world about his new cathode-ray tube. Then quickly came radio. Then, just after the end of World War II, Milton Berle popularized the infant medium called television, primarily because Texaco decided it was good business to advertise in this new medium. So Texaco wrote a check and made it happen. And after that, sponsors and good programs went side by side to bring to the American home both advertising and entertainment.

In 1997, after only about fifty years of television, it came to be that advertisers spent more money in television than any other media, dethroning newspapers which had been king of the hill since the start of the Republic.

I was fortunate enough to be a witness and an active participant in the intertwined meanderings of this young industry's wonderland.

I have always been fascinated with entertainment. As a kid I put on small plays that played to an audience of not more than two or three. But growing up in Brooklyn, New York, I inevitably turned my focus to the Dodgers, Ebbets Field, and occasional games of punch ball on 84th Street.

But when I entered college at the University of Wisconsin in Madison, I had no idea of what I wanted to do with my life. I remembered that my Physics course in high school had seemed to be a snap, so I nominated that as being what I would major in. Thus in my sophomore year on day one, course one, lecture one, I was in an Atomic Physics class -- an introduction. After fifteen minutes of lecture, I slowly got up and left. I couldn't begin to fathom what the professor was talking about. Right then and there I went to change my major.

So I moved over to the Primate Testing Lab, run by Professor Bryce Harlow. This was the Psychology Lab where we tested monkeys. The easy part was hiding peanuts or other goodies under a series of colored blocks, and getting the monkeys to recognize those colors and sequences. The monkeys were smart. We weren't. I was one of the guys who had to clean up after them. One day one of the primates got loose and scampered out the door, up into the trees. It must have been a silly sight when a gang of us, students and staff, moved cautiously down the street, trying to lure the monkey back into his cage. A row of carefully placed peanuts finally did the trick.

Having had enough of that kind of monkey business, I tried my hand selling advertisements for the student newspaper, *The Daily Cardinal*. The '*Cardinal*' wanted someone to create ads and sell them to local merchants. I figured any fool could do that, and the proffered 15% commission would help me pay for my room and board and incidentals. Well, it wasn't easy, but after awhile I got the hang of it. By the time my senior year rolled around I had built a formidable list of "clients." These included various local merchants, the campus student bookstore, and -- always the best of local advertisers -- the several local movie houses, for which the student body constituted an important segment of business.

Fortunately, none of them seemed aware that I was also the movie critic for the newspaper. But this was 1955 and nobody seemed to notice that while I was selling them ads during the day, by night I was writing critical reviews and sometimes biting the hands that fed me. Try that today!

As we got closer to graduation, members of the newspaper's staff received a letter from an advertising placement bureau in New York, inviting "All those seeking a career in advertising" to call them. I figured this was a good connection and so I followed through -- but not until after I had bummed away the summer. Then when I went to visit them in September I was offered one of two jobs, both mailroom entry jobs at ad agencies. One was at Dancer-Fitzgerald-Sample and the other at BBDO. Since the DFS job was immediate, I opted for it and was told my starting salary would be $35 per week.

I started in the mailroom on Wednesday, September 7, 1955. From my weekly starting salary they deducted the usual taxes, plus Blue Cross, Blue Shield, Major Medical, and all the other deductions that are customary. Got my first check and went to the teller at Chase Manhattan Bank at 347 Madison Avenue. The teller looked at my check -- then looked at me -- then looked at the check again and said, "How do you want it -- heads or tails?"

And that was the start.

Years later, when I had achieved executive status at DFS, one of the agency's major clients was General Mills. With one of their primary products being a strong line of cereals, they targeted many of their ad dollars at children. To assist in this effort they had, over the years, acquired a library of cartoon programs, and our job was to place those programs on the best local television stations catering to children in each market.

It worked like this: the stations which took the shows didn't pay money for them. Instead they gave General Mills two minutes of free advertising time for each half hour they agreed to take. This process is called barter. However, the big benefit to the TV station was that General Mills would also agree to spend a significant amount of spot television advertising dollars with the station which took their programs. In essence, this was truly a win-win situation for both the advertiser and the television station.

This also brought many adventures. In 1975, it fell to me to place these cartoon shows in the Los Angeles market. At that time, four of the seven major (VHF) television stations were carrying children's programming and so each of the four was a viable candidate. The key to the puzzle was to determine which station had the best ability to reach children with their own programs, and thus deliver the largest share of the children's audience.

Television ratings are the industry tools that tell would-be buyers what percent of television homes are watching a particular program. But to the researcher and the time buyer, the more significant number in determining how well a program will do is to ascertain that program's share of audience. This pits one program versus the others in that time period. As an example, if we know how many total homes are watching TV at any particular hour (households using television, or HUT), by determining the share of audience for each program, we'd know what the rating would be. The formula is simple...rating = share x HUT. You just place a percentage against each of the programs running in any given time period, and be sure that it adds up to 100%.

On this particular excursion to Los Angeles, each of the four candidate TV stations gave me their own "share estimates" for the programs they were planning to run in the upcoming new television season. Optimism ran high. Extraordinarily high. If we took all the share estimates and added them up, we knew the numbers would come to over 100%. We had seen that in the past. But this year the stations were overtly optimistic. In fact, they outdid themselves. Not only were their total share estimates over 100%, they were over 200%!

Now the ball was in my court. It fell to me to analyze the material and determine what the true numbers might be, and I knew I needed help. Fortunately, DFS had an expert Research Director, Dick Weinstein, in our New York office, so I telephoned him and gave him all the information I had, along with each of the station's reasoning for their opinion. I was confident he could crank out the numbers I needed, especially as he had not been exposed to the influence and hype that usually surrounds these things.

Dick said he'd have his results "tomorrow" and asked where he could send the revised numbers. Since this was late Friday, I decided to go to Las Vegas for the weekend. I asked Dick to send his findings to me at *Caesar's Palace*.

It was early Saturday evening and I was just about ready to go down to dinner when there was a knock on my door. When I opened it, there stood a '*Caesar's*' hotel security man holding in his hand a long piece of printed paper which I could see was a teletype. (In the 70's these were called TWXs -- still several years before faxes.)

He said, "Mr. Butensky, I have this teletype for you."

I said, "Yes, I've been expecting it."

The '*Caesar's*' man said, "There's a lot of numbers on this teletype. I need to ask you -- are you planning to put any money on these numbers?"

Wow, I thought. What does the hotel think is going on here? I paused and then replied, "Not in the way you think."

We shared a good laugh after I explained the nuances of television program buying and was happy to convince my new friend that we were not involved in some weird betting scheme in Las Vegas. But then again, maybe we were.

Television marketing has always been an intense people-to-people business. No matter what a given person's job, they always had to sell something to another person, be it an idea, the purchase of advertising time, the clearance of television shows on America's TV stations -- it was always an arm wrestle between combatants.

But television has always had a unique aspect. It deals with a perishable commodity -- *time*. If 10:00 p.m. comes around tonight and your show is not ready to air, or a commercial doesn't arrive at the station on time -- guess what -- the time goes blithely on without you. If you were involved in selling shoes or cosmetics and didn't get it done today -- well, your commodity is still available and there's always tomorrow. In television there is no tomorrow.

Because of this perishable aspect of television, the quest for advertising time is always highly negotiable. The price charged for a particular segment of time is always a function of supply and demand. If everyone wants something, the price goes up. If nobody wants it, the price goes down. So if a TV station sales manager got close to airtime with unsold time available, the asking price would fall -- sometimes very quickly.

In the "good old days," when *All In The Family* reigned as America's number one program, advertisers stood in line to pay top dollars to place their spots in that program. Then some clever person created the idea of '*orbiting*.' Instead of selling that spot to the same advertiser every week, the design was created so that an advertiser got that premium spot only once every four weeks. In this manner, four different advertisers got to air in the number one television show, while settling for less desirable positions for their spots during the other three weeks. All of which meant more revenue for the TV station.

The techniques of pricing advertising time has so many differentials. For example, on any given late news show on any station, with all the commercials you would see in such a telecast, it is almost certain that none of the advertisers paid the same price as the other. The fellow who paid the highest price may have paid almost double that paid by the fellow paying the lowest.

But even the universal law of supply and demand isn't always the controlling factor in placing TV advertising. I'm reminded of a scene from several years ago.

The five men who were sitting in the anteroom off the main conference room had, between them, consumed a pack and a half of cigarettes over the last few hours, and now they were contemplating a multimillion dollar recommendation from their two advertising agencies. The company's Chairman, the popular southern gentleman, Bowman Grey, was giving his perspective on what he and the others had been listening to: two presentations, one from the William Esty Company and the second from Dancer-Fitzgerald-Sample. These were the two agencies which had been given the task of telling Bowman Grey's company, the RJ Reynolds Tobacco Company, how they should spend their nearly 80 million dollar national TV advertising budget for the upcoming new season.

At the time I was a senior media executive at Dancer-Fitzgerald-Sample (DFS) and our agency had just recently been assigned to handle the *Camel* cigarette brand for Reynolds. This was a big "win" for us because up until then all of Reynold's advertising business was handled by the Esty agency. It was only when Reynolds branched out with new brands (*Winston* and *Salem*) that they decided to employ us as a second ad agency in order to widen the spectrum of creative ideas. And although the use of two agencies was relatively common in corporate practice, it was a new phenomenon to Reynolds.

As we approached the time of the year when it was necessary to purchase network time, an activity now referred to as "the upfront," Reynolds had to decide which agency was going to do this. The plan was for a single agency to place the entire budget for all brands, thus ensuring that the agency would have more "clout" in negotiating rates with the networks. And, not so incidentally, earn the bulk of the commissions attendant thereto. Needless to say, each group was aggressively urging the client to select them for this task.

But Reynolds decided to test each of us. They wanted each agency to select a list of programs where their spots would appear and to negotiate with the networks broadcasting those programs regarding the cost of the spots to be placed within those shows. Then, after we had done the necessary groundwork to assemble the data, we would come down to their home offices in Winston-Salem, North Carolina, and present them with our proposals.

This challenge was calculated to stir our juices, and it certainly did. Our point person in network negotiating was a little guy out of Oklahoma, Mel Connor. If Mel was anything, he was extremely thorough. He knew every nuance of every TV program, he had an uncanny knowledge of which programs would reach a specific demographic and, most importantly, he had the great ability of negotiating with the networks to extract every ounce of media value from what he bought. Even as late as the morning of the day of our pitch to the client, Mel was on the phone with CBS, doing some last minute adjusting and fine tuning. I knew we couldn't lose.

And then came pitch time, with both agencies sitting in the conference room and able to hear the other side's presentations. A very rare situation.

DFS went first. We showed all the programs, the costs, the costs-per-thousand viewers for each show, and all the other major numbers. We closed with the secure statement that the DFS package was clearly the one to buy.

The Esty people followed. We knew they were the old-line favorites, having serviced Reynolds on an exclusive basis for so many years. But in listening to their pitch, I was convinced that we had all the horses. Our selection of programs seemed to make more sense. We had a more targeted audience, somewhat better numbers, *and* we had a cost advantage. We were confident.

When the presentations were over, the Reynolds executives left the room to huddle, then returned about thirty minutes later and stated that Board Chairman Bowman Grey would announce the verdict. Tension filled the air in the quiet, attentive moments that followed.

Bowman Grey started slowly. He complimented all of us for our thoroughness and for doing such a great job. But then, in his soft southern accent, he said that since the Esty package included *Petticoat Junction* in the mix of programs and ours did not, and since '*Petticoat*' was his wife's favorite program, Reynolds would opt to buy the Esty-recommended package. And that was that!

Costs, ratings, demographics, all took second position to spousal loyalty. And with that went the nearly $80 million budget.

Shortly thereafter, cigarette advertising was banned from television.

It was probably about ten years later when I was working for a media buying company, Ed Libov & Associates, that our major client was the store chain, *Toys 'R Us*. It fell to me to make the annual presentation to their top executives as to where we proposed they spend their budget.

It was during the 1983 presentation when their Board

59

Chairman, Charles Lazarus, complained to me. He said, "Ave, we give you guys nearly $18 million for television and I never see my commercials."

I said, "Charles, the target market for these campaigns is to reach children and to reach mothers with children. You are neither."

I then went on to ask him what he watched and how often. So then, having determined his viewing habits and to keep the Chairman happy, we placed a spot each week in *Eyewitness News*. Just so he could see his commercials. (Sounds a bit like our friends at RJ Reynolds, doesn't it?)

Long ago, both broadcasters and advertisers devised a way to cope with a *preemption*...a situation when a paid commercial doesn't air when and where it was scheduled. Sometimes this occurs when the station cuts away to a breaking news story and all the ensuing programs get *preempted*. Sometimes there is a simple technical error, a glitch if you will. And sometimes, when a time buyer purchases a spot at what is called a *preemptible* rate, well, that means an advertiser willing to pay the higher *non-preemptible* rate gets the spot...knocking out the buyer with the lower cost. Time buyers know that when they buy a spot at the preemptible rate they are gambling...betting that no one will come along and bump them. But sometimes in a tight market an advertiser who feels strongly about the need for a certain spot will pay the higher rate.

When the spots are preempted, the station almost always offers the advertiser a *make-good*. To entice the buyer to accept that make-good the station must give comparable value to the spot that was preempted, often even greater value. When this happens the buyer wins because they get greater audience value for their spot and the television station gets to keep the money.

And then there are the *planned preemptions*. A most classic case happened with a buy I was making for Toyota in the New York market. The head of NBC Spot Sales, Bud Hirsch, came to my office and said, "Ave, how would you like to buy the overtime break in the *Super Bowl?*" He added that such a spot would no doubt be the highest rated part of the game, and probably the highest rated spot for the entire year. It sounded like an offer that couldn't be refused.

Now, as every football fan knows, there has never been an overtime in *Super Bowl* history. Bud explained the cost would be $25,000 for one thirty second spot, and that only one such spot would be aired. Bud also went on to explain that in the event there was no overtime break, WNBC-TV would still keep the $25,000 but would offer a package of make-goods to run over the next few weeks as part of a bushel basket of other spots. But he showed that the overall value of those make-good spots would exceed the value of the one overtime spot in the *Super Bowl.*

I heard enough. We agreed. That night while going home on the Long Island Railroad, I met another time buyer who worked for another advertising agency who told me that *he* had bought the one overtime spot in the *Super Bowl.* I had the feeling that something else was in play here. How was it possible that Bud had sold the same single spot to two people?

And then it came to me.

I called Bud at home and asked one simple question. "Bud, to how many advertisers did you sell that one overtime break in the *Super Bowl?*"

Bud answered, "TWENTY-FIVE."

This was Zero Mostel and *The Producers* all over again, but this time it was television. Bud was betting there would be no overtime. And he was right. Every one of those twenty-five advertisers paid for a bushel basket of other spots, all sucked in by the notion that each might have that special overtime break in the big game.

During his retirement party, I gave Bud the "chutzpah" award

61

and today we both laugh at that great initiative in marketing.

The protocol of positioning advertising spots on television has changed drastically from the way it was in the late 1960's. Today, in a single commercial break you might see a spot for Ford, followed immediately by one for Chrysler. Or another break with ads for Budweiser, then Snapple. But not in the old days. Exclusivity for their type of product was guaranteed by each station's traffic department so as to avoid such conflicts. One of the most critical functions of staff employees at a TV station is the preparation of the daily operating log. This task is performed by the traffic department, which generates a sort of road map for the broadcast technicians, showing what programs or commercials or promotional announcements they should be airing every hour, every minute, even every second.

I think it was around 1968 when I was still at DFS, working on the RJ Reynolds account when they decided to introduce a new product. It was a small cigar called *Winchester*, and it was decided to *test-market* the commercials. The purpose of test-marketing is to take your national advertising plan and run a micro-version of it in several small markets to see what works and what doesn't. One of the chosen markets for that test was Chico-Redding, California.

But we were experiencing a problem with the TV station in that market. We tried to get them to adopt what was, in the 1960's, the new way of scheduling commercials, called "the orbit." This meant that a given commercial would rotate over four different programs during a four week period.

But the station in Chico would have none of it. They were still doing it the old fashioned way. Their number one advertiser had a weekly spot in their highest rated show, and the next guy the second, and so on. Each advertiser laid claim to the same spot every week. In the science of advertising that made no sense. It was proven that by rotating, by "orbiting" the commercials over a variety of programs, the advertiser would reach more people, and usually do so more often. It made good marketing sense. But the management at the Chico station said they couldn't handle that.

It was given to me to fly to Chico to see what I could do. I arrived at the station at about 2:45 in the afternoon and was ushered into the office of the General Manager. One wall of his office was an impressively large window which looked into a conference room, empty at the time.

I launched into my most persuasive mode, detailing for him the advantages he could offer his clients if he would adopt the "new" method of orbiting their spots. Even though he allowed me to continue my pitch, I had the uneasy feeling that he wasn't really buying what I had to say. Then, about ten minutes after 3, the side door of the conference room opened and in came about a dozen high school girls. Each of the youngsters took their schoolbooks and equipment and stuffed them into a drawer which was tucked in under the table in front of every chair. Then each girl took out what we used to call a "column pad" -- those long graphic looking pads with the funny green lines.

I became intrigued at what was going on on the other side of the GM's glass wall, so I asked him, "What's that all about?"

He said, "Mr. Butensky, that's our traffic department."

And that was that. Using part time high school students to do station traffic for about ninety minutes every afternoon explained why all those newfangled scheduling schemes weren't going to happen in Chico.

But with the advertising of tobacco banned shortly after that, the campaign for *Winchester* went by the wayside anyway.

I didn't spend my entire career working for advertising agencies. I also worked on the distribution side...companies which are also referred to in the lingo of the trade as *syndicators*, and whose traveling staff were truly early television's Willy Lomans.

In 1978 I was President of Enterprises at a distribution company called Viacom. In those days it was pronounced "*Vee*-a-com," but years later, when Sumner Redstone became CEO of the company he decreed the pronunciation would be changed to "*Vy*-a-com." The company was a spinoff from CBS and thus owned distribution rights to an impressive list of programs which had formerly aired on that network, including the sitcom which was one of the industry's all time great hits, *All In The Family*. And it was that classic Norman Lear production which led me to become involved in the largest money deal of my experience.

Viacom owned the rights to sell reruns of *All In The Family* on a market by market basis...i.e., syndication rights. But even though we had those rights, we couldn't commence selling it to local stations until whenever Norman Lear said it was O.K. to do so.

The conflict arose because Lear, as he was churning out other hit series such as *Maude, The Jeffersons,* and *Good Times*, and for which he owned the distribution rights, had decided to establish his own distribution company (T.A.T. Communications) and was looking for ways to recover the syndication rights to *All In The Family* so as to have that series as the star attraction in his own stable. I was told he had even gone to court twice in past attempts to get the series, but failed. So things were at a stalemate.

When I got to Viacom and read the file on what had previously transpired, I decided it was time to make another effort to spring the series loose so we could start selling it. As a result, Viacom gave Norman Lear a huge guarantee. Out of the revenue from the first cycle of sales of *All In The Family*, his share would be $100 million! Guaranteed!

In the history of television this still stands as a record.

This was the first time that a non-producing company *guaran-*

teed that amount of money to a producing company.

And the management team of Lear's company was certainly clever enough to put that bundle of dollars to work for them. 1978 was the year that bidding was opened for entities to submit their offers for the telecast rights to the *1984 Olympics*, scheduled to take place in Los Angeles. Jerry Perenchio, who owns Univision, was then running Lear's company. And the very day after the Viacom contract was signed, Jerry pledged their newly acquired one hundred million dollars as that company's bid. But ABC's bid was even higher and they were eventually awarded those rights. So while we established a record in one arena of programming, the *Summer Olympic Games* proved to be even more expensive than Archie Bunker.

Over the years I've probably personally visited well over 600 television stations in all fifty states. Many of the television stations are modern edifices, well constructed and sharp looking, and others are really old. Years ago, the station in High Point, North Carolina, was a converted old *Sheraton Hotel*. Every other office had a connecting room with a bathtub.

Even the parking lots were telling. Most of them had assigned parking slots, with spaces designated for *Staff*, then *Visitors*. A few of them even offered three choices: *Staff*, *Visitors*, then *Syndicators*.

The mention of parking lots reminds me of an incident that occurred while I was working at the *Television Bureau of Advertising* (TVB), an organization which acts as a lobbyist. Our mission was to convince advertisers to place their advertising dollars in television, as opposed to radio, magazines, newspapers, outdoors, and all those other guys.

On one occasion we called on a mid-sized retailer in the Southeast. Right at the get-go the store's owner met us at the front door, escorted us through the entire store, through the back door and into his parking lot. I figured it was the biggest "bum's rush" I'd ever experienced.

But then *Mr. Owner* said, "Do you see my parking lot? It's rather full, wouldn't you agree? If I shift a bigger percentage of my advertising into television, where am I going to put all those extra cars?"

Go figure.

One of the burdens borne by the traveling salesman is to prepare his weekly expense account and then have it approved by the home office. Over the years I have developed a system that results in a fairly accurate accounting. I simply note how much cash I have in my pocket when I start a trip and then recheck it when I return. So I know exactly how much I spent out of pocket. Then by adding that to the accumulated chits from Amex and Visa, I have an accurate total of the trip costs and of the amount I should be reimbursed.

But sometimes the process causes some creative accounting. I remember on more than one occasion when a salesman who regularly called on me would telephone me in the afternoon to say that if his boss called, to confirm that we had had lunch that day, when in fact we had not. When two or three salesmen do that on the same day, well, that gets touchy. I remember one day in the late '70's when I got four such calls in one hour. If the IRS ever checked with me, they'd expect to see a seriously overweight person.

Perhaps the most bizarre situation in that regard occurred to some friends of mine way back when Jerry Marcus (who recently retired as General Manager of Fox's KRIV-TV in Houston, Texas) was working for Metromedia's Jim Coppersmith.

Jerry was barely on the job when he submitted a luncheon voucher, putting down that he took Barry Greene to lunch on Tuesday. (Greene is a fictitious name.) Jim Coppersmith, in going over the voucher remembered reading something about Barry Greene, and sure enough, in rereading the newspaper he saw that

Barry Greene had died on Sunday, two days before he allegedly had lunch with Marcus.

Jim summoned Marcus to his office and confronted him dead on. He told Jerry that he had just read that Barry Greene had died, and did so two days *before* Jerry had lunch with him.

Marcus, without batting an eye, said, "You know, I thought he was rather quiet."

Now, you gotta love a guy like that!

Fridays With Art

"Forget everything you've heard about getting up early, working hard and being conscientious. The most important thing in our business is to be lucky. If you're not, then marry someone who is."
                                                    ...Art Greenfield

Hits, Misses, Kings, Jacks & Jokers
by Dick Colbert

It was in February of 1942 when the California Employment Service sent me to the San Francisco branch office of the Universal Pictures Film Exchange, where to my surprise and delight I was hired at the munificent salary of $12.50 per week. I was also given the grandiose title of Accessory Sales Manager which, I suppose in retrospect, was designed to help make up for the puny pay. Actually, I was just a clerk, in charge of furnishing the posters and materials to theatre exhibitors which the studio used to promote and advertise its movies.

But before long I was promoted to Apprentice Booker and given a $5 raise, both events being due to the arrival of a man transferred to us from Los Angeles. Brought in as our office manager and head booker, his name was Art Greenfield.

I was just 18 and he sort of adopted me, spending evenings

every week, after office hours, teaching me the ropes and educating me about the functions of the accounting department and the booking department and the weekly reports requested by our New York head-quarters' executives. He taught me how to commit to memory lines from various Shakespeare plays, even going so far as to gift me with his own set of Shakespeare's work. But the most demanding task he assigned to me was to memorize both the title and "release number" of every movie Universal handled. I can still rattle them off to this day, though this outdated talent is useless today. Nobody seems to care that *The Egg and I* was number 613 in 1946, or that *Singapore* was number 622 in 1947. What Art was doing of course, was culti-vating my youthful mind to the advantages of education.

Art was a very large man who tipped the scales at various num-bers ranging from 275 to 300 pounds. On many Sunday mornings we would take bicycle rides through San Francisco's Golden Gate Park, and with my skinny 150 pound frame, we must have looked like Laurel and Hardy. Art was then living in a high-class boarding house, the *Carrolton Residence Club*, an old mansion on Powell Street. His rent included a room with breakfast and dinner each day, but they finally asked him to leave during the food rationing days of World War II because they could no longer afford to feed him.

But Art's appetite was a pleasure for my father. Dad was a tiny fellow who loved to cook Sunday morning breakfasts for Art. The menu consisted of hot cereal, pancakes, bacon and eggs, brittle toast from the oven and potatoes, all prepared on a wood stove in our home in the redwood forested community of Boulder Creek, California. Art would eat every proffered bit, then we'd all go to the nearby forest and chop firewood, burning up our calories with an ax, saw, sledge hammer and wedge.

While in the service during World War II, Universal paid me a week's salary every month, a generous gesture that was both surprising and appreciated. I rejoined the company after the war as a *book-er* and was soon promoted to a salesman, after which I shortly found myself elected to become President of what was essentially a union: the *Coliseum of Motion Picture Salesmen* for the San Francisco area. It was a national organization representing film salesmen from all companies (except Paramount who felt their salesmen were too good for us) designated to negotiate with the studios for salaries, benefits, etc. It worked and our situation improved.

But Universal unexpectedly created the new position of *Sales Manager* for the San Francisco branch and offered me the job! So, as management, I had to resign my presidency of the '*Coliseum*.' To this day, I'm not sure whether this promotion was the result of my allegiance to the '*Coliseum*' or Universal's belief in my ability.

Art, in the meantime, after assignments to various other branches, had been promoted to Branch Manager in Portland where he helped oversee the world premiere of a movie which had been filmed in Bend, Oregon, and thus titled *Bend of the River*, starring Jimmy Stewart and Rock Hudson. Art arranged for the film to open simultaneously and with heavy promotion at theaters all across the state, and as a result, won first prize in Universal's sales drive for that year. He and his wife, Irma, were sent off on an all-expenses-paid tour of Europe, where they were wined and dined by all of Universal's representatives stationed in various European cities. Art would recall details of their wonderful trip at every conversational opportunity during the next 48 years.

When Art was later promoted to manage Universal's Seattle branch, he would spend many of his evenings reading to and teaching blind students at the University of Washington. Every Wednesday afternoon he would haul his sizable bulk into the sailboat of his friend, Fred Danz, and they would go for a pleasant spin, then finish the day with an evening of bridge, a game at which Art so excelled

71

that he was awarded the title of *Tournament Master*. I suppose that achievement is not too surprising, considering his Master's degree from the University of Southern California. Truly a versatile genius.

I trailed in his wake for several years, replacing him in Portland and later in Seattle. In 1958, he resigned from Universal to tackle his first entry into the world of TV syndication by becoming a sales representative for Screen Gems, a subsidiary of Columbia Pictures. His change of focus from selling theatrical films to selling television programs soon inspired me to follow in his footsteps. So, after 18 years with Universal, I too joined Screen Gems, moving my family to Omaha.

My boss was the infamous Stanley Dudleson, head of the company's Central Division. He was a sloppy and porky guy with an eternal cigar in his mouth, the ashes of which would frequently soil his shirt. He was a crude and profane man, and in every way the antithesis of the intellectual and gentle Art Greenfield, who had been my mentor for so many years. My entire sales training under Dudleson consisted of loading the trunk of my used company Chevy with a few 16mm film prints, a projector, plus promotion and press material covering the various Screen Gems shows, then handing me a highway map showing the way from Chicago to my new base in Omaha. The map also covered my new territory, which included North and South Dakota, Nebraska, Kansas, Iowa, Missouri and eventually Oklahoma and Minnesota.

Talk about flying solo! I blundered out into those unfamiliar territories, as green as the trees which dotted their riverbanks, and only gradually realizing that I was undergoing an ideal learning experience.

As a newcomer, I was the lowest paid salesman in the entire midwest when there was a sudden downturn in the economy. The movie companies in their collective wisdom, including our manage-

72

ment at Columbia Pictures, all rationalized similarly in what they felt was good economic sense. So, they fired their most experienced and qualified, thus highest paid sales representatives, leaving me as the only "traveling salesman" under my new Midwest District Manager, Bob Newgard. Happily, Bob proved to be a totally different person from the uncouth Dudleson. "Newgie" was a true gentleman with a marvelous sense of humor. And though I sometimes had to drive 125 icy miles from Omaha to have two-man sales meetings with him at his family home in Des Moines, his hospitality and cordial brilliance made the trips a pleasure.

But once in a while a person gets "an offer he can't refuse." So when I was given the opportunity in January of 1962 to return to my home town of San Francisco to join Ziv, which was the largest and most prestigious of all companies in the distribution industry, I grabbed it.

Once relocated, I began learning a new side of the syndication business: besides calling on television stations in the area, I was now calling on the advertising managers of major companies and the heads of ad agencies which handled their accounts. Ziv's General Sales Manager, Len Firestone, was officed in New York but he would frequently fly out to San Francisco whenever I would stir up interest in our product from such major clients as Bank of America, Hills Bros., Carnation, and others. Thus I got to know Len well, which soon led me to order a different set of business cards.

Firestone had been induced to head up a brand new distribution company to be called *Four Star*, and when he invited me to become part of his original sales force, I welcomed the opportunity. The company grew out of the convictions of such top actors as Dick Powell, Charles Boyer, David Niven and Ida Lupino that they were not receiving a fair share of the profits from shows in which they acted or directed because of the distribution fees being paid to outside companies. For example, the customary fee earned by a distribution company was 35% of the amount paid in license fees by the exhibitor. But the producer had to pay all the costs of the actors, writers and technicians who actually make the shows, and do so out of the remaining 65%. Frequently those costs exceeded the producer's share of revenue. The solution was to have the programs distributed by a company which they could own...and not only shows in which they appeared, but every kind of program covering the entire spectrum of entertainment. Dick Powell attracted the very best creative talent, writers, actors, directors, producers, editors, etc.

For example, one of our earliest first run syndication efforts was a series titled *Police Surgeon*, starring Sam Groom and the venerable and ever-popular Jack Albertson. We enlisted the major market stations owned by NBC to be our partners in this venture and with them as a foundation, induced Colgate to come along as a sponsor.

With Dick Powell and Tom McDermott keeping a careful eye on the quality of production, the show was a success and ran in *prime time* for two years...with Four Star retaining the profits as a result of being both the producer and the distributor. Other first-run advertiser supported syndicated shows that followed included *Thrill Seekers*, starring Chuck Connors, through the Ted Bates Agency for Colgate-Palmolive, and John Newland's *X-Factor* for Proctor and Gamble.

We also entered the then-popular genre of musical shows with an original series of productions under the banner of *Something Special*, which featured such talents as Peggy Lee, Maurice Chevalier, Ella Fitzgerald, Count Basie, Tony Bennett and many, many others.

The man hired to produce these one hour shows, Jackie Barnett, did an amazing job of bringing them in for a total cost of between $40,000 and $50,000 per hour-long show. And as the company prospered, so did I, becoming first Sales Manager and then later, Co-

President of Four Star Distribution with Tony Thomopoulos.

But my luckiest break occurred when a man named Jack Barry was hired in 1969 to help develop new programs for Four Star.

At this point a brief recital of some television history is in order. Ten years earlier, when game shows were an essential staple for the networks in *prime time*, Jack Barry was a producer with Dan Enright, and the emcee of the highly popular *Twenty One* in *prime time* on NBC. The format was basically a contest of knowledge between two average people from all walks of life, some of whom became national celebrities as a result of their successful appearances. For example, one of the contestants who vaulted into fame was Dr. Joyce Brothers, whose vast knowledge of boxing seemed far afield from her studies in psychiatry.

But if you saw the hit movie *Quiz Show*, you know of the furor caused when one of the contestants, who had bested every opponent for many weeks in a row, admitted to having been given the answers by a producer of the show prior to air time. And while Jack Barry was technically one of the producers, his function was primarily to be the handsome, genial emcee who voiced the questions during the broadcasts. The primary creative work fell to Jack's partner, Dan Enright who, as shown in the movie, succumbed to pressure from the show's sponsor and the network to make certain the winning contestant was a more attractive personality than the dowdy frump of a nerd who had been winning the contest week after week. So when the young and handsome Charles Van Doren appeared and dethroned the nerd, and then continued for weeks as the winning contestant, he enchanted the nationwide audience with his sweating and tortured struggle to come up with the right answers.

When it was later revealed he had been given the answers in advance, a major scandal erupted, resulting in a Congressional hearing, after which both Jack Barry and Dan Enright became undesirables in the eyes of the TV industry. They were then forced to sell their highly successful series such as *Twenty-One, Concentration* and *Tic Tac Dough* to NBC, and to retire from the public eye.

But now it was ten years later and Jack was eager to make a comeback. He and his partner, Dan Enright, began their resurgence at Four Star with a charming little series called *Juvenile Jury*, which they originally produced for radio in the 1940's, where Jack would interview children, encouraging them to voice their opinions...hilarious concept. Jack managed to convince John McMahon, General Manager of the Los Angeles ABC station, to broadcast the series, and it became such a hit that it was renewed for a second year, resulting in 52 episodes, enough for syndication. So off I trekked, offering *Juvenile Jury* to television stations around the country. Sometimes Jack would join me in those sales pitches because he enjoyed meeting the broadcasters, and those contacts would prove invaluable in later years.

But in 1971, Jack left Four Star when CBS invited him to create, produce and host *Joker's Wild*, a five-per-week series which they placed on their daytime schedule. A remarkable young man named Fred Silverman was then in charge of programming for CBS. He is the only man to have headed up programming for all three of the then existing networks at various times in his career. Silverman was such a hands-on executive that he even spent time in the evenings at Jack's home, consulting with Jack while he tinkered with the plans for the series. But it was purely Jack's vision which finally hit the air, and '*Joker*' thrived for several years until a slight dip in the ratings in the spring of 1975. At that time, Silverman was making many schedule changes and one of the casualties was '*Joker*,' which he canceled just before he departed CBS to become President of ABC.

And in doing so, Silverman created for me the greatest break of my professional career. Jack Barry decided I would be the exclusive distributor of all programs created by his newly reestablished partnership with Dan Enright, so Colbert Television Syndication, Inc. was born! I supplemented their inventory with the rerun rights to the *Lassie* series and an epic western series titled *The Rifleman*, the latter a show which I have been distributing now for 40 years...a record for an independent syndicator.

It was early in 1976 when Jack was notified by friends at CBS that the network planned to erase the tapes of the 700 existing episodes of *Joker's Wild* which were taking up needed space in their warehouse. If he was interested, they would sell these old tapes to him for just their cost of the tape stock, $100 per episode. Jack asked my opinion and being the syndication expert of the firm I told him, with full conviction, that those old off-network programs had absolutely no sales potential in the current marketplace. I cited the experience of a competitor friend of mine, Jack Rhodes, who had suffered failure the previous season with off-network reruns of a game show from the prestigious stable of producers, Goodson & Todman.

Thankfully, Jack didn't take my advice. He went ahead and paid CBS $70,000 for the tapes and then prodded me to call on broadcasters in our home market of Los Angeles to see if any were interested. It turned out that the most immediate opportunity to get the series on the air was at the market's weakest station, Channel 9 (then using the call letters KHJ). They had an available time period at 7:30 p.m., Monday through Friday, and even though their license fee was very low, we made the deal on the premise that it would be an interesting test of whether or not *Joker's Wild* reruns were of any value.

And wow! Were they ever! The show eventually built to an amazing 10 rating, and as a result, we were able to make sales in New York, Chicago, Philadelphia, St. Louis and many other markets where the series became a favorite counter-programming tool against shows on stations affiliated with the networks.

I was aware, of course, of the government regulation which required network affiliated stations to air only first run programming, no off-network stuff, in the time periods which preceded *prime time*. So I began nagging Jack and Dan to produce new episodes of the '*Joker's*' format. They scoffed at the idea, saying in effect, we're doing fine at no cost, so just keep selling the old shows for which we had enough episodes to strip for almost three years before repeating.

But I was excited at the prospect of being able to offer *first-run* episodes of '*Joker's*' to network affiliated stations and the potential for high revenues from that source finally convinced my partners to commence production of new shows for the fall season of 1977. However, we remained loyal to those independent station customers who had helped us get started.

The ratings on those strong affiliated stations were also great, and once again Jack was a major celebrity. He reveled in the recognition by admirers everywhere he went...restaurants, stores, taxicabs and golf courses. I will always cherish the memory of my special relationship with Jack, of his visits early every morning when we were both in town, when he would drop by my office to share his brilliant and creative ideas, of which there was a constant daily flow. He had again become a celebrity, but he was without artifice. There was not an ounce of insincerity or phoniness in his makeup. Just a decent, charming, talented and smart man.

To expand upon the success of '*Joker's*,' Jack and Dan created a new version of *Tic, Tac Dough* and hired the talented and personable Wink Martindale to be its host. The series began airing successfully the following season and generated even higher ratings when programmed back to back with '*Joker's*,' as it was in most markets. We hired additional sales representatives so we could expand our coverage. They included the King brothers, Roger, Michael and Bob, whose previous syndication experience had been mostly limited to selling reruns of *The Little Rascals*, an old film property which had been passed on to them as a family treasure by their father, Charlie King.

The Kings spent five productive years with us before setting up their own company and taking over syndication of some programs you may have heard about: *Wheel of Fortune* and *Jeopardy!* Oh, and a little talk show hosted and produced by someone you may also have heard about: Oprah Winfrey. They became the giants of the industry.

Later they flattered me by inviting me to join their company in the role of General Sales Manager and *partner*, and to bring the shows created by Jack and Dan along to become part of their library. But, that library already included two wildly popular game shows created by Merv Griffin, and I didn't feel I could fairly represent both producing companies. Too much hazard in the area of conflict of interest, whether it might be real or only perceived. By turning down the job I may have missed an opportunity to become quite wealthy, but I could not simply turn my back on Jack and Dan after all the wonderful years of our relationship.

But the King brothers still talk about the old days and our first Colbert Syndication sales meeting at the *Mayflower Hotel* in New York, where I talked extemporaneously from early Saturday until late Sunday without repeating myself. They credit me with teaching and mentoring them, but I contend that my main contribution was preventing Roger and Bob from killing each other. I believe it is widely acknowledged that Roger King, with his unique talents, has long been syndication's number one salesman. But, if in fact I did teach them and/or mentor them, I was simply passing along the kind of affectionate and patient treatment Art Greenfield had given me so many years previous.

Did you ever hear of one TV station using its own airtime to promote the programming on a competing station? And I'm not talk-

79

ing about paid advertising...I'm talking about free spots!

Well, a little history was made in that regard when Evan Thompson requested we release KCOP from its agreement with us to allow them to acquire *Jeopardy!* and '*Wheel*' from King World. We insisted KCOP extensively promote on their air that *Tic Tac Dough* and '*Joker's*' were moving to Channel 9, with which they complied.

And more history was made when Jack Barry persuaded the then head of CBS programming, Bud Grant, who was happily airing *Tic Tac Dough* as an effective entry on his network's daytime schedule, to allow us to sell different episodes of the series in the syndication market, with his only caveat being that it air on the competing stations later than 4 p.m. This breakthrough opened a new and lucrative market for several game show producers who could now supplement their network income with revenue from the syndication versions of their formats.

Sometimes those of us in this business remember our mistakes as clearly as our hits. One such error was when I declined the opportunity to acquire a talk show which originated in the Midwest and which featured an unknown emcee named Phil Donahue. *Wrong!* Instead, I encouraged Jack and Dan to finance Alan Bennett in the production of *Breakaway*, a one hour daytime magazine show which suffered a disastrous failure. Moving on, we produced for demonstration at NATPE, the annual broadcaster's program convention, an excellent 90 minute pilot of a talk/variety show hosted by Bob Crane which was received with overwhelming accolades. Tragically, soon after the convention, Crane was found grotesquely murdered in Arizona. It was rumored to be a Mafia hit because Bob had been fooling around with the wrong lady.

Because he was such a superstar on his morning radio talk show, we taped a pilot with emcee Don Imus, but he exhibited evidence of being very difficult to work with, so despite his talent we decided not to go forward. We produced a series designed to benefit from the popularity of daytime Soap Operas, called *Soap World*, but it flopped. And we had only mild success with some other shows: *Private Investigator*, starring Washington columnist Jack Anderson; *Tales of the Haunted; Purely Personal; Play the Percentages;* and *Bumper Stumpers*, created by Wink Martindale.

It was during this time that I experienced what is now a cherished memory from my years of doing business with the famous Ted Turner, a true innovator and courageous industry visionary who pioneered CNN about 25 years ago.

Ted owned a beautiful mansion near downtown Atlanta with magnificent Tara-like architecture, adorned with huge white columns. I recall, as if yesterday, Ted with all his elegance, striding down the long marble staircase, with his mustache and handsome stately carriage, wearing an ascot and perfectly tailored jacket. In the center of the huge ballroom-sized living room was CNN's first studio. There was a single fixed position camera and cameraman, and a set which revolved whenever necessary to reveal a tiny newsroom, or a cramped kitchen, or a small news interview room, or library...whatever the director called for. Reese Schoenfeld was the creative genius for CNN, who soon after decided to depart following differences with the *Mouth of the South*. It's hard to imagine the now giant CNN springing from such a humble and inexpensive start, not that long ago.

But then, in 1984, Jack Barry, while still in his prime at age 66, suffered a fatal heart attack while jogging near New York's Central Park.

Later, Dan Enright expressed his desire to sell the firm's entire library, which included more than 5,000 half-hour episodes of game shows. After more than a year of negotiations with various interested entities, we finally sold the inventory to Sony's cable network, *The*

Game Show Channel. But sadly, Dan passed away in the interim. At long last, my close, happy and enduring relationship with Jack and Dan had come to an end. And there was never a written agreement between us.

"I have already screwed up in half a day
what it normally takes me all day to do."
...Art Greenfield

Of Pins and Needles
by Joe Siegman

Someone had to do it.

I created *Celebrity Bowling*, one of the early made-for-syndication series, and likely one of the first, if not *the* first, live-taped entertainment shows produced for syndication. It debuted in 1971 and aired for seven years. It was programmed mostly on weekend afternoons, and generally was either first or second in its time period wherever it played. *Celebrity Bowling* was considered by some the poster child of banal programming. Its very name was a frequent punch line for Johnny Carson, and network sitcoms used the title to earn a quick laugh. The only people who enjoyed the series were TV viewers and station managers.

Celebrity Bowling was the first TV series I produced and was born of a seemingly unrelated process. It's a long short story. If you stick with it, it eventually fits together.

My first grown-up employment resulted unexpectedly from a visit to Chicago's *Farwell Beach* in the summer of 1956. In two weeks of job hunting following my University of Illinois graduation, I couldn't seem to find anyone interested in giving me a TV directing position, despite the fact that I had a degree in journalism and a major in television production.

So I hit *Farwell Beach*, my usual summer haunt. While wading through a sea of non-working contemporaries on Farwell's grassy "schmooze-but-don't-get-wet" area, a stranger seated on a blanket stopped me and introduced himself. He explained: he had just graduated from the University of Wisconsin-Madison; had been a member of the Badgers fencing team that faced Illini fencers in Champaign during the past year's U of I homecoming weekend; was taken to the homecoming *Stunt Show* (an annual big deal Broadway-type musical competition between fraternities and sororities) by my roommate - an All American fencer; and saw me perform. "You were terrific!" he said.

It was nice to hear a kind word from a stranger, considering the success I wasn't enjoying in the job market. How he recognized me in a swimsuit after seeing me only once, eight months earlier in costume and make-up, he couldn't explain. But he said it was a relief to see even a semi-familiar face. He had just received the bad news he had been drafted and was leaving for basic training in a week.

"You wouldn't know anyone looking for a job?" he asked. He explained he worked in the advertising department of his family's business, and didn't want to leave without finding a good replacement. "You'd be great," he said.

And that's how my first job found me. Sixty bucks a week writing radio and TV commercials for Polk Bros. "in-house" advertising agency. Polk Bros. (not Polk Brothers) was the first discount department store chain in Chicago to promote its wares via huge purchases of broadcast time. Its president, Sol Polk, made his family business a Chicago institution by introducing not only low, low prices, but everyday giveaways such as free watermelons, pumpkins, bushels of corn, movie tickets, etc., with every purchase of a refrigerator, washer, TV, air conditioner, etc. I never quite figured out why a watermelon or pair of movie tickets valued then at maybe $1 could be a deal closer on a $400 item. But Sol Polk did.

Sol (what everyone called him when he wasn't in the room) was a grass roots merchandiser and knew his market well. And so it was that he installed a full-size bowling lane, including automatic pinsetter, in the front window of his South Side super store. Sol knew his consumer base. An awful lot of Chicagoans were tenpin bowlers, and Chicago was the hub of TV bowling.

Sol didn't actually buy the bowling lane. He *promoted it* from the Brunswick Company for use on the weekly telecast of *Friday Night Bowling*, which was telecast in Chicago direct from Polk Bros. southside showroom window. Competing bowlers were local league keglers who vied for their moment of recognition, and "a chance to win some great Polk Bros. prizes."

The highlight of *Friday Night Bowling* was its last segment "celebrity" feature. A celebrity working in the Chicago area was invited to "roll a bowl" for his or her favorite charity. Polk Bros. donated $10 for every pin the celebrity knocked down...plus a bonus for a strike or spare and other incentives. Celebrities were reasonably easy to come by, if for no other reason than to promote their local nightclub engagement, play or film. And celebrities knew that Sol Polk was a sport. He didn't pay them the chintzy local union scale -- something like $28. Instead, he saw to it that a TV, refrigerator, or other choice of the performer, was shipped to the celebrity's home.

When I was promoted from commercial writer to commercial producer -- my first producing position -- my first night on the new

85

$80 per week job was at *Friday Night Bowling*. Comedian Joey Bishop was the celebrity bowler that night. And, my vision of a celebrity bowling television series was born.

Visions notwithstanding, soon after I requested $100 a week to compensate me for the important duties to which I had been assigned, I was promptly unassigned. I was out of work.

Being jobless wasn't so bad. I was living at home and now had a lot of time to develop my "can't miss" ideas, including what I was now referring to as *Celebrity Bowling*. But, after a few months of dreaming and unsuccessful attempts to stir up interest in the concept of celebrities bowling on TV, and a second passion, getting Chicago Blackhawks ice-hockey on radio, I got a job.

Bud Solk, owner of a small ad and PR agency, was looking for a junior partner-copywriter-leg man, and was struck by the idea of getting the Blackhawks' games on the air. (It didn't occur to me until I started writing this piece that my career began with a penchant for employers with four-letter names that ended in *olk*.)

It's hard to imagine in today's sports crazed climate, a major league professional franchise without an assortment of broadcast arrangements, let alone the broadcast of its games on radio. But the Hawks had not been on the air for years. The team was lousy and drawing maybe 3,500 paying customers on a good night. I had discovered ice hockey in my senior year at Illinois, and Blackhawks' games at the old Chicago Stadium had become a must-see for preppies. Forget about season tickets. You could walk up to the ticket window minutes before face-off and get yourself a primo seat.

I couldn't understand why a big league professional team kept its games *off* radio. Between periods at the Stadium one night I noticed the Blackhawks' business office across from a concession stand. Impulsively, I went inside and found a grungy interior, and two men seated behind ratty desks whom I immediately recognized:

Blackhawks' General Manager Tommy Ivan and team PR guy, former Blackhawks' star, Johnny Gottslieg.

When I told them why I was there they both laughed, and Ivan said with a measure of sarcasm, "We're not on the air, kid, because no one's interested in broadcasting our games." I didn't like the answer and told them why they *should* be on the air, thinking all along it was management that *kept* themselves off radio and TV so fans would have to attend the games.

"We've tried everything," said Ivan. "Everyone's tried. Stations, advertisers. Nobody's interested. How 'bout you, kid. Can you get us on the air?"

"Are you serious?" I asked.

He nodded in the affirmative, as Gottslieg had difficulty keeping himself from laughing aloud.

"Who else is trying?" I asked.

"All by yourself," said Ivan.

"Yessir. Okay," I blurted. "You won't mind if I call you tomorrow to confirm this?"

"I'm here after ten," answered Ivan.

I raced back to my seat to tell my friends of my good fortune. They reacted with about the same level of energy as Ivan and Gottslieg.

The following day I phoned GM Ivan and he confirmed it wasn't a dream.

So I had the rights, but no customers. My sales talents didn't kick in that season. I had a couple of stations willing to carry Hawks' games, with the codicil that I brought in paid advertising with the package. No luck. Next year, same story.

But something unusual occurred in 1959. The Blackhawks qualified for the Stanley Cup Playoffs for the first time in a decade. Forty-eight hours before the first playoff game against the Montreal

Canadiens, frantically wading through the *Yellow Pages* for a willing sponsor, canvassing under "Savings and Loans," I found an S&L whose manager said "Yes!" He'd sponsor the third period of all the Hawks' post-season games. The third period (of three) wasn't a whole game, but Chicago hockey fans had to be thrilled with any coverage. I was.

With a little help here and there, some good guessing and an abundance of luck, the technical musts, talent, station requirements, et als, all fell into place. Sure, the Hawks lost the series in four games. But we were on the air. And I made it happen!

Prior to the start of the 1960 National Hockey League season I sold an 18 game package of Blackhawk telecasts to Chicago's WBKB-TV, and was about to complete a radio deal when team owner Arthur Wirtz, a man I had never met, had his secretary phone my office to rescind whatever media rights I had previously been given.

I was mortified.

WBKB-TV chief Red Quinlan ordered me to somehow make it work. But Art Wirtz wouldn't see or speak to me. So I camped in the hallway outside his office...literally. His office was a suite within the downtown *Morrison Hotel*, another Wirtz property. Annoyed by having to step over me every time he left his office, he eventually granted me an audience. Wirtz said he didn't know who I was and denied the validity of any agreements made by his GM. He told me he didn't need me to get his team on radio or television. Anytime he wanted his games broadcast, said Wirtz, if the sponsors weren't there, he owned enough businesses to sponsor them himself. And, at the moment, he didn't want the Hawks on the air. "If you can't accept that, sue me."

Which I did.

Via a citywide publicity campaign I raised "Blackhawk Broadcast Bucks" to help underwrite my cost of litigation. Of course, the suit didn't cost me much since one of my newly-shingled college

friends was my mouthpiece. Eventually, the gnat and the elephant settled out of court. The most significant portion of the settlement was
bragging rights.

It was about this time that I received an offer from a longtime
friend to move to Los Angeles and join him in his budding advertising PR agency. He would be the artist, me the writer and business
type. I went to visit him for a week in early September, 1960. By the
time I returned to Chicago seven days later, I had committed to making L.A. my new base.

I scheduled my L.A. return for late November because I had
previously committed to working for the *Citizens for Kennedy-
Johnson Committee* and the 1960 November presidential election.
My cousin, Harry Finkel, was the #3 executive at Chicago's
Merchandise Mart. His boss was Sargent Shriver, Senator John
Kennedy's brother-in-law. Shriver and his lieutenants played a major
role in the campaign.

As I understand it, my cousin told Sarge Shriver and the
Kennedy-Johnson people that I was something of a broadcast *wun-
derkind*. After all, I got the Blackhawks on radio and had created the
WBKB package that Mr. Worse (my name for Wirtz) had reneged on.
The Illinois race between Senator Kennedy and Vice President
Richard Nixon looked like it would be a neck and neck finish. While
no one had a crystal ball to know that Illinois would turn out to be
pivotal to Kennedy's victory, the Democrats knew they had to win the
state. The city of Chicago was a lock for the Senator, but downstate
Illinois -- the rest of the state -- was being bombarded by a Nixon
assault, featuring the theme that a vote for Kennedy, a Catholic, was
a vote to put the Pope in the White House.

A few years out of college, I wasn't much of a wunderkind. But,
just like that, I took on the new name, Siegman Advertising Agency,
was given an office and instructed to purchase all the downstate (non-

Cook County) radio and TV time I could dig up for the final week of the campaign. I didn't have an open ended budget, but I had a budget with an open end!

Kennedy narrowly won Illinois (and the presidency). I wasn't offered a cabinet post or even a cabinet, but I received letters of appreciation from the *'Kennedy-Johnson Committee'* and members of the Kennedy family, particularly Eunice Shriver. Two weeks after the November election I left for California, unknowingly to renew my quest to give life to *Celebrity Bowling*.

My Los Angeles partner's crowd of young Hollywood types became my crowd. Only months after dropping anchor in West Hollywood -- it had no reputation for anything at that time -- our crowd began meeting for softball games on Sunday mornings. The games and after-game get-togethers soon became the stuff of legends. Before long we were known as *The Entertainers' League* -- performers, agents, producers, studio executives, personal managers, et als -- a unique group of the famous, powerful, emerging, never-heard-ofs and nobodies that held together for nearly a decade. It is from this affiliation that this "nobody" would develop many of his closest West Coast friendships, allies and contacts.

One such contact was Elliott Kozak, right arm to Jimmy Saphier, Bob Hope's personal manager. We were teammates on the *Entertainers' League 'Ten Percenters,'* the team sponsored by Saphier, and on *'Darin's Demons,'* Bobby Darin's team.

In 1961, Bob Hope's company produced *Celebrity Golf*, to my recollection the first celebrity sports series on national TV. It pitted a good golfing celebrity and a prominent golf pro in a head-to-head match. Key to the entertainment value of the one-hour series was the ongoing banter between the competitors. Sometimes it worked, sometimes it was deadly. Mostly, celebrities tried to be serious about their golf, while the pros attempted to be witty. But Bob Hope produced it, so it stayed on the air for a year.

Somewhere in a conversation with Elliott I mentioned my latent *Celebrity Bowling* idea. He thought it was a magical concept and called his pal, Art Stolnitz, at ABC Television. ABC had just spun off a new production division, Selmur Productions, and *Celebrity Bowling* sounded like it fit right into their game plan.

I met with Selmur, they gave me the title of Associate Producer and handed me a check for $300 for bringing them the idea. But they felt the format I had sculpted was too simple. I was counting too much on entertainment value and there wasn't enough "game show" to it. They would produce the pilot and I could watch how it was done. The producer, however, wasn't interested in my looking over his shoulder. So, never given a desk or phone to at least play Hollywood, I didn't watch very much.

The day I started earning a paycheck I realized I would have to work on Saturdays and certain holidays if I chose to pursue a career in the media-entertainment field. An observant Jew, I made a deal with myself not to work on five significant religious days a year: the two days of Rosh Hashanah, Yom Kippur, and the first two days of Passover.

Selmur scheduled the shooting of the *Celebrity Bowling* pilot on the second day of Passover. The first day of Passover was the setup day. They asked me to book the four required celebrities for their format, which I did. But I told them I wouldn't be on the set to greet them. "I don't work on those days." Stolnitz didn't have a problem with that. But his producer thought I was a nut case.

The celebrities were Nick Adams - star of *The Rebel*, Connie Stevens - starring in *Hawaiian Eye* at the time, Debra Walley - *Gidget*, and Phil Crosby - one of Bing's twin sons.

Wouldn't you know, on the day of production Nick Adams has several of his ribs cracked during a morning karate workout. He can't do the pilot. The producer, who hasn't said ten words to me since I accepted the $300 check, phones and tells me I must find a replacement. I tell him that I don't make phone calls on this Jewish holiday. In fact, it was a stretch for me to even answer the telephone. He yelled a lot of things and hung up. Art Stolnitz called right back to ask if I had any replacement "ideas." I suggested several actor friends of note and gave him phone numbers. I also suggested, if the producers wanted, to ask Phil Crosby to phone his older brother Gary, the best known of the Crosby sons. Perhaps the producer could make something out of the Crosby brothers competing against each other. So Gary became the replacement.

I never saw that pilot. To the best of my recollection, a viewing was never offered. Connie and the Crosby boys told me the shoot seemed to go okay, but Stolnitz who, with his wife would become friends of my wife and I, said: "You don't want to see it."

A year later, relating the Selmur story to a college pal, I picked up another live one. I had stayed in contact with several of my Chicago area college chums, including Kenny Denberg, the lawyer who handled my Blackhawks' case. Inasmuch as nearly everyone not in show business has two business interests: the one that provides their living and 'show business,' Kenny broached the subject of his raising money to do another *Celebrity Bowling* pilot.

And he did...he raised $12,000, my estimated budget, provided by one of Ken's clients. In 1966, I put together a pilot with host Harvey Lembeck, 'Sgt. Barbella' on the '*Sgt. Bilko*' series, and co-host, bowling champion Bill Bunetta. Guest stars were actor Jack Palance, Arte Johnson of *Laugh In* fame, actress Joanna Moore (wife of Ryan O'Neal), and Mike Connors, TV's *Mannix*. The pilot was taped at a neighborhood bowling center.

In the days before videocassettes, you carried around a large kinescope reel to show your wares to potential buyers. Among those who gave me an audience were Dick Woollen at Desilu, Bob Newgard at Paramount, and Dalton Danon at L.A.'s Channel 5. I think I remember these three because meetings with them were more lessons than rejections. My collegiate production experience, coupled with those first positions of employment, provided me a foundation for *producing* for television. But no one had ever mentioned how to *sell* what you produce. Particularly, the role of *advertising* vis a vis *programming*. This pilot (#2) went nowhere and would be another experience to be filed away, to await the next sortie.

Can't say why, but I kept up on technical developments in videotape and associated equipment. Ampex was developing one inch videotape; transistor powered hand-held cameras were in the early stages; home videocassette players/recorders were a reality; and simple, lightweight lighting equipment was coming on the market. Contemporary TV production equipment was very bulky, and often pricey. Seemed to me, if the Hollywood trade papers provided an accurate picture, the studios and Hollywood production community weren't paying attention to technical upgrades and revolutionary changes that would soon be available.

I got the idea of setting up a videotape studio and equipment rental service using this new wave type state-of-the-art equipment. A local attorney friend had a wealthy widow client who "wanted to get into show business." We were a perfect match.

Videotape Productions Studio debuted at 9229 Sunset Blvd., in West Hollywood, a toney address for a production facility. But a brokerage firm had departed the large hunk of prime office space in the middle of the night eight months earlier and the landlord evidently figured some rent was better than none. We did a good PR job and all sorts of industry types stopped by to touch and feel the new lightweight and mobile equipment. We even did a little cash business, too. But the attorney and my financial benefactor had a relationship which was a bit more than client and counselor. When she was upset with him she got even by withholding, among other things, checks for my studio business.

Coincidentally, Bob Hope's manager's office was harbored in the 9229 building. Elliott Kozak, the Hope rep and friend who set in motion my first *Celebrity Bowling* pilot, often stopped in to schmooze. As I was lamenting my investor dilemma, he had an idea. I should close the studio and get into entertainment publicity. Be a press agent. Without giving it a second thought I said, "Call me when you find someone who'll hire me."

He did. Within an hour he phoned to give me two appointments for interviews on the following morning. Next a.m., I met both prospective employers. By 11 a.m. I was working at Gene Shefrin Associates, assigned, among other clients, Don Adams, star of CBS's *Get Smart*, comedian Don Rickles, and recording star Matt Monro. At the time, I was most impressed with Monro.

I was with Shefrin for two years, during which time Eunice Shriver's office contacted me. The Kennedy family's *Joseph P. Kennedy, Jr. Foundation* was a major player in the mental health field -- Eunice had a retarded sister -- and wanted to know if I knew any-thing about organizing a TV celebrity golf tournament. At the time, seemingly every celebrity had his or her own TV golf tournament, or at least the celebrity-pro-am portion of a PGA or LPGA event. Mrs. Shriver and her staff didn't have an event for me to run. They were asking if I could create one. "Of course!" I told her.

Well, I didn't play golf and the sport never interested me. So I asked my friend Elliott about staging a Bob Hope golf tournament benefiting the 'Kennedy Foundation.' He replied that the last thing Hope needed was another golf tournament, particularly another char-ity golf tournament. You're a bowling guy, he reminded. Half in jest (perhaps more than half), he suggested I put on a bowling tournament for the '*Kennedy Foundation.*'

It was a case of "golf/shmolf." The Shriver office thought a televised bowling event was just fine, as long as they could transmit the theme and message of the *Joseph P. Kennedy, Jr. Foundation* to a national TV audience.

Meanwhile, college friend and Chicago PR guy, Mert Silbar, representing the *Bowling Proprietors Association of America*, phoned to ask if I had any ideas to promote the sport of bowling tying in with one or more of the celebrities I represented. Suddenly, all this bowling action. Was there karma in the air? I suggested Don Adams, and we developed the *Get Smart, Go Bowling* campaign. After that, *Even Odd Couples Bowl*, featuring Jack Klugman and Tony Randall, stars of the *Odd Couple* TV series, and *Eddie and His Father Bowl*, featuring the father-son costars of *The Courtship of Eddie's Father* TV series.

Employer Shefrin had been good enough to allow me to have several personal non-entertainment PR accounts. The principals of one of them, the Ira Roberts Galleries, had long been suggesting that I go out on my own. Set up my own shingle. I liked where I was but Bob Kohn and Ira Kaplan offered to fund my startup. How do you refuse an offer you can't refuse?

The '*Kennedy Foundation*' TV bowling event now took on new meaning. I'd be doing it on my own time. Truthfully, I didn't really think a celebrity driven bowling tournament had network potential. But I figured Metromedia, probably the country's leading independent station group, was the place to make a first try. I knew Bob Rhodes, one of the sportscasters there, and in time, was directed to Metromedia's programming boss man, Dick Woollen. He was someone I had met when he was at Desilu during my first round of *Celebrity Bowling* pitches, and was the guy from whom I now needed approval. I pitched *The Celebrity Bowling Classic* -- "just like a golf tournament, only with bowlers." He bought it for his five stations.

The '*Classic*' featured 32 celebrities and was quite an event. With a little more foresight, the '*Kennedy Foundation*' and I might have staged a fundraiser to go along with the TV taping, nonetheless, the team of Don Adams and Arte Johnson won the '*Classic*' and captured "The Hollywood Bowl," a sterling silver trophy presented by a starlet. Someone named Raquel Welch had been recommended as the starlet presenter, but when I called her she told me that, seeing as she was the "billboard girl" on ABC-TV's *Hollywood Palace* variety hour, she feared being typecast. The '*Classic*' wasn't the slickest production ever aired, but the Kennedy's were happy. (Not long after, the '*Kennedy Foundation*' asked me to get involved with Eunice Shriver's newest charitable focus, a sportsfest for retarded children, later named *The Special Olympics*.)

Diane Ginsburg watched the *Celebrity Bowling Classic* on L.A.'s Channel 11. Diane, a capable, loyal and whiney lady, was one of the secretaries at the Shefrin Agency, and the TV special provided a nudge for her to call and ask if I needed a secretary. Soon after she joined me, she mentioned that her brother, Don Gregory, Vice-President of the *Agency For The Performing Arts* (APA), had seen the '*Classic*' and thought it was a great idea for a TV series. I "took" a meeting with Don, using the opportunity to tell him about my "better" idea for a *Celebrity Bowling* series. He said he could sell it. A few weeks later, Gregory left APA to set up his own management firm, partnering with one of his clients, entertainer Bobby Darin. Gregory could no longer be my agent. Now he wanted to be my partner.

A little wiser (though not necessarily smarter) from past experience, I told Gregory that shooting a pilot was a waste of time. A pilot can generate interest but no one seems willing to take the leap into producing a bowling series. I insisted we needed to shoot the entire series in advance. With 13 episodes in hand, we couldn't miss getting it on the air. In fact, I said, if we had 26 episodes in the can, we would be a lock to get on the air. My budget for 26 shows was $52,000.

Don Gregory knew little about production. His was the business side. He wanted to know how you can produce anything on TV for $52,000, let alone 26 episodes. Well, I had this production concept dating back to my job at Polk Bros. On paper it was a "can't miss."

Back when I was working at Polk Bros., we sponsored *Dangerous Assignment,* a filmed action series that was station WNBQ's final programming of its broadcast day. But even after the station signed off, many of the station's staff were required to hang around for another two or three hours because their union contract defined a "shift" as being, variously, 8, 10 or 12 hours. They had to stay until their shift was completed, even if the station was off the air.

What a waste of potentially useful time I thought. I figured if I could install two bowling lanes in a television studio so I could control the venue, hire a crew and staff on ten or twelve hour days, with guerilla scheduling I could shoot six or seven half-hour shows a day. Where does it say, I asked, that when you hire staff and facilities for a day, you're limited to shooting just one show? It was the common practice, but why?

As the publicist for *Hollywood Squares* and all the Heatter-Quigley Productions' game shows, I saw how producers Merril Heatter and Bob Quigley comfortably shot five episodes of '*Squares*' on a single day. I thought we could tape even more episodes with better time management. Yeah, it might be tough on some members of the crew. But as an observant publicist of all sorts of video and film shoots, I was convinced that overwork was not a common condition for most production staffers. Also, editing would be nothing more than a financial blip, inasmuch as two-inch videotape editing at the

97

time was primitive. To edit meant physically cutting the tape. I felt we could shoot everything to time, and thus have to edit only in an emergency.

The *Bowling Proprietors Association* had blended into what now was called the *National Bowling Council.* I was invited to make a pitch for their public relations account in collaboration with Mert Silbar, the friend-PR guy who introduced me to organized bowling during the *Get Smart, Go Bowling* promotional program. My portion of the presentation was the Hollywood side -- getting bowling seen often and positively in motion pictures and TV. My presentation included a $26,000 expenditure for a *Celebrity Bowling* TV series.

The *American Bowling Congress* (men's bowling) representative was against it, saying the idea was "another one of those television game show lotteries." The *Women's International Bowling Congress* rep pictured all sorts of flaky actors and suggestive language, and "who knows what." But AMF's Al Spanjer countered with, "If I have to, I'll go around the country with a projector and screen the shows on the sides of buildings!" Brunswick's Hal Meyers added, "And I'll carry the projector!" I got the PR assignment and the $26,000. I also got commitments from both AMF and Brunswick to provide all the necessary bowling equipment for the TV series, including the studio bowling lanes.

With all kinds of spanking new production office space and non-stressed staff available, a newly refurbished Metromedia/ KTTV/Channel 11 welcomed my production with generous pricing and all sorts of perks. Best of all, they were slow to ask for money.

Gregory and I were comfortable being our own talent coordinators. Between our clients and friends, and maybe a few "favor" phone calls, we should be able to handle getting the guest star bowlers. But we needed an emcee, a show host. And we didn't have the bank account to approach any of the name brand game show hosts. However, one of my PR clients was John Barbour, then host-ing KABC-TV's *A.M. Show*. I asked John and he said yes, but KABC wouldn't allow it. Another client, Jed Allan, one of the stars of the *Lassie* series, was interested in broadening his career reach and offered to do it. Gregory and I were mutually skeptical about an actor's ability to be a game show host. But Jed felt he could easily handle the task and, more importantly, was willing to go along with us regarding compensation.

I hated Jed's approach to hosting, but Don Gregory and most others thought he did a good job. Jed would go on to host all 144 episodes. He was different than the Bill Cullens, Monty Halls, and other staples of game show hosting. My distributor, many buyers and viewers told me that his "difference" added to the attraction of the series.

Episodes of *Celebrity Bowling* called for four celebrities com-peting in teams of two each. That first season we decided we would book at least two celebrities for each show, and if they had friends they wished to have as teammates, famous or not, that would be fine with us. We had no idea that our rapid fire shooting schedule would be incomprehensible to the celebrities, to the point that they hung out in our lively greenroom for hours after their booked appearance. Their day's work, 30 minutes of bowling, came and went in 30 min-utes. Many of them wanted more. And we found that we were able to accommodate them.

Our production plan called for two days for bowling lanes installation; then one day of rehearsal/run-through, during which time we'd tape two episodes (we'd only use them if they were okay); and four days of production to turn out a total of 26 shows. That's how I had it on paper. However, we shot six shows on run-through day by having the time available and the celebrities hanging out, ready for more. We simply mixed and matched the players, changing the combinations from episode to episode. We were then able to squeeze in ten episodes on each of the next two days, making the maximum use of our time and guest stars. What a rush!

Among the unusual amenities we provided to guest talent was a bowling pro-shop. It included a huge selection of AMF and Brunswick bowling shoes, fitted by a bowling pro to size, and a professional ball-driller, so every celebrity could appear with his or her personally fitted and initialed bowling ball (and a carrying bag). The celebrities got to keep this equipment.

My wife and my partner's wife greeted each celebrity upon arrival, ushered them to be fitted for shoes and a ball, had them sign AFTRA (*American Federation of Television and Radio Artists*) contracts, and brought them to a *green room* like few others. The food was nonstop hot and cold deli, a fully stocked bar (including a large English pub bar set-piece that KTTV had in storage), and a couple of fine-tuned loose-looking ladies imported for the occasion by my partner. Which might account for so many celebs sticking around.

We gave our guest talent the payment option of AFTRA scale, about $165, or a selection of appliances and TVs. Format of the shows called for episode winners (members of the studio audience) to win a prize commensurate with that episode's winning score. Prizes ranged from a steam iron for a very low score to an automobile for a very high score. Of the eight prizes offered, there would always be seven un-won prizes. We owned those prizes in return for on-air promotion. We offered a choice of these prizes, generally appliances and color TVs, as compensation. To get the TVs (not one of our show prizes) we made arrangements with a local retailer to trade some of our plugged-but-not-used items, such as refrigerators, washers, dryers, et als, for color TVs. Not one celebrity took the cash. Looking back, I'd have to say that this system of payment was homage to my first employer, Sol Polk. AFTRA didn't like it. But there was no rule against it.

AMF built and installed the show's original pair of lanes and automatic pinsetters in Metromedia's Studio 4. The huge bowling set-piece had to be built two feet off the studio floor to accommodate an under-the-lanes ball return. After 13 episodes, AMF's crew broke down their equipment, logo's, facades, automatic ball return, et als -- and Brunswick's skilled workmen jumped in and installed their company's specialized equipment. We were, frankly, in awe of the process, and the change-over didn't cost us a production second. Mr. Polk would have been proud of the financial arrangement with Brunswick and AMF, in which the pair of manufacturers absorbed all of the equipment and related labor costs. This co-op process continued through the life of the series.

I'll spare you the entire first season guest list, but the very first episode pitted Oscar winner Ernest Borgnine and recording star Bobby Darin and their friend partners. Borgnine was a publicity client of mine and Darin was Don Gregory's client-partner. Other first season guests were Sid Caesar, Peter Lawford, Bob Newhart, Dick Martin, a very young Michelle Lee and then-husband James Farentino, Caesar Romero and Hugh O'Brian.

We shot 26 episodes in three days, plus two days of setup. I wrote a press release about the shoot and it appeared in *Daily Variety* the following day. It helped to be a producer-publicist. A couple of days later I received a phone call from Art Pickens, the midwest TV distributor of the seminal tenpin bowling series, *All Star Bowling*. The '*Variety*' story hadn't mentioned a distributor and, if there wasn't one, he was interested. I sent him a copy of one of the shows. He phoned after viewing it and said if we were okay with a *barter-type* sale, we had a distribution deal. Neither Gregory nor I knew exactly what *barter syndication* was, but we went into business with Mr. Pickens anyway.

Remarkably, I never used up all of the $26,000 seed money provided by the *National Bowling Council.*

KTTV's crew proved old dogs can learn new tricks, although they probably needed a month of R&R following our kamikaze schedule. Nonetheless, most of them were with me for all of the 144 episodes we shot over six years. KTTV's Dodgers baseball director, Bob Heistand, handled the first year's shoot. He was replaced by the venerable Don Buccola, who not only directed all other episodes of *Celebrity Bowling*, but 72 half hours of our *Celebrity Tennis*, which is another long short story.

We did well with distributor Pickens, but he never said anything to us about a second season. When we asked, he was less enthusiastic than at any time in our short association. The series had pulled good ratings and he had brought in some sizable barter sales income. We didn't understand his lack of enthusiasm, but he said he was ready to distribute the next season of the series if we produced it.

Well, turns out Pickens thought *Celebrity Bowling* was such a good idea, he went out and produced his own celebrity bowling series for season #2, called *The Best of Bowling.* I found out about it by accident when one of my PR clients taped a guest appearance on Pickens' series, shot in the midwest. Client Don Grady, Fred MacMurray's oldest son on *My Three Sons,* had agreed to the appearance, thinking he was being booked by my talent coordinator. Although I hadn't said a word about it to him, he surmised I wanted to separate the two hats I wore -- me working for him as a publicist and him working for me on the show. He figured he'd see me on the set of *Celebrity Bowling.* When I wasn't there, he asked about me and was given some sort of vague story. After hearing from Grady, I phoned Pickens who told me he had indeed taken on the other bowling series, but it was nothing like *Celebrity Bowling.* No conflict, he said, and sent me a tape of it.

But there was a conflict. The two shows were practically identical. The format, the set, lighting, and out-of-the-ordinary audio setup were identical. If you weren't involved in the two productions you likely wouldn't know one from the other. To boot, on the credit crawl there was Pickens' name as producer, and his organization as the producing company.

Our L.A. lawyer got us a Chicago lawyer and we moved to stop Pickens. We met with the attorney in Chicago and he outlined a full-service legal attack. On the flight back to Los Angeles, Gregory and I were all pumped up. Having a drink in the Pan Am plane's lounge, we asked a stewardess (that's what they were called in those days) whether or not we should renew ourselves for a second season. She knew nothing about what we were asking and offered a giddy "of course." Figuring she knew as much about renewing production without a distributor as we did, we clinked glasses and renewed ourselves.

The Pickens problem quickly solved itself. Following just one letter from our lawyer, he agreed to cease offering his show to stations in place of ours, to not pursue advertisers who had previously bought time in *Celebrity Bowling*, and to pay us a lump sum for damages. We never heard from him again.

A New York company called CPM, with a close association to the Colgate Palmolive Company, became our second season distributor. Its partners, Len Koch, Shel Boden and Mickey Johnson, would later change their company name to Syndicast and represent us for the life of the series.

Don Gregory and I would continue as "hyphenates" during the 'Celebrity Bowling/Tennis' years -- Don, as a personal manager, and me as a publicist. But we were both making more money producing the series than we earned from our full-time work. Don became a theatrical producer and his first play, with co-producer, Mike Merrick, was *Clarence Darrow*, starring Henry Fonda. And it was a hit. When the show left Broadway and opened in L.A., our friend John Barbour, now an entertainment reporter for KNBC, Channel 4, opened his '*Darrow*' review with: "From the people who bring you *Celebrity Bowling* comes Henry Fonda as *Clarence Darrow*." Barbour liked to make jokes. But Gregory wasn't laughing. He said: "My future is in the theatre." So, we stopped producing the '*Celebrity*' shows.

After all, all we were doing was having fun working a handful of days and making a lot of money as a sidelight to what we really did!

*"The secret of being a successful independent distributer
is to be independently wealthy."*

...Art Greenfield

The Youngest Kid on the Block
by Steve Rodgers

Of the group of television industry veterans who gather for
lunch each Friday, I am probably the least qualified when it comes to
the nostalgia department, because I belong to a different generation.
Being 38 years old at this writing, I am still in the learning stages of
what *was* the business. But I had a father who was well known to all
the others at lunch, and now I am also an active participant in the syndication business, so they have accepted me as one of them, for which
I am grateful.

My father was Peter Rodgers who, for as long as I can remember, worked at a television distribution company called NTA
(National Telefilm Associates). He traveled constantly and also complained about the business every single day, no matter where he was.

As a boy, I recall spending lots of Saturdays and Sundays at the
NTA offices. My dad would set me up in the screening room to watch

old Roy Rogers movies, or Sci-Fi titles, most of which were pretty boring, including such "cheapie" dreadfuls as *Kronos* and *The Beast Of Yucca Flats*. When I got tired of those I would go into the film warehouse where thousands of film reels were stored in tall metal racks, and where I could ride around on the film dollies.

I was too young to realize that my dad was a workaholic and loved to work weekends. One of the people my dad worked with was Marv Gray, who may be mentioned in other pages in this book. I used to play in his office. Later Marv was a supportive part of helping me learn this business and was someone I could call upon and trust if I had a question about syndication. Ken Harris, who was managing the warehouse I played in as a kid, later owned his own business which he called Imperial Film Services, and which even today houses all of my film elements. (The place is now called Bonded Film and Ken has long since retired.)

In 1974, my dad left NTA and decided to go on his own, and in 1976 formed The Peter Rodgers Organization (PRO).

I'm not sure exactly when my dad and Art Greenfield met each other, but from what I understand it was back in 1974 when NTA bought the company that Art worked for, an entity called "M & A Alexander." At the time, I lived in Northern California with my mother, she and my dad having been divorced in the late 1960's. I've always suspected that my dad's heavy travel schedule was at least partially responsible for the breakup, because I'm sure he deemed constant travel an essential part of his duties, and maybe in those days it was.

It was only about two weeks after I had moved back to Los Angeles when I first met Art Greenfield. My dad asked me if I would like to earn $25 for installing some shelves in the office of an associate of his...Art. By then I had long since outgrown the film dollies as a source of entertainment and was enjoying the role of being a wild teenager, so a visit to dad's office held no particular charm. But the proffer of $25 was very attractive. When I arrived at the office I encountered a grossly overweight man who was on the phone, laughing and telling jokes. He was a 180 degree opposite of my father's totally serious disposition and I could hardly believe that two such different personalities could become associates. And I noticed that instead of a library of films including such recognizable stars as Roy Rogers, the film titles in the inventory included items such as *The Corpse Grinders, Touch of Satan, Blood Orgy of the She Devils,* and *The Incredibly Strange Creatures Who Stopped Living and Became Mixed Up Zombies.*

"Who watches this crap?" I asked myself. I had certainly never heard of any of these titles in my life and couldn't imagine anyone making a living off of selling these films!

Art did the acquiring and the schmoozing with people and my dad did the selling. The two of them and a secretary, plus a salesman named Jules Gerlig, were jammed into a 300 square foot office. I didn't understand how they made a living. But I do know my dad worked every day, every weekend and every holiday, selling those films. He was even mugged one night leaving the office at 8 p.m. on a Christmas Eve.

As I grew into youthful manhood, I would be drafted by my dad, usually in January, to help him prepare for a convention he always attended called NATPE. This was an annual program market attended by television station executives from all around the country and also by every salesman who had programming he hoped to sell to them. So it was a big deal for my dad and required that flyers be made, cassettes inventoried and posters packed for the trip to Las Vegas or San Francisco, whichever the site might be that year.

I would join him in the cavernous halls where the event was staged, and was fascinated to get an inside look at the process which at least partially determined what it was that the whole country would be watching on their TV sets during the upcoming season. I was totally fascinated by the huge scale of it all, and the sensationalism of some of the participants. The place crackled with energy from opening to closing, and I decided then and there that this was where I wanted to be. This, despite my father's frequent warnings: "Stephen, don't ever get into this business!" But I was hooked.

In the mid 1980's, things at the office changed for the better. My dad and Art started acquiring shows that I had actually heard of. Gone were the days of being embarrassed by the programs my dad sold to TV. Oh sure, he still had the "B" movies, but he also handled series like *Flipper* and *Gentle Ben*. Plus a series which was the most desirable of all, *I Spy*, which starred Bill Cosby and Robert Culp. As I visited the office more, I not only became even closer to my dad, but also began to better understand the relationship between him and Art. Though different as night and day, it was that difference that helped them function so well as a team. Laurel and Hardy, or...if you prefer a more contemporary reference...Penn and Teller.

To my great sorrow, Peter S. Rodgers died of a cerebral hemorrhage on Sunday, February 21, 1988, at the age of 67. It was the first funeral I had ever attended, and I was impressed by the number of top executives in the entertainment industry who were present for the ceremony.

On Monday, April 4, 1988, my role in this business and my effort to continue my father's legacy began. I was then 24 years old.

Up until this time I had worked as a heating and air conditioning installer in the San Fernando Valley. I had been dealing with plumbers and electricians, not program executives and General Managers of television stations. One group was not necessarily smarter than the other, but they certainly spoke in different languages. Early in my transition from one job to the other, I would end my day of construction work about 3 p.m. and head over to my dad's office and help sort out matters for the attorneys handling the estate. Both my father and Art kept a lot of things only in their heads...they did not have a computer. But Art was tireless in his efforts to educate me, advising me of procedure and explaining the mechanics of the business. He also told me who in the business I could trust (a short list) and who I should stay away from.

Previously, I had been just a viewer of TV, unaware of how the crap that my friends and I were watching on TV actually got there. I discovered that it really didn't matter *what* viewers wanted to see, it was all about *economics*. Even today, station and cable programmers are airing shows that they have to take for money reasons, not necessarily what they want to take. And of course, the whole world of TV revolves around the 5,000 or so "Neilsen homes." Ratings. Advertising. Those are the things which matter most to programmers. Not content.

The challenge of being an independent film salesman was not easy. As Art often would say, "Forget everything you've heard about getting up early, working hard or being conscientious, the most important thing in life is to be lucky. And if you're not, then marry someone who is!" Sometimes, just being around Art made me feel lucky.

After a few months of working together, one day Art invited me to join him for lunch with a group he called *The Dinosaur Club*. About a dozen or so of the group I mentioned earlier would meet every Friday at various restaurants and talk about past and future business and frequently relate wonderful stories of their past experiences. Listening to them, I often wished I had been active in their day.

But I also had my share of memorable experiences involving Art. I still find it hard to keep back the laughter when I think about the time when Art and I were returning from a luncheon. In those days Art would usually leave the office right after lunch, so as we returned to our office parking lot I asked him if he would be going straight to his home, which I knew to be only about 7 minutes away. But Art, who usually drank at least five or more glasses of iced tea at lunch, said, "No, I'm coming up with you. I'm afraid I won't be able to make it home to the bathroom." So we got out of the car and headed to our building's sole elevator.

Of course the indicator showed the car to be at the top floor, so we waited patiently for it to descend to the lobby. When we got on we were joined by three women whom we did not know, and each of us selected our floor of choice. The doors closed and the car started to go up, but in a few seconds it came to an abrupt stop. It took a moment for us to realize that we were stuck. In disbelief, Art reached around and proceeded to push every button on the panel, to no avail.

So we used the emergency telephone and some distant voice told us to remain calm, assured us that we wouldn't run out of air, and comforted us with the proclamation that a technician would come to rescue us in about fifteen to twenty minutes.

I looked at Art who looked at me and with his knees slightly together, squatted somewhat and motioned, with his hands crossed over his bladder area, to the effect that running out of air was not really his primary concern. Minutes went by with no sign of a technician. To pass the time, the three women who had accompanied us on the elevator were discussing a new maternity shop which had opened across the street. One woman was compelled to tell the others about the wonderful products they carried. She then took out of her shopping bag a multi-compartmented diaper bag she had purchased which had the feature of being waterproof in case of spillage. At hearing this, the now desperate Art piped in, "How much do you want for the bag?" When the technician finally arrived about 30 minutes later, it was all we could do to stay out of Art's way once the doors were opened.

As I became more and more involved in the syndication business, I frequently recalled and appreciated the wry wit of another of Art's statements, which was: "The secret of being a successful independent distributor is to be independently wealthy." Fortunately, that's not literally a requirement, but the activity does have its demands and its hazards. First you have to make your customer, the broadcaster, happy with the deal you're offering. Then you have to please the owner of the product you are representing about the terms of the deal you have put together on his behalf. And when they are both happy, you have to hope there's a little happiness left over for yourself. In the interim, you hope that neither side louses something up to the point where the deal falls through. Sometimes negotiating a deal can be like breaking up a fight between spouses or friends. That is, both of them can turn on you, leaving you to look like the enemy.

For example, a few months ago I received a phone call from a program executive with whom I had made a number of program sales deals when she was at BET (Black Entertainment Television). She told me she had left BET and now moved on to join Quincy Jones' new network, NUE TV (New Urban Entertainment). We chatted for some time and I listened to her programming concerns and wishes for this new network. After some time, I had secured her interest in a number of programs from my library which I felt would be attractive properties.

One of these was the first series to bear the title of *The Bill Cosby Show*. Not the series which aired under that name and ran on CBS in the mid 1980's. Ours had originally aired on NBC in the early 1970's and Bill Cosby had retained ownership of every episode for many years, and my company owned the distribution rights.

I happened to know that Bill Cosby and Quincy Jones were

111

good friends so I was perplexed by this situation. If I owned a television network which needed programming and my buddy owned a show that had been sitting around on the shelf for over a decade, I would just ask him if I could use his show on my new network. Why didn't Quincy just pick up the phone and call Bill? What did they need me for?

Now I learned where the term "have your people call my people" came from. Suddenly I was one of "Mr. Cosby's people." NUE-TV, which was planning to launch in January of 2000, sent my office a letter of intent which offered a license fee of around half a million dollars. And when I advised Cosby's agent of this offer he instructed me to close the deal. So I sent contracts to the network and they executed them and returned my copies.

The time approached when we should commence physical delivery of the tapes to the network and only then did I discover that we would need to begin transferring the tapes from their current 1" format to the Digi-Beta format which had become the new industry standard. To my horror, I found that none of the episodes had been prepared and that the necessary materials were scattered at various locations on the East Coast. Nothing had ever been done to prepare them for delivery.

Fearful of being in breach of our contract with the network, I pleaded with Cosby's agent to speed up the process of locating all the needed elements. This chore was apparently delegated to Mrs. Cosby who, because of her stature, wasn't concerned about this deadline. After all, out of the license fee of $500,000, after deducting my 35% commission, the Cosby's would net about $325,000, which, in their world, would probably be the equivalent of $100 to you and me. But then, after payment of the various lab fees out of their share, it was clear I would be the only winner in this deal.

But nobody would win as long as Mrs. Cosby took no action. It was exasperating.

I was secure in my contractual rights to offer the series for licensing for broadcast, and was very aware of my contractual obligation to deliver the shows to NUE-TV. So I sought relief from the only arena available to me. I commenced legal proceedings against the Cosby's, well aware that I was '*David*' going up against a '*Goliath*' who was reputed to be the wealthiest man in television. It was kinda scary. It was the first time I had ever been forced to resort to using the legal system to enforce my rights, and I would have much preferred a much lighter contender.

Two months later, my attorney reached a settlement with their representative. The Cosby's were very unhappy, but they had given in and commenced delivery of the tapes.

Ironically, later that same month NUE-TV filed for bankruptcy. They never paid me or the Cosby's a dime. I was informed that Mr. and Mrs. Cosby were mad at me, even though it wasn't my fault. I wonder if Bill and Camille were mad at their good friend, Quincy, too.

I was learning that it's not uncommon in this business to spend a lot of time on something for nothing.

However, there are also occasions where you *can* get something for near nothing. Like the time I got a phone call from The History Channel inquiring on several *public domain* films listed in our catalog. (Public domain films are those on which the copyright has expired.) They were interested in titles like *Aerial Gunner*, a 1943 pic with Richard Arlen, *Against The Wind*, a 1948 film with Robert Beatty, *The General*, with Buster Keaton, and a few other World War II titles. Typically, we don't have masters on all 750 titles in our library, so sometimes I have to source these titles from collectors, PD houses or rental outlets. Anyway, when the conversation turned to price and the executive asked me to quote them a cost per title for these films, I told him that I'd have to get back to him the following morning. You see, I had not ever previously done business with The History Channel and wasn't quite sure what to quote them. I knew my cost to purchase materials from the sources mentioned above might run between $400 to $500 each, and that from other cable channels I was able to turn them around for as much as $2,000 to $5,000 per title. But what should I charge them?

I decided to let them come to me with an offer. I expected to haggle a $5,000 price per title. Imagine my surprise and delight when they came back with a $20,000 per picture proposal! Sometimes silence can be a powerful negotiating tool. And, as Art would often say, "Our business is like sex. Even when it's lousy, it's still pretty damn good!"

The Friday luncheons for me became a history lesson, where I could listen to the often humorous recollections of a very talented, experienced and respected group of men from all aspects of the industry: programmers, producers and syndicators. I began to realize that TV, compared with a media entity such as newspapers, was really an infant industry, and that many of the players bounced from one side of the industry to the other. Or, if they stayed in one category of work, then they changed from one company to another with surprising frequency. I also learned that it's a relatively small industry, with most of the veterans knowing everyone whose name might be mentioned during the conversations.

I regret to say that I feel the climate of our industry has changed since the days of TV's growing years. Gone are the days when a single program executive could make a decision instead of being required to first assemble a committee to ponder the deal. And severely diminished, if not gone, are the comradeships between competing syndicators, of afterwork sessions of drinks and/or dinner and the swapping of news and gossip.

Today, getting a time period for a TV program on a station or cable system is like the bitter battle for shelf space among the suppliers of grocery stores. A distributor must do or give whatever it takes to obtain one of those precious slots.

But lest I sound too negative about the way things are today, I must admit I have been blessed. I've been involved in producing for major cable networks, I have a syndicated show running in 80% of the U.S.A., plus another series on PBS, and am becoming increasingly active in the expanding market of DVD. And learning every day.

Fridays With Art

"50% of something is better than 100% of nothing."
...Art Greenfield

Full of Tvog
by Jack O'Mara

It wasn't just the Cobb Salads and the grapefruit cake that made Bob Cobb's Vine Street *Brown Derby* the entertainment industry's most popular restaurant in Hollywood. It was many things. The interior walls were decorated with 1100* caricatures of celebrities, all identically sized and framed. A summoned waiter could bring a portable telephone to any table and plug it into a plug located between booths. In those years before cell phones, the voice of the '*Derby's*' telephone operator was heard over the P.A. system as

---

Actually there were 1104, and I know that because one time I got Bob Cobb's permission to cover each of them with an image of Bing Crosby for one day to promote the switch of Bing's radio show from NBC to ABC where I was then working.

frequently as 10 or 12 times each lunch hour, advising one and all that there was a phone call for this or that individual. I think film composer Dimitri Tiompkin held the daily record, sometimes managing to get his name blared out three or four times a day, and there were suspicions his secretary was his only caller, and that he had ordered her to do this just for the publicity.

But the only time in my life I was ever paged at the Derby was a few months after I started working for Dick Moore, the Vice President and General Manager of KTTV, Channel 11 in Los Angeles. I was embarrassed at the attention called by the paging, but I quickly ascertained that Moore was steaming.

He was calling from New York where part of his mission had been to meet with high level ad agency guys to gain attention for and to establish a more favorable attitude toward KTTV when buying spot TV advertising time in L.A. As an independent channel in a seven station market, we were a different animal than these guys. The country was blanketed with three station markets, each affiliated with a network, and so when buying time in a seven station market, the ad agencies tended to play it safe and buy avails adjacent to the network shows with which they were all familiar.

When I started at KTTV in October of 1952, Dick had specified my title as "Director of Merchandising and Promotion." Merchandising was anything the station could do to build good relations with the retail trade, especially the food chains, to get them to give store displays, etc., to products advertised on KTTV. He talked vaguely about finding some way to use our open air time to favor those who favored us.

Now, on the phone, he was angry about a stinging rebuff he'd had from an agency V.P. and said, "I want to go ahead right away with that thing we talked about." "That thing" was the idea of doing a daily half-hour program from a supermarket, drawing a crowd to the market, etc., with the market giving us what we wanted. This could give us a plus with advertisers so that agencies would give us more favorable treatment.

Within hours, Program Director Bob Breckner and I huddled and came up with *Star Shoppers*, a Monday through Friday half-hour. It was an audience participation show with folks playing games that used our advertised products as props, like "how many cans of Hunts Tomato Sauce can you stack before the thing falls down?" As emcee, Bob named Bill Welsh, expert in special events who had an easy and engaging personality. I hired a Merchandising Manager, Jack Duffield, and he and I made a bunch of pioneering calls on chain ad managers. In a few weeks the first show was on the air from a Compton supermarket. The series ran for more than 1,400 broadcasts, and helped get national business. We made detailed reports of the "shelf talkers," "end displays" and other favors the stores did, and built relationships with the chains and the L.A. managers of the advertiser. The whole thing gave our sales guys and our reps a new dimension to talk about.

We used the story of this show as the focus of one of a series of one-column ads we placed in *The New York Times*, aimed at educating New York's ad agency personnel about KTTV and about why Los Angeles was totally different from the only other existing seven station market: New York.

One ad's headline read: *"Los Angeles is...well, it's...Okay, we'll say it..."*

CONTRARY

Can you imagine a flock of Jersey City housewives gamboling in an outdoor TV show in January? In Los Angeles, it happens. Five days weekly, for more than 2 years, KTTV's 'Star Shoppers' has been staged from supermarkets -- a different store

119

each day. The crowds (sometimes a thousand people) soon drove us outdoors to the spacious parking lots. In the past year, 'Star Shoppers' has been rained in only 3 times.

Many agencies would like to buy 'Star Shoppers,' and small wonder: it clobbers network opposition in its time period, gets an audience bigger than 233 programs now on L.A. television.

But it's not for sale. It's one of the merchandising plusses given free to KTTV food advertisers. Doing a high-rating show from a different supermarket daily, and giving rather than selling it to advertisers is only one of many different things about Los Angeles and KTTV.

The fellows who can best help you understand Los Angeles are at Blair TV. Call Jack Denninger, Otto Ohland, Bill Vernon or any of the crew at Murray Hill 2-5644. They represent us, and they're supermarket men.

Another such ad's headline read: *"Los Angeles is...well, it's...Okay, we'll say it:*

Full of Tvog

And what's Tvog? You didn't know? It's the strange invisible mist which surrounds the Los Angeles television viewer, and causes advertisers to wonder why L.A. TV is so different from New York's.

When Tvog is present (which is often), its effect makes the L.A. viewer choose his own local programs in preference to national TV fare. For instance, there's a fellow here in New York (sort of a king in his way) who gets 15 ratings for a full hour every morning. But out in Los Angeles he gets a Tvog-bound 1.5. (That's one POINT five!)

Those same mornings, several local personalities are getting as much as six times that rating on KTTV.

That's Tvog at work.

Does Los Angeles Tvog cause you headaches? Then take the

local cure. Use KTTV, the station with the amazing knack for reaching and selling Los Angeles. Call Jack Denninger, Ralph Allrud, Frank Martin or any of the Blair TV crew. (Murray Hill 2-5644) They represent us cogently.

Yes, Los Angeles is different from any other market..and the difference is KTTV."

Dick Moore was a perfect boss, best I ever had. He was a big, affable, redheaded Irishman, a graduate of Yale Law School and straight-arrow as they come. He entered TV by being with the New York law firm that represented ABC, then later joined that network as a staff attorney. It wasn't long before ABC transferred him to Los Angeles to run KABC-TV, Channel 7, and he did such a good job with that station that he attracted the attention of the *Los Angeles Times*, which owned KTTV, Channel 11. The '*Times*' people were experts in newspapers, but neophytes in TV. They had previously accepted an operating agreement with CBS whereby the latter ran the station and the '*Times*' looked on, and (hopefully) would rake in the money. This jerrybuilt arrangement collapsed when CBS bought W6XAO, a pre-broadcast experimental station, from the Don Lee Broadcasting system, then were granted their own license, and named the channel KNXT, later KCBS. Understandably, they moved all their CBS programming to their new Channel 2, which left the '*Times*' bereft of any TV knowledge, but in charge of programming and everything else. So they offered Moore the job of running KTTV and he soon began to bring the station from nowhere to somewhere. He had a razor-sharp mind and a colossal memory, but at times, for his own purposes he affected a somewhat bumbling role, as when sparring with film salesmen or fencing on the phone with Hugh Hefner while explaining to him why he would not air *Playboy's Penthouse* on the channel owned by the ultraconservative '*Times*'.

The only time I saw him flustered involved the previously mentioned *Star Shoppers*. Moore, Breckner, GSM John Vrba and I were lunching at *Lucey's* when Dick got a call from his secretary, saying the Ad Director of Brown and Williamson Tobacco (*Raleigh* and *Kool* cigarettes) and B&W's local agency head, had stopped by unexpectedly so that their Ad Director, whose name eludes me, could visit a bit.

Dick told his secretary to seat them in his office and to turn on the TV because *Star Shoppers* was coming on and the guy would get a taste of the plusses he was getting by advertising on KTTV, and that we'd be back as quickly as possible.

I jumped on the phone to KTTV engineering and they patched me through to Ernie Collings, producer of *Star Shoppers*, in the remote truck at show site. I explained, and asked him to be sure some of the games would involve B&W products. We wolfed down our meals and raced back to the station.

We walked into Dick's office as the show was ending, and after the introductions and apologies for the delay, Dick said he hoped they had enjoyed *Star Shoppers*. The Ad Director, who was a pompous little ass, replied in a rich Southern accent dripping with sarcasm, "Very nice, Mr. Moore -- but we're advertising *Kools* on your station, not *Raleighs*." I realized that Ernie Collings was working from information a couple of weeks old, at which time *Raleighs* were on our schedule. They switched brands from time to time.

For one of the few times in his life, Moore was truly flustered. In his confusion, he fished around in his coat pocket and pulled out a pack, offering the Ad Director a smoke.

They were *Parliaments* -- a Phillip Morris product.

It wasn't one of our better days.

When I started at KTTV, my wife Peggy and I were living in the

L.A. suburb of Whittier. We had moved there in 1947 to raise our kids in a small town environment. It was a lousy 22 mile commute over surface streets -- no freeways then -- and took nearly an hour. There was some relief when a smidgen of the Santa Ana Freeway was opened, linking up with the Hollywood Freeway, but it soon was jammed and I found I could drive it in -- nearly an hour!

So I was just getting home after seven one night when Peggy said to call Dick Moore at his home right away. He then told me he'd just had a gloomy call from Johnny Vrba who was in Chicago, telling him the Leo Burnett agency had just decided to put the new syndicated '*Superman*' series, for its client, Kellogg, on KABC-TV, Channel 7.

To us it was stunning -- and ludicrous. We were offering them 7 p.m. Tuesdays. Channel 7 was offering them 8:30 p.m. Mondays -- one of those few time periods in early television where a network had an open half-hour they could dole out to stations for local sale. Its lead-in was the new *George Jessel Show*, which we all felt would bomb.

Johnny and Harry Smart, Blair TV's Chicago manager, had exacted a promise from Burnett that they would hold off until morning to give us one last shot. Now, the question was, what could we shoot with?

Dick and Johnny had hatched the idea of a telephone survey of parents to verify when their kids went to bed. '*Superman*' obviously would be a big hit with kids. So wasn't 8:30 p.m. too late for a lot of them? Dick had tried in vain to reach Roger Cooper, manager of the ARB-Teleque rating service, to make the survey -- it was after business hours and ARB was closed. We all knew Roger lived in East Whittier, and Dick requested that I go to his home and get the survey under way. Roger's house was dark, and neighbors (a little suspicious) told me the Coopers were vacationing. On the way back home an idea came to me. We could use the phone-answering services, which took calls to the station responding to on-air offers, to do an on-the-air appeal to parents, asking them to call and let us know what ages their kids were and what was bedtime for them.

Dick said okay and we teamed up. He called George Putnam, our 10 p.m. newscaster and also Jackson Wheeler, who hosted a movie after the news. He explained the pitch to them. I called our wonderful Sales Service Manager, Val Conte, to get spots cleared out for these messages and to arrange with the phone answerers. And I wrote copy for the guys to use and dictated it on the phone to Lenny Blondheim, the producer of the news show, to transcribe for George with a copy for Wheeler. Then, finally, about 9:30 I ate my dinner.

The guys of course did the spots beautifully, especially Wheeler, who had a gift for this kind of thing. He expanded on my copy until the 60 seconds became more like 120, and pleaded that station management needed people's help in deciding how to schedule a new program with strong children appeal -- not naming the program -- and urged folks to phone this number right now and tell us the ages of their kids and when the kids went to bed. We stressed they should give only the info specified, and to make the calls as short as possible so as to open the lines for other callers. Then I got on the phone with the supervisor of the phone-answerers and worked out the routine of how the crews should organize the parents' answers by half hours and by childrens' ages. I left my phone number with her and sat to watch the rest of Putnam's news and Wheeler's movie.

By 2 a.m. I was able to call Western Union (remember them?) and dictate a long telegram to Vrba, based on about 200 phone calls, showing the bedtimes of kids by half-hours and by age groups (7-11 and 12 plus). I got to bed about 2:45.

So we got the business, right? WRONG!

Even though the survey results supported our offer as being better, the agency was still dazzled with being in *prime evening time* and picked Channel 7. But six months later, when 'Superman' was struggling and the Jessel show did its belly-flop, they moved to our 7 p.m. spot and we quickly got the show the 17 rating points it deserved.

Another evening phone summons from Dick Moore in early 1956 resulted in a more extensive odyssey than East Whittier and caused me to spend most of the first half of that year in Washington and New York.

When I returned Dick's call upon getting home, he said he wanted to talk about an important matter and could I drive over to his house? I swallowed hard -- La Canada was an hour's drive from Whittier. But I said yes, gulped dinner and got to his home around nine. We talked out on his chilly patio and I think my hands were blue by midnight. A notorious night person, he was blooming and so full of his subject he never even noticed the January night air.

The problem, as Dick articulated, was the scarcity of nighttime programming for KTTV. Much of our *prime time* programming flowed from syndicators, either shows of their own which they produced, or off-network reruns. Most of the shows were bought by stations and some by advertisers, such as Kellogg's *Adventures of Superman* and Standard Oil's *Sea Hunt*.

But only a handful of U.S. markets had more than three stations. The FCC had imposed a construction freeze around 1950, after 108 channels had been allocated, because of such uncertainties as to whether the future broadcast system would be VHF or UHF, etc. Each station in those three station markets had a network affiliation. A condition of the affiliation was the station's agreement to reserve its *prime evening time* for network shows. That time period was designated by the FCC as 7:30 to 10:30 p.m. Eastern, etc., and thus non-network shows were blocked from those high-audience hours.

So producers were shying away from producing shows for syn-

125

dication because in most markets they were relegated to weekend daytime or 10:30-ll:00 p.m. weeknight half-hours. Even the latter was no safe haven as networks began scheduling one-hour shows at 10 p.m., effectively increasing "network option time" to 3-1/2 hours a night. This shrinking supply of syndicated programs posed a real programming threat to KTTV.

Moore's legalistic mind identified network option time as a *collusive agreement* between the network and the affiliate which blocked non-network *prime time* shows from most of the country. Further, he thought the so-called "must-buy" arrangement, whereby a network advertiser was forced to buy a minimum of 50-60 specified markets, was a collusive agreement not only between each affiliate and the network, but also collusive between one affiliate with each of the others. For example, it could result in a case of a Detroit station, in effect, saying to a network advertiser, "If you want to buy my Detroit station, you also have to buy Houston," even though the advertiser's product might not even be distributed in Houston.

Dick had been talking this out with an old buddy, Lloyd Cutler of the Washington law firm of Wilmer, Cutler and Pickering (in later life, White House counsel in the Carter and Clinton administrations), and was intending to testify at a hearing of the Senate Interstate Commerce Committee regarding network policies and practices in spring, 1956. He wanted me to be his aide.

He finished, told me to think about it, and sometime around midnight I rubbed life into my numb fingers and drove home. Next morning, Peggy, ever the dutiful wife, said okay and I signed on.

The Senate hearing was scheduled for late March, so we headed for New York about a week ahead to commandeer an office at our rep firm, Blair TV, to write and polish his statement. Testimony ready, we trained to Washington and checked into a suite at the *Mayflower Hotel* where I quickly recognized that part of my assignment was get-

126

ting Dick out of bed in the mornings. As already hinted, he was very nocturnal. The bulbs glowed so bright late at night that it took almost a minor explosion to awaken him in the morning. And this morning it was crucial because the Senate hearings were gaveled to order at 9:30 a.m.

He was the first witness, and his testimony filled the entire morning. *Variety* might have termed his appearance "Boffo!" Lee Jahncke, ABC VP, whom we both knew from our ABC days, was the first afternoon witness. Shocked by Dick's testimony, he had gone to lunch, got slightly sloshed and scrapped his prepared statement and made an ill-prepared and sluggish rebuttal -- not one of his finer days.

The KTTV testimony was a bombshell; considerable interest from senators, and the lead story in *Broadcasting* and other industry trade papers. The networks retreated into their bunkers to prepare for the next round, a followup hearing in July, at which they would marshal various stations to assert their happiness with the option time arrangement, etc. I was back in Washington a few more times that spring, meeting with Lloyd Cutler's crew. One night I roamed Washington with Kenneth Cox, the newly-appointed Commerce Committee counsel (and later a member of the FCC), cluing him in on our view of the option time setup.

The networks had mobilized their affiliates for the July followup hearing. Moore and I checked into our hotel and beside us at the registration desk was a prominent midwestern station manager, pro-network. As the bell boys took us to the elevator, this manager recognized Dick, insulted him, cast doubt on his parentage, and generally made it clear he didn't want to be on the same planet, let alone in the same elevator, with Dick. Moore's red hair took charge as we exited and the elevator door closed behind the three of us. Our suite was on the 6th floor, and I was halfway down the hall before I realized I was alone. Dick had become verbally combative, challenged the guy and pursued him to his room, eventually experiencing a slammed door in his face.

The upshot of it all was option time was untouched, but the must-buy lists were eliminated by government order. A minor victory, perhaps, in view of all the excitement caused by Moore's testimony. Eventually KTTV's program requirements were fulfilled by a stronger flow of syndicated programs, a growing number of off-network reruns, and movies, including the 714 titles of the MGM library which Moore managed to snatch from under the nose of CBS.

Moore unknowingly created one new program for us. He was a speaker at a convention of the *American Association of Advertising Agencies* and he departed from his text to comment about a current agency development. The media department of a major agency had just adopted a policy against "triple spotting" -- placing three spots in a break. Any availability considered by them had to contain not more than two ads. Dick rebutted that the quality, not the number of spots, determined public acceptance. Good commercials, no matter how many, would be accepted like good programming was accepted.

In the bristling Q & A after his speech, he impulsively said he'd prove his point by presenting, on our station, a series of programs that would draw a respectable audience and that would consist of *all* commercials. Then he came back to us and said, "Okay, I said we'd do it -- now do it!"

Dick Woollen, then KTTV's Assistant Program Director, and I produced a half-hour of nothing but commercials called *Cavalcade of Spots*. It ran thirteen weeks at 6:30 p.m. Saturdays, was 2nd in its time period in our seven station market (behind only *Lawrence Welk*), drew nearly 4,000 letters, pulled 1800 entries in a one-time contest involving commercial recognition (for a $50 savings bond prize) and its audience was four-fifths college educated and triple the national average in upper income level. It also got coverage in *Time, Reader's*

Digest, *TV Guide*, *Variety* and the trade press as well as various U.S. newspapers, plus a lengthy piece in the Melbourne, Australia *Herald*!

We used, of course, only good spots that entertained as well as sold, including creative contest winners in this country as well as England, France, Japan, Canada, Mexico and Germany. The triple-spot tempest was quelled. That was 1959. Today a break with only 3 spots would be an oddity -- but sadly, agencies didn't get the message. They are still making spots that are loud, banal, fast, boorish and demeaning to TV.

If much of this sounds like a tribute to Dick Moore, so be it. He was a great boss, a great friend, a great judge of people, and he surrounded himself with a most competent and convivial group. We were good and each of us knew the other was also good, so there was minimal politics or backbiting. And we were all caught up in the kick of transforming a floundering enterprise into a viable, profitable business.

Dick was also a great party animal. And the bunch was so empathetic that we had many memorable parties at each other's homes and elsewhere. Two stand out.

The first: Four years after starting at KTTV, Peggy and I surrendered to the commute-monster and built a home in the Los Feliz hills, 10 minutes from KTTV. We were just getting settled when Dick and Jane Moore invited us to dinner at *Perino's*. He said we'd be joined by Don McGannon, President of the Westinghouse station group, and the talk would probably turn to Dick's Washington crusade -- and McGannon could be an important ally.

I was flattered to be included and we primped up pretty good. We met the Moores at the restaurant and Dick said McGannon had phoned regrets -- he was detained in San Francisco, but at least it would enable the four of us to have a good visit.

Which was true, and toward the end of the meal the talk turned to our new house. He said he and Jane were dying to see it, and since it was still pretty early -- with no McGannon discussions to prolong our dinner -- could they maybe follow us up the hill and have a look at the house?

I had designed the house and was bursting to show it off. So we led them up the hill and walked in the front door -- to the wildest, wackiest housewarming imaginable. The walls were straining with the KTTV crowd who had conspired with our teen daughter, Pat, to sneak in, being careful first to park their cars distant from the house, which was no mean feat in those hills. I realized the whole McGannon thing was a ruse and we had a ball. Many times since, I've thought of how casually and gently Dick had steered the conversation to the subject of the house.

The second: KTTV's farewell party to us -- turning a dismal evening into a riot of fun. I really felt punk about leaving KTTV. From such a great group I was going into a one-man office representing the Television Bureau of Advertising in 13 western states -- lots of travel, and mostly telephone friendships with our New York guys.

Why did I move? I felt dead-ended. As KTTV emerged from the red, Dick had started thinking expansion and proposed various station buys to our owners, the Chandlers, of the *Los Angeles Times*. Any such purchase would have opened management opportunities for several of us. The one I had the hots for was KFSD-TV, the NBC affiliate in San Diego.

But the conservatives at the '*Times*' were accustomed to big bucks from their newspaper, and choked on the asking prices for TV stations. So when San Diego followed the earlier proposals into the ashcan, I concluded the door was closed and started looking. (I was vindicated two years later when the '*Times*' sold KTTV.)

So my last day at the station was pretty gloomy. My department had an afternoon office party. When that wrapped up and I was finally alone, I wandered down memory lane across the sound stages and down to the newsroom for the last time.

By the time I got home I was really feeling sorry for myself and was wishing we hadn't accepted a dinner invitation from our friends and neighbors, Don and Kathy Arvold.

We crossed the street to their house for drinks, which stretched out interminably, full of aimless small talk. I was almost uncivil and anxious to get the damn dinner over with and wondered why Don didn't take us to the *Hollywood Athletic Club* as planned. Further, I was irritated that he frequently absented himself from the room.

Suddenly he came back into the room and said, almost brusquely: "Well, how about we go eat?" and hustled us out the door -- where stood a Greyhound-size bus full of reveling KTTV'rs in search of a party. They'd gotten lost for 45 minutes, which was why Don had disappeared so much...to look out the window in another room. I pity the bus driver who had to herd this monster through the narrow, winding hillside streets.

They'd zinged us again -- conspiring with the Arvolds and our daughter Pat (by now pretty good at this sort of thing). Dazed, we got on the bus and were transported to the *Fog Cutter Cafe* on LaBrea for one hell of a party. Three remembrances stand out.

1. A tribute from George Putnam that aired on his 10 o'clock news (it was a tough job quieting the crowd to watch the monitors set up in the room).

2. A hilarious tape of phone "interviews" of some of my former associates: Frank Tooke in Philadelphia; Rollo Hunter in New York; Bud Edwards in Fresno -- with the producer of the *Paul Coates' Confidential File* show, Herb Golden, posing as Personnel Director of my new employer, wanting their opinions about my char-

acter, etc. They ranged from very tepid endorsements to the outrageous, scurrilous and defamatory -- with Golden playing perfectly the role of the dismayed personnel man.

Then Paul Coates came on the tape, phoning my jazz idol Benny Goodman, wanting to check my supposed background playing piano in the Goodman band. Benny, who'd been clued in very little, was cautious and noncommittal, but Coates' expertise fashioned it into a daunting and funny "interview."

And lastly: At some point I noticed guys with music cases coming into the room. I looked closer and one of them was Ziggy Elman, the super trumpet man in the original Goodman band. They had hired him and four other legendary jazz players, such as clarinetist Matty Matlock and drummer Jack Sperling, to play for this party. And at one point I was dragged up to sit in with them at the piano.

So right up to the last, the KTTV party animals -- Dick Moore and his henchmen Reavis Winckler and Dick Woollen -- had added another event to their epic gatherings.

Is it any wonder I hated leaving such a bunch?

"I feel like the south end of a north bound horse."
...Art Greenfield

Still a Loodmouth After All These Years
by Dalton Danon

I was just finishing a round of ad agency calls and was returning to my office at radio station KHJ in Los Angeles when I encountered two men leaving the building, one of whom, Dick Feiner, I knew well. We stopped and chatted briefly, and Dick introduced me to Erwin Ezzes. Jokes were exchanged and personas exercised in the manner of salesmen worldwide and eternally. Later Feiner told me that Ezzes was the Executive V.P., Sales, of Motion Pictures For Television (MPTV), a major distributor of programs to TV stations, and that I should give Ezzes a call. Feiner explained that Ezzes had asked, "Who is that? He's the type of guy we need with us." Enticing, I thought. So I called him. He said I would soon hear from John Cole, V.P., Western U.S., with whom I shortly negotiated an exciting opportunity.

That was in 1953. Those were pioneer years for both broadcasters and people like me who were interested in selling programs to those new businesses called TV stations. My immediate supervisor in the Los Angeles office of MPTV was John Cole. To commence my syndication education he took me with him to first visit stations in San Francisco, then in Seattle. Cole was a tall, highly articulate charmer with natty clothes and a constant smile on his face which could (but only rarely) slide into a smirk if he didn't like the person he was talking to. I was fascinated with the completeness of his dazzling presentations. First he impressed the potential customers with every detail about what a major and successful company MPTV was and only after this elaborate buildup did he, with an almost conspiratorial air, reveal to the customer the identity of the product he was giving them an opportunity to acquire. It was called "The Station Starter Plan" and consisted primarily of movies, about 365 of them, plus a couple of theatrical Saturday afternoon serials such as *Flash Gordon* and *Buck Rogers*. Movies of any kind were a relatively rare availability in those days as major studios were fearful of theatre owners who were convinced TV would destroy them. Our fees were on the basis of so many dollars per hour, depending on the size of the market we were selling.

After I had dutifully witnessed and absorbed Cole's presentations in San Francisco and Seattle, John said it was almost time for me to start making the pitch on my own, but first we would go together to the tiny market of Great Falls, Montana. Then, after a few such visits, I could solo. At that time, Great Falls did not even have a TV station on the air. John called it a $150 rate card station, based upon what the station would charge for one hour of *prime time*.

So I was nervous as we boarded the old WW II C-54 aircraft late at night to go from Seattle to Great Falls. I wasn't nervous about flying. I had done plenty of that as a B-25 pilot in the Air Corps during World War II, where I flew combat missions in the Pacific

Theatre. But I was nervous about whether I could properly emulate Cole's expertise and vitality in constructing my pitch.

But I should have worried more about the flight. It seemed to take forever as we crossed over the high, wide mountain range of the Cascades. We were in the midst of one of the most violent thunderstorms I had ever encountered, and for over an hour were in severe turbulence as the four groaning propellers fought their way through an awesome display of nature's might. So Cole and I were both a little green around the gills as we finally made it to the Great Falls airport where we dashed through a downpour to grab a taxi. By the time we reached our hotel John had extracted from the driver a history of Great Falls, as well as a list of the best restaurants in town.

Next day we met with Mr. Joe Smith, an impressive man who had made his money as a miner and who was now going to own and operate the town's new TV station. He already owned the town's top radio station.

John launched into our presentation with full bore energy and enthusiasm. He explained that we were offering him 3,000 hours of programming, and that we were asking only $35 per hour for the right to exhibit the material over a three year term, starting at whatever date Mr. Smith's station eventually went on the air. We also told him that he, naturally, would pay the cost of shipping the films to and from his station. But John minimized these items in passing, assuring him it was "standard in the industry." And Cole made a point of the fact that even though the episodes of the serials each ran approximately 20 minutes, each would be considered as only a quarter-hour for purposes of calculating the debit against the 3000 hours. Each movie telecast would be calculated as only one hour. "Another bargain."

Joe Smith may have been a hard-scrabble miner but he was wise in the way of business customs and gracious enough to take us

135

to dinner that night at *Dempsey's*, a rather good restaurant, decorated with autographed photos and old boxing gloves hanging from the walls, all as a shrine to the former heavyweight champion, Jack Dempsey, also known as the "Manassas Mauler." I believe he had lived in Great Falls or had once owned the restaurant. But the decor didn't distract Joe Smith. Joe knew how to calculate, and pointed out that Cole's asking price was over one hundred thousand dollars, more than the cost of his transmitter and a huge sum for such a small market. And Cole responded with one of his favorite counters: "Mr. Smith, you can't stand in front of the camera all by yourself and wave for an hour at less cost than we're asking!"

The next day was a Friday, and even though Smith hadn't yet said "Yes," he also hadn't yet said "No." Cole sensed he could close the deal later that day so he sent me on to Idaho Falls to handle that market alone. At that time there was no TV station on the air in that city, either.

By phone, I managed to persuade Roy Southwick, who was to be Program Director of station KIDK when it signed on the air, to have dinner with me upon my arrival in Idaho Falls Friday night. He and I quickly established a rapport, partly because he had previously worked at a radio station in town and I had just left radio station KHJ in Los Angeles. So he was polite enough to listen to my presentation during our two and a half hour dinner, but also clever enough to let me know about competitors of my company who were also eager to sell his station a large group of programs. And he rattled off their names: Ziv, Flamingo Films, Hollywood Television Service (Republic Pictures).

Then he arranged for the man who would manage the station, Rosie Lane, to meet with me on Saturday morning where I repeated most of my pitch which I was already polishing. To my delight, he responded favorably and we commenced negotiating. He rejected the concept of 3,000 hours of programming as much more than what he could handle, but sounded like he might agree to less. At 2,200 hours, I agreed to lower my asking price from $35 per hour to $32.50 provided he would agree to buy a new weekly half hour show we were producing featuring well known liberal newspaper columnist and network radio commentator, Drew Pearson. Despite the fact that Mr. Pearson's liberal politics were not at all popular in conservative Idaho, Rosie Lane finally agreed to accept the deal when I said I would cut another fifty cents per hour from my asking price. Rosie and wife Mary provided a sumptuous Sunday brunch before I left town. Wow! What a thrill! I had closed a deal in my very first solo market. My first sale in syndication!

The following week I closed a deal in Butte and then went on to Billings, Montana, another $150 per hour *prime time* market. Billings was another of what were referred to as "one engine stops," because the twin-engined DC3 airliners would only kill the left engine when they landed. That was because the left side was where the door was located which allowed passengers to board and/or disembark and the airline didn't want to risk decapitating anybody or blowing them away on the icy tarmac. But they were never on the ground more than a few minutes, and with one engine still running and providing cabin heat, they were ready for a faster takeoff once everybody was on board.

Commercial aviation was a young industry in those days and not everybody considered it to be very safe, including those in the home offices of my company. So the standard instructions under which we operated were to always get two copies of a 12 page contract, with details filled in and initialed and signed before leaving town. Put one in an envelope and mail it to the headquarters office and put the other in your briefcase. That way, if your plane crashed, the company would still have proof that the station had made the commitment. Not exactly a warm and cuddly thought from the home office.

The manager in "one-engine stop" Billings was a fellow named Bud Clark, who was an enthusiastic outdoorsman and who looked a lot like my favorite uncle back in Iowa. Bud was a bright and genial fellow, but he allowed me only about 30 minutes in his office before he grabbed me by the elbow at 11:15 in the morning and steered me to the nearby *Northern Hotel*, where he bellied up to the bar and ordered himself a straight-up gin martini. It was obvious this wasn't his first such visit because the bartender had started mixing the drink as soon as we entered, so the fact that he verbalized his order was just for effect. In the hope of keeping a clear head, I uneasily joined him for one, with no previous experience in a.m. imbibing of martinis.

Later we were joined by Clark's Program Director, whose first name was Cliff. At this point I should explain that Billings sits in a rather wide valley, with sheer cliffs on both sides. One of those cliffs bore the legend that it was the place where Indians formerly threw maidens off the cliff in ancient rituals to their gods. I was surprised when both men proudly told me that Cliff was planning to host their Western movies using the moniker of *Sacrifice Cliff*. They were both pleased with this, and I complimented their cleverness even though I thought it sort of macabre. I was invited to have dinner with them at the *Skyline Cafe*, which sat on top of one of those cliffs, overlooking a breathtaking view of the town. And I later closed a deal with them for the whole package.

Even before the menus arrived, Bud Clark was extolling the qualities of antelope meat, urging me to try out this exotic dish which I had never tasted before. So I joined them in ordering it...when in Rome, do as the Romans, etc. I found it to be delicious and similar to veal. I must admit however, that I was somewhat distracted by the entertainment provided by the restaurant. It was a young woman who enthusiastically sang songs while accompanying herself on the accordion and pumping away at a foot pedal which was connected to a pair of cymbals. She was one *busy* performer.

Red haired and freckle nosed, she was cute, so we invited her to join us for a drink. During introductions I flashed her my business card showing I represented MPTV, a big Hollywood TV company on Sunset Boulevard. It turned out that she and I were both scheduled to fly out of Billings that night. We weren't too concerned about the seemingly light snowfall which had started during dinner, but after collecting our luggage and finding a cab to get to the airport, we arrived only to find that the snowfall had become a full-blown blizzard and the airport had been closed. No more planes that night.

We were lucky to get a cab back down the side of the slippery cliff into town and managed to reclaim the rooms we had just checked out of. Snowed in, we then went back down and into the bar, staying there until it closed. Now, if this had been a movie, say with Tom Hanks and Meg Ryan, a romance would have ensued. But I was just recently married and the girl singer, accordionist and cymbalist, was a married lady. So we went to our separate beds, pure as the driven snow which continued throughout the night. The snow, that is.

At this point I had made sales in three of the three markets where I soloed and I began to think "This business is great. A walk in the park!" But soon I was confronted with the sober realities when I was unable to make a deal in either Boise or Twin Falls. Blanked. Rejected. Turned away, but cordially.

I was in Yakima, Washington, another one-engine stop, when I got a message to call my big boss, Erwin Ezzes, in New York. He was inviting me to accept a promotion and move from Los Angeles to Detroit to become head of that regional office. Inviting me, hell! He was making it clear he wanted me to accept the transfer, especially after I made an overnight trip to New York to iron out details of a new deal. So I did, despite John Cole's expressed desire to keep me under his wing to cover the West Coast. As I settled into Detroit I began to understand and accept the truth that those of us who labored in the field of program sales were like chessmen on a board, moving wherever the master hand of headquarters ordered us to go.

This thought was reinforced just a year later when my company, MPTV, merged with Guild Films, with the result that there were suddenly too many employees and I feared I might be deemed excess baggage. Instead, I was complimented by an offer to make my choice of running one of three regional offices: Minneapolis, Detroit or Philadelphia. Not being a fan of frigid winters and having already tasted enough of Motown, I opted for Philadelphia, which had the bonus attraction of "Preview" openings of Broadway shows such as *My Fair Lady*. But it was only a year later when John Cole was promoted to V.P. of U.S. Sales in New York and I was ordered to return to the Los Angeles office and replace him as Regional Sales Manager. That was an offer I couldn't refuse.

It was in 1957 when I was hit with an attack of air travel flu and was left with a lingering bad case of laryngitis. I was calling on KING-TV in Seattle when their Program Director, Lee Shulman, observed my strained whisper and asked me how long I had been having problems with my voice. When I told him three months, he immediately called a local throat specialist he knew and then committed me to go to that doctor's office that afternoon. That doctor examined me and said I had an ulceration on my left vocal chord. When he discovered I lived in Los Angeles he recommended I see a Dr. Sam Kaplan and said I should see him as soon as possible. Once back home, Kaplan took a biopsy and reported I had *insitu carcinoma.* Scary words. I underwent several surgeries during the following nine months and also 13 weeks of cobalt bombardment, but neither approach was successful in conquering the cancer. One day, when I attempted to shout a "hello" to a friend of mine, my vocal chord ruptured, and the doctor concluded my condition had become life threatening. The only solution would be the complete removal of my larynx.

As if my health problems weren't enough, my employer, Guild Films suffered financial collapse and went out of business. Fortunately I was soon hired by my good friend, John Ettlinger, President of Medallion TV, but my voice was becoming so thin and whispery that I decided I couldn't properly represent any company any longer in sales, so I resigned. Unable to properly speak, I eagerly accepted a job at $1.75 an hour from my friend, Fred Sutherland, who operated an electronic aviation supply house near the *Burbank Airport*. I functioned as a general handyman and stock clerk, doing chores which required little or no speaking.

But my health continued to deteriorate. If a boxer has no arms, he can't fight. If a runner has no legs, he can't run. And if a salesman has no voice, he can't sell. And it was either let them remove my larynx, or accept the inevitable.

The surgery had left an open hole in my throat, a tracheotomy, through which I was supposed to breathe. The first night after my surgery, the special registered nurse who was supposed to be watching over me fell asleep in a nearby chair. The device, called a canula, a short curved metal tube which was inserted into my stoma to keep the airway open, became clogged and I couldn't breathe. I had no voice with which to awaken her and was becoming desperate for help, so I started beating on the metal bedside rails, finally attracting the attention of a male nurse from across the hall. He came over and awakened my nurse just as I had managed to expel the blocked canula with a big spasm of air from my chest. The drowsy nurse saw the expelled canula lying on the floor, picked it up, rinsed and wiped it off on her uniform, and inserted it back into the wound in my throat.

And as a result of this unsanitary process my wound was infected with staph, the dread of all hospital patients. It required heroic doses of various antibiotics to finally knock out the infection and it also extended my hospital stay to a total of thirty days.

The only nourishment I could consume was provided via a feeding tube into my nose, and to the stomach, and my weight plummeted from 210 pounds to 160. For six months I could take no solid food, and then, at my first taste of a dish of cherry *Jello*, I wept at the thrill of the taste.

In those days, people who had been subjected to a laryngectomy were usually taught to communicate verbally through use of a device which they held against their throat while they formed the words and it croaked out a buzzing, mechanical version of speech. But my doctor would not allow me to even experiment with such a device. He did not want me to become dependent upon the "buzzer."

Instead, he sent me to a speech therapist after healing and removal of the feeding tube. This man, Dr. Harrington, asked me what I thought was an odd question: "Do you know how to burp?" He couldn't have known that when I was in L.A. High, we used to stage burping contests, and I sometimes won. At that time, we were doing it mainly as a prank designed to gross-out our parents and teachers. When the therapist explained that I could relearn to speak if I would just capture air and burp while forming words, I was sure it was something I could do because of my previous contests. And I did. In fact, the therapist subjected me to only three lessons and then declared me ready to verbally communicate. He also pronounced me the best student he ever had which raised my spirits mightily.

I spent a couple of months at home, regaining my strength, and then returned to my thankful chores at Fred Sutherland's Coast Air, Inc. where my strange new way of speaking was readily embraced by a caring and supportive staff. The consideration and warmth of fellow employees and Fred were major factors toward coming back to life. But, grateful as I was to have any kind of job at all, I sorely missed the interaction with the people I had worked with in the TV industry.

One of a number of friendly calls I had received during my recuperation had been from a colleague from the days when we both worked for Guild Films in New York, a man named "Stretch" Adler, another colorful character. At the time of this call however, Stretch was General Manager of KTLA, Channel 5 in Los Angeles, and his message to me was "when you feel ready to go back to work, call me." So when I regained my vitality and improved speech I called, and to my astonishment and delight he hired me immediately and gave me the job title of "Film Director" for this powerful independent station.

What a joy it was to return to a functioning role in the industry which I loved! Eventually the station expanded my responsibilities to "Director of Film and Tape Programming and Syndication" and I found myself in the role of a customer for the syndicators of the programming rather than a colleague as I had been before. Because of knowledge and experience previously gained, I felt comfortable in this job and especially so when I found that my ability to communicate, even in a voice best described as "throaty," was unimpaired. I could talk and I could "wheel and deal" just as well from this side of the desk as I had from the other.

Then, after five good years at KTLA, a new General Manager arrived on the scene and decided to merge some positions for cost efficiency and mine was eliminated.

Again, friendship rushed to the rescue. As I was packing my belongings to clear out my office I was offered a job by a distribution executive, George Mitchell at Olympus TV, and I accepted over a breakfast meeting the next day. My mission was to go market by market to sell the videotaped coverage of *Boxing From The Olympic*. Even though I felt vocally comfortable when working behind my KTLA desk, I was unsure how my speech and I would be accepted by TV station personnel who didn't know me. I quickly discovered they listened even more carefully, and I was uniformly greeted with warmth and respect. A great confidence builder at an important time of rediscovery for me.

The job offers continued to reach me. Dave Sachs, the General Manager of the ABC-owned station in San Francisco, KGO, offered me the job of Program Director of that station. He even arranged for me to fly, at ABC's expense, to Chicago for a meeting with two top executives of the O & O stations group, Phil Mayer and Elton Rule. And while they offered me the job, they advised me that as a matter of company policy, they could not pay any loss I might incur in selling the new home I had just bought in Los Angeles. Such financial assistance was available only to current employees, not to new hires. So I reluctantly could not accept.

Then an old friend, Bob Newgard, called to tell me he had just accepted a new job as head of sales at Paramount Pictures Worldwide TV Syndication and was resigning his job as VP at Teleworld. He said he had strongly recommended me to his Teleworld boss, Bob Seidelman, whom I knew, and urged me to call him. Shortly thereafter, we met in New York and made a deal.

Teleworld's product list was comprised mainly of feature films and I soon established a close and friendly relationship with Bob Seidelman...a relationship which lasted a full eleven years in business together. This close friendship endures to this day.

In 1979 I joined Columbia Pictures Television, headed by Norman Horowitz, and later followed Norman to Polygram Pictures when he was recruited to head worldwide television. But Polygram went out of the television business after only 18 months. I then moved to Lorimar, where after eight wonderful years, I again had to have my business cards reprinted when Lorimar was absorbed by Warner Bros..

But I am proud to say that I spent the final twenty or so years of my career as a marketing and sales executive of these fine companies, and in roles where I had constant contact with broadcasting and cable program executives all across the nation.

Had fate deemed otherwise I could have wound up a mute and embittered man. But...and you can ask anyone who knows me...I am anything but! I'm still a loudmouth!

As tribute to the many whose names I could not include in the above, but who especially contributed to my rewarding experience over 39 years, please see the addendum on the final pages of this book.

Fridays With Art

Can You Have Your Secretary
Call a Taxi for Me?
by Al Sussman

In the early days of television (1953) I was hired by the Crosley Broadcasting Company to be the Program Director for their four TV stations They owned stations In Cincinnati, Columbus, Dayton and Atlanta. The three Ohio stations were all affiliated with NBC and the Atlanta station was an ABC affiliate.

Three or four weeks into the job, my boss came into my office to say that the Atlanta station was ranked as a bad third in the market and we needed to come up with programming to increase their ratings. He said he and I needed to fly down to Atlanta, but not to tip off that station's General Manager in advance that we were coming. What we would do is just sit in our hotel room and watch all three of the Atlanta stations and hopefully we could come up with some kind of solution as to how to strengthen our station's position.

We reserved a two bedroom suite and arranged for the hotel to

147

provide us with three TV sets which were hooked up in the living room. For the next 36 hours we had all our meals sent in to our suite while we studied the output of each station. It didn't take too long for us to realize that our station was a real turkey. As an ABC affiliate in those days, the network didn't provide us any programming until the 7 p.m. *Evening News*, so we had many daytime hours to fill with either syndicated shows or live local shows produced by the station itself.

One of those locally produced shows was a daily hour-long show which started at 11:30 a.m. where the host, a tall skinny man, would lip-sync popular records. Then he would talk to the audience of about 35 to 50 women, run around the studio doing pratfalls, sit on (usually the fattest) women's laps and make silly or allegedly funny comments. The show was atrocious.

My boss, Bernie Barth, who was the second highest ranking executive at Crosley, asked me what I thought we should do with the schedule. The first thing which came to mind was that we had to get rid of that 11:30 a.m. show.

At our three Ohio stations we had a very successful movie slotted in that daypart. Ever since I was awarded the job of programming four stations, I had been swamped with telephone calls and requests for meetings with various syndicators because I represented such a major potential customer for them. At that time I believe I was the only program executive handling more than one station.

Among the distributors who wanted to talk to me was Erwin Ezzes, then sales chief of MPTV, a company with a large library of feature films which were unsold in all four of our markets. So when I returned to my office, I was able to make a very attractive deal with Ezzes which included a very lowball price for Atlanta. Bernie agreed that we should replace that dreadful 11:30 show with a movie and that I should fly back down to Atlanta to revise that station's program schedule.

So the following morning I went to the station and fired the host, Dick Van Dyke!

Perhaps my weakness in not recognizing talent when I saw it is why I spent most of my following career as a salesman for various distribution companies.

In 1956, when I was working for AAP (Associated Artists Productions), I was sent to the Norfolk market to sell the newly acquired Warner Bros. feature film library of 754 features. I was at WVEC-TV in Tom Chisman's office, the General Manager, extolling this fantastic feature library, the first major Hollywood studio to sell their library to a television distributor. AAP's advertising department prepared a very eloquent hardcover catalogue describing each picture with photographs, story lines, and listing any Academy Awards the feature may have won. In addition, we had a lengthy flip card presentation which could test the patience of our prospective customers.

Half way through my flip card presentation, Tom Chisman started to look at his watch. I knew I was in trouble. Anytime your audience starts to look at a watch, or yawn, or look out the window, you knew you were losing them and you were dead, as far as making a deal. I continued my pitch when Tom finally said he had an appointment in town and he couldn't listen to the end of my presentation. Well, as all salesmen would do, I said I could come back tomorrow to finish up. He advised that he would think about the features and I should call him the following week.

That is the kiss of death. I knew I had no chance of making a sale at WVEC-TV, so I asked Tom if he would ask his secretary to call a cab for me so I could go to my hotel in town. He asked where I was staying and said he was going right by there and he would take me. When in the car, instead of making small talk, I started my pitch again, telling him what a terrific opportunity he had to capture the

149

market with my fabulous features. I could see he was getting agitated with my pitching and couldn't wait to get rid of me. When he dropped me off I knew I had lost him.

This was mid November about 4 p.m., and it was cold and raining in Norfolk that day. When I got into the elevator there was an advertisement for the guests to consider using the hotel's steam room, sauna and massage facilities. When I got to my room I immediately called to see what time I could have a massage. When I got to the health club, I got undressed and went into the steam room. Who should be sitting there, wearing nothing but a frown, was none other than Tom Chisman. The first thing he said was, "Al, not a word. Do I make myself clear? Not a word!"

I sat there...quiet...not making a sound when an attendant came in for Tom for his massage. About ten minutes later they called me in for my massage. And where did they put me? At the next table to Tom. He glared at me but said nothing.

Some ten minutes later, in walks a friend of his who apparently was a booker for a chain of movie theatres. Tom looked up and after some greetings asked the man, "Sam, if you had to book features for a television station, which studio's pictures would you buy?" (The following is absolutely true!!) Without missing a beat, the man said something like, "For their star value, Academy Awards, writing, directing, I would go with the Warner pictures."

Tom turned to me at the next table and said, "Al, can you be in my office tomorrow at 9:30?"

And during that meeting I sold him the entire 754 feature film library!

Years later I found myself in Peoria, and I'm sure it must have been because my then boss at a distribution company called ITC had given me firm orders to go there.

I was in the office of Bill Mueller, the General Manager of

WEEK-TV, pitching him on *The Saint*, using a voluminous flip card presentation as elaborate as only ITC could create. Halfway through the presentation I looked across the desk and saw that Bill was fast asleep. I was beginning to get a complex. Earlier I recited how I had lost an audience when my prospect started looking at his watch, and now this one had fallen asleep. What should I do? So I dropped something heavy on the floor and made a loud thump.

Bill Mueller was startled awake and opened his eyes widely in an effort to convince me he had been wide awake during the entire presentation. He then said he had a lunch date and would have to leave, but that he would think about *The Saint* and I should call him next week. Since I hadn't even gotten to the point of quoting him a price for the series I knew he had no intention of buying it.

I asked him to ask his secretary to call a taxi for me. And, as had earlier happened to me in Norfolk, he said he was going into town and would drive me to my hotel. When we got into his car I knew I had a captive audience and so I started my pitch again. He seemed a little perturbed but was a perfect gentleman and listened silently. Twenty minutes later he dropped me off.

Several years later the scene shifts to a NATPE convention in Las Vegas. In my company's exhibition area on the floor of the convention center was a group of people from Storer Broadcasting. During the course of pleasantries with them, Bill Flynn mentioned that he got his start in the television business as a salesman with WEEK-TV in Peoria. Well, I then began to tell them ironically what a terrific salesman I was, and how when I tried to sell a show to Bill Mueller he fell asleep in the middle of my presentation. But I told them that he was at least kind enough to drive me to my hotel.

Upon hearing this, Bill Flynn shouted, "What? You got into a car with him? You could have been killed. He suffered from narcolepsy!"

Fridays With Art

Pioneers Were the Ones with
Arrows in Their Backs
by Dick Block

In late 1961, I was running the broadcast division of Kaiser Industries at our Oakland, California, headquarters when I came up with the idea to apply to the FCC for open UHF allocations for stations in Chicago, Detroit, Los Angeles, Philadelphia and San Francisco. Programming would be patterned as it was on the handful of independent (non-network) VHF stations, clustered mostly in New York and Los Angeles.

I had been transferred earlier that year from Honolulu where I had managed our TV and radio stations there since 1958. The Hawaiian stations were quite successful and my new mandate was to replicate the Hawaiian experience, but I soon discovered that the price tags for established stations on the mainland were more than the company had in mind to spend at that time. On the other hand, for little or no risk, Kaiser's financial strength could support the applications, even though it might opt out of the project down the line.

The idea to apply for UHF franchises had been planted while attending a speech by Newton Minnow, President Kennedy's high-profile FCC chairman. Minnow waxed optimistically about the impending federally imposed requirement to add UHF tuners to all new TV sets, beginning in 1964. It's hard to believe today, but in those days most TV sets could only tune in to channels 2 through 13. Minnow hoped that the new stations would possibly create oases in the "vast wasteland," a term he had used to describe the state of the medium when addressing the shocked aristocracy of the business the previous spring during the convention of the *National Association of Broadcasters*.

The announcement six months later in the *Oakland Tribune* about the Kaiser UHF initiative elicited a formidable wall of skepticism and eye rolling from most of our company executives who didn't take kindly to the idea of such a project on the grounds that it just didn't fit our corporate culture. The internal questioning was buttressed by a consensus that UHF was so inferior electronically to VHF that failure was all but certain anyway.

Kaiser at that time controlled aluminum, steel, engineering, cement, automotive (*Jeep*), real estate and health (arguably the first HMO) companies. Its founder and Chairman was industrialist Henry J. Kaiser, an indefatigable septuagenarian, who had gained prominence during World War II by building ships, which had previously taken years to construct, in just a few days. Kaiser had built the Hawaiian stations against the advice of his staff, primarily to promote his *Hawaiian Village Hotel*. Because the hotel was about a mile from Waikiki Beach, it would benefit from broadcast promotions. And because the brash malahini (newcomer) was hardly being made to feel welcome by the local power structure, the ruling kamaaiana (literally, Hawaiian born) Mr. Kaiser felt that he could do an end run around their dominant local media to counter a campaign of negativism.

A few forward looking Kaiser executives, however, noted that other heavy-industry companies such as GE and Westinghouse had balanced their portfolios with broadcasting assets. Additionally, Kaiser's ethos was to meet needs by creating new players in ostensibly saturated industries. The UHF project, as it was to be called, certainly resonated with "Together We Build," the legend imprinted on company cornerstones, plaques and service awards. The public service aspects of such a major company supporting the UHF initiative was also important to some at the highest levels who justly prided themselves on the high principles of the company.

I soon became known as "The UHF Apostle." At the slightest provocation I would point out...to mostly deaf ears...that UHF was working just fine in places like the United Kingdom, where the switch to UHF went hand-in-hand with color and a higher definition picture. Additionally, there were UHF "islands" in the United States, such as Grand Rapids and South Bend, where the monster had been tamed by technicians and the public, who had no alternative for reception of the three networks other than snowy distant signals pulled faintly in by fifty foot high antennas. I also knew from personal experience in the Sacramento-Stockton market and the Hawaiian island of Kauai that UHF's bad rap was overstated.

Eventually a law was passed requiring that all TV sets in the future must be able to receive both VHF and UHF channels. Without such a requirement the ABC network would not have been able to develop fully, or in the cases of networks known as Fox, The WB and UPN, to exist at all.

I had learned the importance of syndicated programming and the necessity of using aggressive tactics in acquiring it while working in various staff capacities at KCRA in Sacramento and KRON in San

Francisco, both of which were NBC affiliates. Management would study ratings in other markets and track the development and launches of new shows that they thought would be crucial to the success of their local 7 p.m. time periods, areas which they needed to program themselves, ahead of the network programming feeds which commenced at 7:30 p.m. Half-hour syndicated shows featuring B-movie stars such as Preston Foster in *Waterfront* and Broderick Crawford in *Highway Patrol* were eagerly sought after.

Movie packages were also intensively evaluated, particularly after the so-called "pre-1948's" were released for television by MGM in 1956 and Warner Bros in 1957. For the first time, TV stations had access to some of the biggest pictures of all time. The respective packages had hundreds of films. Consultants, such as ex-film buyer for movie theatres, Sid Cohen of Salt Lake City, would establish local values for each picture. Decisions to buy a package involved big money at the time. In fact, so big that Norman Chandler, patriarch of the family that owned the *Los Angeles Times* and also independent station KTTV, Channel 11 in Los Angeles, gave MGM a one quarter equity interest in that station as a way to reduce the cost of acquiring their films. As an illustration of what that transaction would be worth in 2002 terms, independent KCAL, Channel 9 in Los Angeles, was sold to Viacom for $650 million!

My tie to the above was that Mr. Chandler was also on the board of Southern California based Kaiser Steel, and a confidant of "Mr. Senior," the in-house appellation for the founder and Chairman, to distinguish him from his sons, Edgar, Chairman, and Henry Jr., who was tragically dying from multiple sclerosis.

Chandler's bragging to "Mr. Senior" about the big ratings of the pre-1948 films on KTTV resulted in the decision to construct an independent TV (and a radio) station atop Kaiser's *Hawaiian Village Hotel*, complete with surrounding walkways for the public to watch the action in the glassed-in studios. Other than the radio antics of Hal Lewis ("J. Akuhead Papule"), the reigning morning DJ and, to the horror of Kaiser officials back in Oakland, also a partner of "Mr. Senior" in the radio venture, there wasn't much to see. Especially after "Aku" complained that the spectators interfered with his artistic concentration.

Mr. Chandler had also recommended that if the two movie packages were acquired, then there would be no need for such costly items as studios or cameras. But at that time, live in-studio commercials for car dealers were the bread and butter of TV stations. Perched on the 14th floor of the hotel, with nothing larger than a passenger elevator to reach what was then called the penthouse level, effectively placed Kaiser's Channel 13 out of the running for the lucrative car business and other clients who needed live commercials. So a 16mm Auricon sound-on-film camera was purchased to fill the gap. Unfortunately, the quality of the film and sound equipment plus the cost of film stock and the time consuming difficulty of editing, all resulted in a poor substitute for the live facilities of the competing stations. Videotape wouldn't come to Hawaii for another three years But even then it would require "big rig" trucks for mobility.

A footnote is that in 1971, I finally met Mr. Chandler at a Kaiser Industries function attended by board members of other affiliated companies. Mr. Chandler told me that it was impossible to make money with independent stations. His KTTV in Los Angeles had launched in 1948 as the CBS affiliate. It subsequently lost the network when CBS purchased Channel 2 and KTTV became an independent. In 1967, Chandler sold KTTV to John Kluge's Metromedia. By that time, many independents such as WNEW, New York, WGN, Chicago, and WTTG in Washington, D.C. were quite profitable. And the fact that Chandler sold KTTV to Kluge for $10.4 million, when viewed through the prism of the aforementioned sale of another Los

Angeles VHF independent station for $650 million, underscores the adage that patience is a virtue. I trust that my rejoinder to Mr. Chandler at the end of our conversation, to the effect that pioneers were the ones with arrows in their backs, was adequately diplomatic.

As the 1957 launch of the Kaiser TV station in Honolulu approached, "Mr. Senior" himself took charge of the campaign to acquire the two feature film packages, plus the wonderful Chuck Jones cartoons featuring such beloved characters as Bugs Bunny and Pepe LePew. By then there were management and financial problems with Kaiser's radio partner, so it was decided that even if an MGM or Warner Bros. partnership was a possibility, it would be declined on the basis that one such arrangement in show business was quite enough. And while the film packages would command a premium, as attested to by the Los Angeles experience, neither of the studio TV marketeers, in their fondest dreams, imagined what the preemptive offer from Kaiser, in tiny, far-off Hawaii, would amount to. Four to five times the going price for that market, was what I heard from the respective sales managers several years later. In fact, both were so astonished that they risked running afoul of the antitrust laws when they spontaneously called each other to see if the offers were for real. While they didn't collude on price, both had instinctively withheld immediate confirmation, avoiding the appearance of being overeager to accept.

It should be noted that those pre-1948 feature films proved to be critical building blocks in the ascension of Kaiser Broadcasting in Hawaii. With Kaiser's purchase of the stronger ABC affiliate, KULA, Channel 4, from Jack Burnett and cult-movie producer Albert Zugsmith, they turned their independent Channel 13 back to the F.C.C. Now broadcasting from a superior facility with inter-island coverage, the 10 p.m. *The Big Movie* dominated late fringe, especially after ABC's young skewing *prime time* programming was rolled back an hour to start at 6:30 p.m. in order to better match the local prevailing work patterns. Upon purchase of Channel 4, Kaiser changed the call letters to KHVH, an acronym for *Kaiser Hawaiian Village Hotel,* which was of course the reason for erecting a TV station on the island in the first place. The November ratings sweeps showed KHVH with a 56% total day share -- highest among all ABC affiliates in markets with 3 or more stations. This dominance, abetted by strong news initiatives that competitors had wrongly concluded would not generate interest in the island culture, lasted many years. In 1964, the stations (a repeater in Hilo on the Big Island counted as one toward the FCC limit of seven stations at that time) were sold for $4 million in order to make room for the pending mainland group.

The first Kaiser UHF was WKBD, Detroit. Channel 50 was launched on January 10, 1965, as "All Sports," a label that encompassed hockey's Red Wings, the NBA Pistons and University of Michigan basketball. It was a wonderful positioning statement for about half the year, but woefully weak in the summer and fall because rights to Tigers baseball, Lions football and Wolverines football were firmly held by VHF affiliates and networks.

Actually, "All Sports" masked doubts that the station could achieve viability, either financially or electronically. Success of a UHF in a market which also had four VHF signals from competitors (including CKLW, Channel 9, in Windsor, Ontario, managed by RKO General which also had independent stations in New York and Los Angeles) was a longshot to many experts. The station was to debut without any programming other than sports, which at times stretched to such obscure offerings as high school coaches lecturing physical education classes.

John Serrao, WKBD General Manager, had come up with the sports theme and seemed to understand the corporate caution, despite his general aura of optimism bordering on the possessed. When John called me about a month prior to air to tell me he had contracted to acquire telecast rights to *The Little Rascals*, a compilation of theatrical short comedies generally known as '*Our Gang*,' I went ballistic. It wasn't the $10,000 (payable over three years) that he had spent. It was that the rules had been broken. He had not been given authority to make such a commitment. After pledges from John never to sin again, I came back to earth.

And, oh yes, there was one more wrinkle in the deal which Serrao told me about. Charlie King, the film's salesman (and a double for Sidney Greenstreet, the corpulent misanthrope in Humphrey Bogart's movie classic *The Maltese Falcon*) promised that we would have the option to buy '*Rascals*' at all Kaiser stations at similarly low cost when and if they were constructed. I was further underwhelmed by Serrao's gleeful recital of this aspect of the deal.

Detroit was one of the few markets that was locally rated in January. This was many years prior to general local meter ratings, so calculations were based on the diaries kept by selected viewers. One of the Nielsen managers had agreed that he would call me as soon as there were any advance ratings showing the performance of the stations. The call came in early February. "Mostly scratches (no viewing)," were the words that landed on me like a doctor saying that I needed emergency surgery for a life threatening condition, but then he added, "except for a couple of *prime time* hockey games and *The Little Rascals* weekdays at 5:00 p.m., which had solid one and two ratings."

Prior to that call I was prepared to pull the plug in case of disaster; to sell the 55 acres of land and donate the tall tower to the public TV station. I was certain I would forever be labeled as the clouded and failed visionary of UHF. But when I heard that the station was being viewed for other than high-interest sports, that news lifted my spirits to the heavens. I knew then that we had a success on our hands, even though it was to take several years to fulfill, and would still require constant defense vis-à-vis the nay sayers.

Charlie King's company, King World, went on to be a dominant force in syndication with shows such as *Oprah* (Winfrey), *Wheel of Fortune* and *Jeopardy!*. True to his word, we were later able to acquire *The Little Rascals* in Los Angeles, Philadelphia, Boston, San Francisco and Cleveland, the five additional stations we activated between 1965-1968. After Charlie's untimely death a few years later, King World went on under the aegis of his sons, Roger, Michael and Bob. To this day, they will introduce me as the guy who got their company going with the purchase of '*Rascals*' in Detroit, despite my protestations that I would have refused to authorize the deal if John Serrao had called me prior to making the commitment

Relations between buyers and sellers were mostly good. Certain buyers would sour on an individual salesman -- few if any women carried the heavy projectors and film from market to market -- and/or companies. And vice-versa. But for the most part it was a fraternity, and help would be extended in both ways in times of crisis or need. But there were some salespeople who were less welcome, especially the hard-driving ones whose minds never entertained the thought that a property they represented was anything but perfect for the station they were pitching.

In November, 1970, I took my family to Europe for their first time. There was a great deal of preparation and excitement for Julie (14) and Nick (10) stemming from several orientation meetings we had with the "club" that made it possible to book a low-cost charter flight. This was before "mileage" and airline deregulation. The distance would hopefully offer me an opportunity to share experiences with my brood rather than be off physically or mentally on the never-ending problems of the stations.

The itinerary included a nonstop flight from Oakland to

London, followed a few days later by a flight to Paris. Despite the mostly gray skies, Paris looked more beautiful than ever. The usual sightseeing destinations were taken in, including the Eiffel Tower. The cold and wind seemed to be increasing the day we visited the 'Tower'. Regardless, the tradeoff was that there were few other tourists to absorb the beauty and solitude from the observation platform. It was a rare opportunity for me to truly relax and savor life, and reaffirm that there were more important things in life than ratings and revenue projections.

My reverie was interrupted by a hand on my shoulder and a familiar voice saying, "You should really reconsider *Ripcord* (a first-run half-hour show) for San Francisco." Without turning around, I looked up at the skies and said, "Dear God, what have I done to deserve this?"

The voice behind me then added, "Nice view, huh?"

The voice was that of Dick Colbert, who was a living symbol of Ziv, a distribution company which trained its salespeople to "walk through walls" to get orders. Fred Ziv went from radio to TV syndication from his Cincinnati location, and was the force behind half-hour shows such as *Science Fiction Theatre*, *Sea Hunt*, and *Highway Patrol*, all of which were produced on bare-bones budgets but were the mainstays of early fringe time periods in those pioneer years.

Colbert, by the way, was only one of several industry types in Paris at the time, having signed up for a tour conducted by the same Sid Cohen who evaluated movie packages. Dick went on to run the distribution company for Jack Barry and Dan Enright, as he relates elsewhere in this book. Dick and I both hailed from San Francisco and had a great deal in common, which along with experiences such as Paris, has kept our friendship strong through the years.

Except for a brief hiatus when I was Executive Vice-President of the Metromedia stations just prior to their sale to Fox's Rupert

162

Murdoch, I have been a consultant since 1975 to the *National Association of Television Program Executives* (NATPE) for their annual convention. While the organization has changed and grown over the years to international status, my function of coming up with ideas for some of the convention sessions hasn't changed all that much.

Program Directors working at stations in the U.S. made up the largest contingent of NATPE delegates up until the industry consolidation and economic conditions of recent years. The job title of "Program Director" is now extinct for all effects and purposes, with buying decisions completed well in advance of the conference and done at a handful of station group headquarters. Of course the "film peddlers" were also at NATPE.

I thought it would be appropriate to have a session in San Francisco one year when the buyers and sellers could exchange uninhibited criticism of one another. It was certainly a subject that was discussed at the drop of a hat, and to recognize its importance would be useful. To symbolically reinforce the desired uninhibited aspect, Lone Ranger type masks were distributed at the door and required to be worn prior to admission by the nine hundred audience members. In the convention's program booklet, even the promotional ad about the session showed the moderator, John Goldhammer, wearing a mask stretched across his eyes, with neither his name nor those of the syndication executive panelists listed. Anonymity was the key. As the lights dimmed, John's introductory remarks emphasized that this was a once-in-a-lifetime opportunity for the frequent adversaries to exchange ideas with no holds barred. John then said that the session would start off with a question from the floor. The silence was interrupted by a huddled masked figure at an audience mike booming out the words, "I want to thank NATPE for zis opportunity of anonymity that will protect me from offending my customers." A roar of increas-

163

ing laughter filled the room almost from the first word, because the speaker was the well-known and universally loved salesman, Pierre Weiss, who at that time was the only person at NATPE with a heavy French accent.

In 1973, Metromedia decided to bring Merv Griffin back to syndication after Merv's late night network show failed to make a dent in Johnny Carson's hold on the time period. I had followed Metromedia's lead in first-run programming, and was almost an automatic sale for them if they desired, having bought such of their offerings as *The Woody Woodbury Show* and *The Joe Pine Show*.

Al Krivin, who ran the Metromedia stations, told me that we had a good shot at acquiring Merv in several of our markets, including the key ones of Chicago and Philadelphia. Al suggested that I set a meeting with Ken Joseph, the head of syndication, and that Ken would be briefed in advance that the company wanted him to make a deal if at all possible. I subsequently learned that Ken would be bringing along with him his second-in-command, Pierre Weiss.

The meeting was set for Los Angeles in the space Kaiser rented from Metromedia for our KBSC, Channel 52, parenthetically a station that was the antithesis of selecting underserved markets. It owed its existence to the public relations wishes of the local Kaiser steel company. Uncharacteristically, Barry Thurston, Kaiser's VP of Programming, who was an excellent negotiator (and later went on to lift Sony/Columbia's TV syndication arm to great heights), asked me to attend the meeting with him. I think that Barry felt uneasy, not only because of the importance of the programming -- it would fill ninety minutes of *prime time* every weeknight -- but also because he didn't want to be blamed for failure under the circumstances if that should come to pass.

KBSC was managed by Bruce Johansen, whom I had originally known at Kaiser's KFOG-FM as an announcer, and who later, until his recent retirement, was President of NATPE. Bruce speaks French fluently, having lived there for many years, and had even acted as our guide when I took the family to Paris.

Unknown to anyone but Bruce and me, I arranged for Bruce to barge into the room after thirty minutes or so, and insult Pierre in French as "a low-life person of questionable ancestry with a penchant for raping and pillaging whenever the opportunity was at hand."

Bruce arrived on cue and began his tirade. Ken, who wasn't given to levity, was clearly nonplussed. Barry, on the other hand, immediately sized-up my invisible hand in the proceedings. Pierre, arms crossed, remained serene. Pierre let the dramatically proper time elapse between Bruce's final words and his reaction. He then turned to me and said, "Dick, your friend speaks French very poorly."

We made the deal for Merv.

My plan for the independent UHF stations was based on the simple premise that independent stations were attracting 20-30% of the general audience in multiple-station markets such as New York (six stations) and Los Angeles (seven stations.) Even where there was only one indie, such as Chicago, Minneapolis and St. Louis, their share of audience was high enough to achieve profitability.

The Kaiser stations were to emulate those independents in markets served primarily by network affiliates. Additionally, the stations would be in major markets not only so as to tap larger revenue pools, but also to be affiliates in a possible future network. Another motivating factor was that the Kaisers had been badly treated by the networks, with programs such as *The Kaiser Aluminum Hour* subjected to unilateral time period changes, and they would like nothing better than to be competitors to those networks someday. Plus, the concept also fit the Kaiser pattern of building from scratch.

While I realized that UHF was initially less desirable than VHF, the history of broadcasting had been that over time, the difference in reception of broadcast frequencies, such as between AM and FM in radio, would be eliminated or largely overcome by the skill and expertise of technicians who would refine the transmissions. I also organized the *Council for UHF Broadcasting* (CUB), a consortium of commercial and public broadcasters, which had the narrow purpose of physically and technically bringing UHF tuners up to VHF standards. I also supported cable, contending that it did more good than harm, and expressed this last view to the chagrin of many of my fellow broadcasters.

I believe that today, however, each of those broadcasters are in agreement that cable is a great boost for them because of its ability to deliver to the home, pictures and sound of excellent quality for VHF and UHF stations alike.

"The food was excellent, but only half as good as the service."
                                                    ...Art Greenfield

Through The Looking Glass
by Tom Piskura

Forty-nine years ago, my first temptress was a television station in my hometown of Cleveland. That station was one of the first to go on the air in the entire country. She succeeded in seducing me.

It all began in earnest for me outside a big window which was in the lobby of television station WEWS. If you stood in the lobby you could look through the glass to the "innards" of the TV station. I was mesmerized. It was 1953. I was fifteen years old. Although my eye was right up against the window, I couldn't see much.

All kinds of stuff was stacked inside the cavernous room on the other side of the glass. The stacks of materials blocked my line of sight to the right and left. I could only see a few feet either way. It was frustrating, but what I could see was tantalizing.

Day after day, in the late fall of 1953, that is how it went. I'd leave James Ford Rhodes High School, on Cleveland's west side, shortly after three o'clock in the afternoon. I'd hop aboard the West 25th Street bus to Public Square and walk the thirteen blocks to 1816 East 13th Street. That was the address of television station WEWS-TV. That TV station, which at the time had only been on the air for a scant six years, had a magnetic appeal.

Inside the lobby entrance, lining the walls, huge windows had been installed to allow spectators to watch television "happen!" However, inside the hallowed, seemingly magical studios beyond those windows, no one seemed to care that the view was completely obliterated by stacked-up scenery. Nevertheless, my almost daily pilgrimage to catch a glimpse of the WEWS-TV studio action continued for months.

Specifically, my obsession with television began on December 17, 1947. That's the day WEWS- TV first signed on the air. I was nine years old. Girls were not yet on my radar. And baseball, despite my grandpa's encouragement and hopeful expectations, was just not going to be part of my future. I would never be the next Bob Feller.

My very first seductress was television. All those many years ago, when I was a skinny kid in Cleveland, I would spend hours watching the WEWS test pattern. And the actual programs were only slightly better.

I knew the brief evening schedule by heart. And, because we could not afford a television set, I was forced to make friends with the freckle-faced girl next door. We were the same age, but that's about all we had in common. I could barely tolerate being in the same room with her. However, she really liked *Captain Video* and at her house I could get my nightly fill of TV. More like a nightly dose; I was hooked.

On December 17, 1947, Cleveland's WEWS-TV became the twelfth commercial TV station to go on the air in the United States. It seemed that the station was making up the rules as it went along.

And as I look back on it now, there's no doubt that it was in fact making it up as it went along. In those very early days WEWS would show lots of behind-the-scenes stuff and most of the programming was very informal.

Everyone seemed to be having a great time. There were lots of insider jokes and infectious fun. I loved it. Eventually, because I was watching WEWS habitually, I knew all the cameramen by name, as well as the directors, engineers, boom men, and others. And I certainly knew the names of the personalities who spoke into the camera, including the inimitable Dorothy Fuldheim. She seemed to be on-camera all the time. In the early days of WEWS-TV she became the living embodiment of the station.

Right from the start, it was clear to me that I wanted to be part of the action. I had to be a part of this wondrous new thing...television. In Cleveland, the arrival of television began to change everything. At first it was subtle, incremental. But things accelerated quickly and television soon had a powerful impact on my hometown, a place that from my then-youthfully optimistic point of view, was a Norman Rockwell painting come to life.

When WEWS went on the air in 1947, television very quickly became the dominant force in Cleveland. Very soon television seemed to determine what people talked about at school or at the water cooler at work. It was genuinely transforming the community.

I knew I had to be involved in the magic that was WEWS-TV. At the age of fifteen, in late 1953 and early 1954, I found myself hanging out in the WEWS lobby all the time. Looking back on it today, it is clear to me now that this was the reason why I found myself dashing to the studio every day after school. I wanted to see if I could capture just a bit of the thrill that television represented just by hanging out in the lobby of that brand new television station. One day, after a kids' program, the crew broke for lunch. They opened the large studio doors and gave me a strange look. One of the guys, who introduced himself to me as Dick Bodnar, asked why I kept showing up in the lobby day after day?

As I think back on it now, I mumbled some awkward answer. I said that I wanted to get a job, any job, at WEWS. Dick shot me a friendly smile and asked if I wanted to join the crew for a Coke at the *Allerton Hotel* next door. It was an offer I couldn't refuse. I was that much closer to being part of the magical world of television. I was told there weren't any openings at the moment, but they'd keep me in mind.

And so it went for weeks. I'd show up after school and the crew would invite me to join them for a Coke. Eventually, I was introduced to Jim Kirkey, the production crew boss. Mr. Kirkey made it clear that they had no openings. However, he promised to keep me in mind.

He was true to his word.

One day in 1954, Jim Kirkey called and asked if I would like to come to work part time. He didn't have to wait for my answer. As I look back on it now, nearly fifty years later, I think I answered "yes" even before he finished asking the question. In 1954, part-time work paid a dollar an hour, up from about seventy-five cents per hour just a year earlier. Jim Kirkey, I am certain, knew that I was underage. However, he never brought the issue up and I never volunteered information that would confirm that I wasn't quite sixteen, Kirkey said that only one last hurdle remained before I could be officially hired at WEWS: I had to meet and be approved by James C. Hanrahan, the Vice President and General Manager of WEWS. He was "Mister Big." Yikes! I was petrified just *thinking* about the meeting.

When the day came I put on my best suit. As a matter of fact, it was my only suit. I showed up at Jim Kirkey's office at the appointed time. I was already in a sweat. Jim explained that I would be meeting *alone* with Mr. Hanrahan and promptly led me to the outer office of "The Boss." I was instructed to sit and wait until I was called. At the time I would have sworn the clock on the wall was operating in slow motion. The five minutes I waited seemed like an hour.

Eventually, I was led into Mr. Hanrahan's inner sanctum. My legs felt as if they were made of *Jell-O*. I steadied myself, holding on to the back of a chair, until I was mercifully invited to sit down. James C. Hanrahan was respectfully referred to as JCH (Jesus Christ Himself) by his staff. They respected him and were fiercely loyal to him. But even though they admired him, they were careful to only utter the "Jesus Christ Himself" reference behind his back.

He had been a Lieutenant Colonel in World War II, serving under General George Patton on the General's headquarters staff, Third Army. Patton, of course, was known for his exploits during World War II and was regarded as an imperious and intimidating figure. As I sat there listening to Mr. Hanrahan, I had the feeling that more than just a little of General Patton had rubbed off on JCH.

Although I must say, as I got to know him, I found him to be a kind and generous man. As time went by I learned that he was tough on the outside but compassionate on the inside. I am in his debt for getting me started in a wonderful career that has spanned nearly fifty years.

Back then he was in his early 50's. As I sat in front of him, Hanrahan's presence seemed to fill the room. His smile was disarming, but he seemed to never take his eyes off me. He barraged me with questions. Who was I? What did I want to do with my life? Why television? How were my grades? Did I intend to go to college? Where? I recall hesitating and struggling to answer his questions. He wanted answers to questions I had not even considered, much less decided.

The interview went on for about twenty minutes, during which I seemed to be growing smaller and Hanrahan and his office seemed to be growing larger. I felt a bit like Alice, when parts of Wonderland would seem to grow gigantic as she shrank. Suddenly, he got up from his chair behind his desk, came around the desk, stuck out his hand and said, "Welcome to the WEWS family. I am going to expect a lot from you." I stood, shook (no, *pumped*) his hand, and we walked toward the door that led out of his office. As we reached the door, he abruptly stopped and turned to look me directly in the eyes. He said, "Tom, I will expect to see your report card for each grading period...anything less than a "B" and you won't be allowed to continue working at WEWS." Double yikes! And he made it clear that after high school I had to go to college if I planned to continue working at the station.

As I look back on that day all these many years later, I am grateful that he forced me to commit myself to getting an education. Hanrahan and WEWS provided the opportunity. However, it was his insistence that I stay on track to get a solid education that provided me with the real key to success.

So it was that I went to work at WEWS in 1954. I was assigned to the production crew. The production crew set up scenery, trimmed curtains, set up commercials, poured beer on close-up shots during commercials, installed overhead scenic flies, and did just about everything *except* touch a camera.

Being a cameraman, I was to learn, was a relatively exalted position and becoming a cameraman involved a rite of passage. It was not until almost a year later that I was allowed to stand behind a "locked down" camera. I was told to not touch anything, to just stand there. I did my very best to look like a professional as I stood there. As I recall, the regular operator just went to the restroom for a few minutes. I discovered that I was just a placeholder, but for me, oh it was a glorious beginning.

During the next three years I became good friends with my

boss, Jim Kirkey. Jim was born in 1910. Just to put things in perspective, 1910 was the year the Mexican Revolution began. It was the year the *Boy Scouts of America* was founded. It was the year the electric toaster was first sold. And 1910 was the year tennis shoes first hit the market. Jim was full of fascinating stories about how he had worked as a construction boss on Hoover Dam, high-voltage towers, skyscrapers like the Empire State Building and tall transmitter towers. Jim was like a second father to me. Not that my dad fell short in any way, but Jim was able to put a lot about growing up into perspective.

He was patient and was somehow able to put up with my inexperience and occasional bumbling. Jim Kirkey was a fine mentor. He helped me to grow from a kid to a young adult -- without too many accidents. I will be forever grateful for his patience and friendship.

In 1955, the chief of operations at WEWS, Ernie Sindelar, asked my boss, Jim Kirkey, if I would be interested in joining the WEWS remote crew. The remote crew did special broadcasts live, on-location, and sports events such as baseball and football games. The remote crew was regarded as the elite team of the WEWS production staff. Being a cameraman on the crew was a coveted position. For me, a wide-eyed kid of seventeen, it was a great honor to be invited to join the crew. Regrettably, my invitation to be part of this elite crew was taken as an insult by others who believed that they belonged on the crew -- at least before me.

The Cleveland Indians were not in the pennant race in 1955. They weren't in it in 1956 either. However, as a remote crew cameraman, I was thrilled, on many occasions, to be an eyewitness as 75,000 or more Indian fans literally shook Cleveland's *Municipal Stadium* as they roared their enthusiastic support of all-time great Bob Feller and the rest of the Tribe.

Later, when autumn signaled the start of the football season, I operated a TV camera on the roof of the stadium for our station's coverage of the Cleveland Browns games. A stiff twenty-mile-per-hour wind blasted us while we manned our camera positions. The wind shot out directly over frozen Lake Erie, creating a wind-chill factor of minus fifteen degrees. It was fifteen degrees warmer on the field which was sheltered a bit by the walls of the stadium. On the roof, our camera positions were completely exposed to the relentless freezing wind. I was a popsicle.

Nothing I have ever experienced was as cold and uncomfortable as those icy afternoons during which I was hanging onto that TV camera on the stadium roof for an entire football game. But it was worth it that year to witness the Cleveland Browns (with such great players as Otto Graham, Dante Lavelli, Lou Groza and Ray Renfro, under the direction of head coach Paul Brown) put together a thrilling season for Cleveland Browns' fans. I still remember those days fondly, despite the bitter cold.

And, I was steadily gaining experience about all aspects of broadcasting, thanks to the opportunities at WEWS. I was also discovering that I was pretty good at it.

In 1958, Don Perris, who was now Assistant General Manager at WEWS, appointed me Executive News Producer. At that time, WEWS had almost no news personnel, no news-gathering equipment, and, except for Dorothy Fuldheim's fifteen minute news program, WEWS had no other regularly scheduled newscasts on the air. At age twenty, it was a stunning challenge for me to be put in charge of building the WEWS news operation.

At the time, my promotion was not even a blip on the radarscope. However, it did represent the first step in a long journey aimed at making WEWS news a top contender in the market. It took almost twelve years of hard work by many talented people, but eventually TV5 News became a solid number one in Cleveland. And for me, that promotion was a start in management -- something that set the course for the remainder of my television career.

In 1966, I was hired by Group W, Westinghouse Broadcasting Company, to be Executive Station Producer at KPIX-TV in San Francisco. I was a bit nervous, but WEWS had prepared me well for my new responsibilities. When I left WEWS, I was making $14,000 per year. I was hired by Group W at $35,000 plus a yearly bonus. That was a lot of money then, and particularly for someone who still regarded himself as just a lucky, eager kid from Cleveland. WEWS was always very fair to me, and even with Group W's huge salary increase, it was very hard for me to leave my family at WEWS.

I soon discovered that, unlike chummy WEWS, Group W, Westinghouse, did not care much about being a "family." Group W was about being an aggressive "number one" in each of its markets. It was ruthlessly aggressive about budgets, about making the highest profits, and about being the very best broadcasting company in the United States. I learned a lot about television at KPIX, and a lot about being successful from Group W.

In 1969, Fred Walker, former General Manager at KPIX, joined Reeves Telecom and asked me to join Reeves as Vice President and General Manager of WHTN-TV in Huntington, West Virginia. I quickly discovered firsthand that there is nothing about Huntington that even faintly resembles San Francisco! Huntington is to San Francisco what Perris, California is to Paris, France. Truth is, I should have had my head examined for making the decision to leave beautiful, intoxicating San Francisco and take a job in Huntington, West Virginia. I suppose I had a kind of tunnel vision at that time, focusing only on climbing to the next management rung: TV station General Manager, Vice President, maybe even the head of a network. That's what I thought I wanted at the time, and that's why I packed up and moved to West Virginia, thinking it would help me climb up the management ladder.

What a mistake!

I shall never understand how I managed to hire really talented people from Chicago and New York to join WHTN and move their families to Huntington, a sleepy, off-the-main-track, antebellum town on the Ohio River. It certainly was not the meager salaries I offered.

Unfortunately, after eighteen months of trying to build too fast, Reeves suddenly found itself out of money. In one sobering weekend, all of us were fired. We had done a good job rebuilding WHTN, but none of us really regretted the opportunity to get the heck out of town and back into the "real world." I loaded up my '67 Mustang and headed west. Way west.

I don't recall exactly where it happened, but somewhere along the way, heading west, I stopped to see David Lean's *Lawrence of Arabia*. It was nothing less than a life-changing experience for me. By the time the film had finished, I realized that I really didn't want to devote my life to calculating the cost per thousand, film deals, what I was going to schedule at 4:00 p.m., and whom I was going to get to anchor the six o'clock news. I didn't really want to climb that television management ladder.

What became clear, all at once, was that conventional television was never going to give me an opportunity to touch the hearts and emotions of people as they can only be touched, seated alone and within themselves, watching a movie in a dark theater. I asked myself if I had wasted almost eighteen years in pursuit of my dream in television? I was terribly saddened at the possibility.

I decided that I wanted a career producing films.

But the questions descended on me: how was I ever going to get a start at making films? Where were the big lobby windows to view the studios? Where was the crew to help me get a start over a Coke. Where were my good friends Jim Kirkey and Jim Hanrahan when I needed them most? My outlook was bleak and I was discouraged. I headed for scenic Huntington Beach, California, where I did a lot of sitting on the beach and thinking about how to make a new start.

Eventually, I'd had too much sun and I'd done too much thinking. In 1970, I traded in the beach for a one-bedroom apartment in West Los Angeles. While there, I happened to read a small note in *Daily Variety* that tipped me off to a Film Fellowship and Grant-in-Aid that was being offered by the *American Film Institute* (AFI). Following up, I was instructed to write a paper on what interested me most about movies as compared to television. Although I don't really fancy myself a writer, I gave it my best shot.

Imagine my surprise when I was informed that I had won the award: to be an AFI intern on one of several theatrical features that were about to go into production. I selected *Silent Running*, an MCA/Universal Pictures science fiction production made in association with Douglas Trumbull Productions. To help solve mounting budget and production problems, Doug Trumbull appointed me to head his company and to help bring the picture in on budget and on time. That was pretty heady stuff for me, but I drew on all the experience and resourcefulness that I had acquired at WEWS. It paid off. We brought *Silent Running* in on budget and on time.

I was in the movie business! Well, not really in the movie business, but at least I had a solid start.

Later I became Associate Producer on *Magnum Force,* a Warner Brothers movie starring Clint Eastwood. I was the Unit Location Manager on *Streets of San Francisco*, Assistant Director on *The Book of Numbers* and worked on films for Disney, NBC/Hallmark Hall of Fame, and ABC-Circle Films. Assignments kept coming. I was combining my knowledge of television with my love of movies.

In 1972, with what I later learned was a solid recommendation from Don Perris, I was hired by the ABC Television Network (ABC Entertainment). At ABC, I was eventually promoted to Director, *prime time* Dramatic Program Development, and special assistant to Michael Eisner and Barry Diller. These men, of course, are giants in the world of entertainment today. While at ABC, I learned that the media of film and television could coexist and that they could both have emotional impact as entertainment. I was fortunate at ABC to be involved in the successful series development of *Starsky and Hutch, Wonder Woman, How The West Was Won,* and *Matt Helm.* The experience of working with Eisner and Diller was one for which I remain extremely grateful.

Later I joined Marcy Carsey and Tom Werner at Carsey-Werner Productions as Executive Vice President. Carsey-Werner produced *The Cosby Show,* and I oversaw program development at their West Coast office.

In 1987, the perfect job opportunity came along in the form of a management position at USA Networks. As Vice President, Programming-West Coast, USA Networks, I was put in charge of making as many as fifteen made-for-television movies each year.

USA Networks was primarily based in New York, so building a West Coast office, staff and network presence was a startup operation in every respect. It was not entirely unlike the task of building WEWS news from scratch. It was my job to do those things and start producing movies. Over the next ten years we produced nearly 150 movies for television. Luckily, made-for-television movies were experiencing something of a revival. Overall, our USA movies did very well in the ratings and were considered a hallmark of USA Networks. One of our films, *The China Lake Murders,* was the highest rated cable movie ever produced -- a record which stands to this day.

But good things don't last forever. In 1997, heading into my second kidney transplant, it was time for me to leave USA. I was pleased by our success, but I was tired and my health was interfering. After almost 45 years in broadcasting, it was time for me to rest.

Now, at age sixty-four, with my health very much improved since my second kidney transplant, I am still trying to figure out what I want to do when I grow up! I still carry that boyhood dream of piloting my own beautifully restored P-51 Mustang. However, movies and television and the opportunity to touch the hearts and emotions of people, as they can only be touched, seated alone and within themselves, experiencing a movie or television event in a dark theater or home, still have a very strong pull on what excites me most creatively.

The reality is I have a shoe box filled with Post-It Notes, each with a different movie, TV show, or entertainment idea scribbled on it. My idea box is starting to overflow. It is time to open it up and evaluate its contents seriously. I am determined to get busy and complete the four or five projects I have been mentally tinkering with. I have promised myself to get them done. And I am committed to doing so. That said, I had better get busy!

Fridays With Art

"Excuse me waiter, but this must be the child's portion."
...Art Greenfield

I'll Lie on the Floor, Open My Mouth, and You Pour the Beer In
by Jack Jacobson

I suppose you could call me a sports junkie, but you can understand my addiction when I explain that I spent many years of my life as a producer and director of TV broadcasts of sports events. Some of those efforts were on behalf of an entity called the Hughes Sports Network but most of them were on behalf of my primary employer, WGN-TV, in Chicago.

I "did" telecasts of the Chicago Cubs, the White Sox and the Chicago Bulls, and became acquainted with the athletes who comprised those teams and with many of the players representing the teams they competed against. I even got to know some of the players of the great Chicago Bears football team of the 1960's.

But of all the athletes I met during those years, the least assuming and friendliest were the men I knew who wore the uniform of the Chicago Blackhawks hockey team.

In the beginning of my hockey travels (1960) there were only six teams that made up the National Hockey League. They were: the Chicago Blackhawks, the New York Rangers, the Boston Bruins, the Detroit Red Wings, the Toronto Maple Leafs and the Montreal Canadiens. Rivalry among the teams was very intense. Hockey fans were rabid followers and knew the names and numbers of every player on each team. This was not that difficult at the time as there were less than 130 roster players in the entire league because each team was allowed to dress only 18 players, plus coach and trainer, for each game.

Interest in hockey in the United States was basically limited to the cities which had "home teams," unlike Canada where the sport was nearly a national religion. Of all the players in the League, about 99% were natives of Canada. These were men who had sprung from rural farming communities or small towns with such colorful names as "Moose Jaw." Very few of them had the opportunity to go to college, and their entry into hockey came at a very young age. It was and is my feeling that this background made them the unassuming professionals they were, totally unlike some of the spoiled celebrities that now populate our sports arenas.

Maybe it was because I was not much older than they were at the time, or the fact that I traveled with them, stayed at the same hotels, and rode the same team bus that made them feel and act as though I was part of the team. In fact, there were times when I was introduced as such, squirming lest they discover I could barely stand erect on skates.

I was accepted as one of their own. I became part of the pranks they played on each other, and the recipient of a few myself. I was also privy to and assisted in some coverups when they broke training.

Of course another factor that helped our relationship immeasurably was that I was on an expense account from my TV station and thus could pick up the beer tab once in a while. Hockey players of my day were the greatest beer drinkers in professional sports. They expended so much energy and sweat so profusely while playing the game that they needed great amounts of liquids to replenish their dehydrated bodies when the activity of the game ended. Beer was the major choice of replenishment.

One night my wife and I entertained the entire team and their wives at our home. I had anticipated their love of beer and ordered a full barrel of the brew. To my complete dismay, that night they drank nothing but my finest liquors...Crown Royal, Seagrams V.O., Captain's Table, J&B, Johnny Walker and Cutty Sark scotch, and other assorted vodkas and gins that I had accumulated over the years.

We became particularly friendly with Stan Mikita and his wife, Jill. One Saturday afternoon on the plane back from Detroit where the Blackhawks had just lost an afternoon game to the Red Wings, I found myself seated next to Stan. On the spur of the moment I said, "Stan, you know we taped this afternoon's game and it will be played back tonight starting at eight o'clock. Why don't you and Jill come over for dinner, we can have a few beers and watch the replay of the game."

"Great," said Stan. "I've never seen myself play."

So they came over and after dinner we turned on the TV and started watching the replay. Stan was one of the most competitve athletes I have ever known, and during the telecast he became so excited that I had to remind him the game had already been played hours ago and we had lost.

"Yeah," he said. "But wouldn't it be a real kick if we scored and won on the replay!"

After dinner we went down to our basement recreation room for an after dinner drink. We had installed a ping pong table there. Mostly for the kids, but also for me to help maintain some of the proficiency

I had developed playing the game in my youth.

"Oh great," exclaimed Stan when he saw the table. "Let's play *"Ganip Ganop."*

"What did you call it?" I asked.

"Ganip Ganop," he replied. "Just listen to the sound the ball makes when it bounces off the table." He was right, as anyone who has ever played the game would agree.

We began playing while our wives watched. I won the first game and was ready to quit, but Stan would have none of it. "No you don't! I'm just getting my rhythm!"

I kept beating him and he kept refusing to quit unless and until he won a game. It was getting quite late when my wife took me aside and whispered, "It's getting quite late. Will you stop being a baby and let him win a game!"

"No way," I replied. "I'm playing a great professional athlete, an All-Star, and you want me to let him win? Stan must have over-heard us because he mumbled, "If I'm so great how come I can't win a game from this out of shape old man?"

When Stan and Jill left sometime during the a.m. hours he had yet to win a game. And I am able to brag that he never beat me. I suspect that if it had been up to Stan we would still be playing.

But it was only a few weeks later when he obtained some degree of revenge.

Remember, please, that hockey is a winter sport, and played (in those days) only in frigid cities such as Montreal, Toronto, Boston, New York and Chicago...none of which were famous for balmy weather during the hockey season. Thus we all had appropriate heavy clothing in order to survive when we had to go outside.

It was routine for the announcer and me to leave our winter coats in the team's locker room before going up to the small announce booths we worked in, which usually had no space for us to hang such bulky garments. Then, following the game, we would retrieve our coats from the dressing room prior to joining the team for the bus ride back to either the hotel or the airport, depending on the demands of the schedule.

We were in New York, televising a New York Ranger, Chicago Blackhawk game back to Chicago. As a neophyte television producer, I tried to look the part. I had a light green waterproof trench coat that was extremely warm and offered me protection from whatever winter weather I might encounter. And I was certain I looked very chic in it.

Our team bus arived at *Madison Square Garden.* We followed the team into the dressing room, hung up our coats and began the standard process of asking around for any information that might make the telecast more interesting to the fans at home. Who had a birthday, who was getting married, who was having a baby, who was hurt and might not play...any tidbit that might give the fans a closer insight into the players. Then we left the locker room and proceeded to our assigned booth in the upper reaches of the '*Garden.*'

I don't remember who won, but I do know that the post game show ran rather long and we just made it back to the Blackhawk locker room in time to pick up our coats just as the team was boarding the bus for the long ride to the airport. Knowing the bus would not wait for tardy television personnel, I threw my coat over my shoulder and scurried out to the parking lot just in time.

Once on the bus I realized that the trip from the heated '*Garden*' to the parking lot had made me chilled. As I put on my fancy trench coat I felt a bulge in the pockets. Reaching down and putting my hands into the pockets I discovered to my dismay that the pockets were filled with ice cubes and full beer cans.

"Who is the idiot that ruined my new trench coat by putting ice cubes and beer cans in the pockets?" I screamed. No one answered.

Then I noticed Pat Stapleton who was seated behind Stan Mikita, pointing to himself as to say 'not me,' but pointing to Mikita who had a very innocent look on his face.

"Was it *you*, Mikita?" I yelled.

He stared at me with the same innocent face, then finally said: "Okay, I did it. I didn't think you would care."

"Not care?" I said, trying to keep my voice down so that the coach would not overhear our exchange. "How could I not care? This is a very expensive coat! What made you do such a thing?"

Stan, who is really a wonderful guy (and now a member of hockey's Hall of Fame), but who at the time I perceived as having a rather distorted sense of humor, replied: "You know how long the ride is from the '*Garden*' to JFK. And there's no beer provided on the bus so we usually bring some along to drink until we get to the airport. But it gets warm during the ride and warm beer has a rotten taste. So when I saw your waterproof trenchcoat in the locker room, it gave me an idea of how to keep the beer cold during the bus ride. Now, if you will just stop the shouting and making an ass of yourself and pass me a cold beer, you can have one for yourself if you want it. Your coat will dry out before we get to Chicago."

Then he reached over and took two cold beers out of a pocket, gave one to Stapleton, and we quietly continued our ride to the airport. I was too steamed to remember I had a chill. But it was the last time I left my coat in the locker room. Small announce booth or not, nobody was going to repeat the trick of putting ice cubes and beer in *my* pockets. Let somebody else be their thermos bottle.

One night, after a road telecast from Detroit where the Blackhawks had beaten the Red Wings, we were all in the Detroit airport waiting for the plane home. The weather between Detroit and Chicago was very bad that night and our flight was delayed. Knowing the great love hockey players had for beer, it was only natural that

Art Greenfield
(1917-2000)

Jim Stern

Jim Stern pitching the *Billy Budd* feature at the
first NATPE, 1963

Jim Stern selling at NATPE, 2001

II

Dick Woollen

Dick Woollen, circa 1960

Dick Woollen, current

Norman Horowitz

Dick Colbert

Dick Colbert (left) with the star of *The Rifleman,* Chuck Conners at the 1963 NATPE convention

Dick Colbert, current

Ave Butensky

Cover of January 1967 Mediascope Magazine, from left: Dancer-Fitzgerald-Sample advertising agency Senior Associate Media Director, Ave Butensky; Shel Pogue; Ken Torgerson; and Media Director, Lou Fischer

Circa 1968-1969, from left: Jimmy Neale, Ave Butensky, NY Mets Manager Gil Hodges, and Bill Shehan

Ave Butensky, current

Joe Siegman

Joe Siegman, current

Joe Siegman and Sammy Davis Jr.
on the set of Celebrity Bowling

Steve Rodgers

Steve Rodgers and his father, Peter
Rodgers, at their exhibition booth at a
NATPE convention

Jack O'Mara

Jack O'Mara, 1965

Jack O'Mara, current

Dalton Danon

Dalton Danon, 1944

From left to right: Bob Newgard, Dick Woollen
and Dalton Danon, 1980

Dalton Danon, current

Al Sussman

Dick Block

From left to right: Dick Block, Bill White and the late
Russ Stewart at WFLD-TV, Chicago, 1973

Dick Block, current

Tom Piskura

Tom Piskura, current

Tom Piskura, cameraman on WEWS
Christmas remote, 1956

Tom Piskura, Vice President and
General Manager of WHTN-TV, West
Virginia, 1970

X

Jack Jacobson

4 time Emmy Award winner and
one time National ACE Award winner

Jack Jacobson when he was producing and directing sports

Jack Jacobson, current

John Vrba

John Vrba with "Exercise Guru" Jack Lalanne

John Vrba, current

Dick Feiner

From left to right, circa 1963-1964: Tom McDermott, President of 4 Star, ???, Dick Colbert, Dick Feiner, Len Firestone (standing), Jerry Weisfeldt, Mickey Sellerman

Dick Feiner, current

Alan Silverbach

Alan Silverbach, current

Alan Silverbach (far left) and Herb Lazarus
next to him at NATPE booth, 1980

Left to right: Jim Weathers, Alan Silverbach,
Charlie Keys, Pierre Weiss at Kaiser Golf
Tournament, San Francisco, 1981

Herb Lazarus

Sandy Frank

John Serrao

John Serrao, 1951

John Serrao, current

XVI

Don Dahlman

Don Dahlman (left) with Fred Ziv at the
Frederic W. Ziv Awards, Cincinnati, Ohio, 1988

Don Dahlman, 1975

Mel Smith

Father and Son at NATPE

XVII

Rob Word

Rob Word (center) with Dale Evans (left) and TV's *The Lone Ranger,* Clayton Moore (right)

Rob Word, current

Steve Bell

Steve Bell and Liz Wrublin on the set of *Meet the Manager* at
WLVI-TV, Boston, 1980

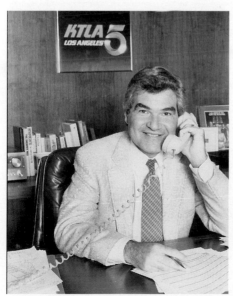

Steve Bell, current

Steve Bell at KTLA

Bob King

Armed Forces Radio on Guam, 1947
L-R: Don Hansen, Radio Engineer; Lt. Hal Miller, Station Manager;
Bob King, Announcer & Program Director

L-R: Gene Nichols, P.R. Maven for Capital Cities; Charlie Keler,
Head of Capital Cities TV Productions; Shannon King and Bob
King, Exec. V.P., Television Division, Cap Cities

Lew Blumberg

Lew Blumberg, 1944

Lew Blumberg, current

Herb Farmer

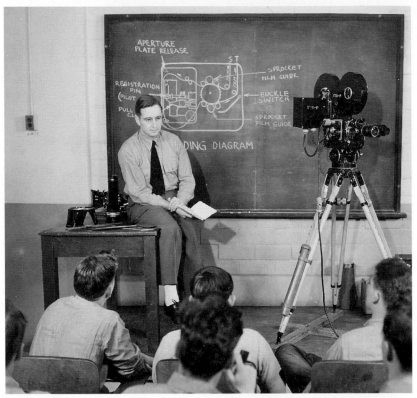

About 1945, lecturing to photo students at the US Navy Motion Picture Camera School, Pensacola, FL

About 2002, Emeritus Professor and Archivist for the U.S.C Motion Picture Technology Collection

Arthur Gardner

L-R: Arnold Laven, Jules Levy, Arthur Gardner, Robert Taylor

L-R: Jules Levy, Arthur Gardner, Arnold Laven

Arthur Gardner

XXIII

Fridays With Art

Seated, left to right: Loring d' Usseau, Art Greenfield, Jim Stern
Standing, first row: Dick Colbert, Lou Blumberg, Jack Jacobson
Standing, back row: Marv Gray, Dalton Danon, Steve Rodgers, Dick
Woollen, Dixon Dern, Bill Clark

they would gravitate to the airport bar.

During that night's game, Glen Hall, the Blackhawks' goalie, had been hit in the mouth by a deflected puck during the second period of play. He finished the period, but fifteen stitches were required to sew up his mouth and lips after the blow. The surgery was done between the second and third periods by the trainer, who at the time doubled as the team's doctor while on the road. And amazing as it may sound to fans and participants of other sports, Glen Hall started the third period in goal for the Blackhawks and played the rest of the game with his mouth occasionally dripping blood from the stitched area.

As announcer Lloyd Pettit and I moved toward the airport bar to join the players, I noticed that Glen was walking slowly behind me. His lips and cheeks were swollen and covered with medication and small bandages. I slowed and allowed him to catch up to me.

"Glen," I asked. "How do you feel?"

"Sore," he mumbled. "It hurts to talk."

"If you could drink, it would be my pleasure to buy you a beer," I said.

"I can drink," was his distorted reply.

I looked at him and asked, "How will you be able to put a glass or a bottle to your lips? Your mouth is all swollen and stitched up."

He stared at me and in a pained voice delivered words that will forever be etched in my annals of great sports quotes: "I'll lie on the floor, open my mouth, and you pour the beer in," he muttered. "There is nothing wrong with my swallowing, but be sure you pour slowly or I'll drown."

I swear to you this story is true. He did lie on the floor. I did slowly pour a bottle of beer down his throat. He did not drown. In fact, he went on to set an NHL record of 502 consecutive games played by a goalie. And he did it without wearing a mask or helmet!

I have vivid memories of the first time my job took me to Canada, the Mecca of Canadian hockey. The assignment was to handle coverage of the Chicago Blackhawks vs. the Montreal Canadiens in the old Forum in Montreal. Canadian television covered all the games and in those early days my station, WGN-TV, simply borrowed their pictures but replaced the CBC announcers with our own.

I had been in my Montreal hotel room the night before our scheduled telecast and noticed something strange as I watched a Canadian Broadcasting Company telecast of a game from Toronto. Eight o'clock was the scheduled start time for the game and to my surprise, the referee dropped the puck fifteen seconds after the hour and the game action started. The Canadian announcers did no opening chatter or commercials, as we did in our telecasts. They just introduced themselves, told the viewers who was playing whom and went right into the play-by-play. In our U.S.A. telecasts, games scheduled to start at 8 p.m. would be delayed by three to five minutes so that television could do introductions and opening commercials.

Fearful the same conditions would exist in Montreal, I approached the officials for that night's game and asked for the opening delay. I was surprised to be informed that they could not delay the start of the game unless the home team gave them permission to do so. I quickly sought out the management of the Montreal Canadiens who were owned at the time by the Selke family. I could not find Mr. Selke, Sr., but his son Frank, an officer of the team, was available.

I respectfully requested of him that he inform the officials that a three minute delay of the start of the game was okay by the Canadiens. I also told him that when his team visited Chicago we would gladly reciprocate. Much to my surprise and dismay, his answer was: "No, we drop the puck at 8:00:15 sharp. I'm not concerned about Chicago's television commercials. This is Montreal and we have our own way of doing things."

No coaxing or talking could change his mind. I explained to him that this courtesy was extended to television in all of the cities we visited.

He said, "You mean cities in the States. This is Canada."

With Selke's refusal I was at a loss. If I could not get a delay we would lose our opening and the first two commercials. It would cost the station money and I would get chewed out. Since such delays were honored in other cities, my management people would believe I had just goofed off.

Suddenly I had a thought. Almost all of my team's Chicago Blackhawk players were Canadian born. Maybe one of them would have an idea which could help. The first player I cornered for questioning was young Stan Mikita.

"Stan, I've got a problem and maybe you can help." I then proceeded to tell him about the conflict in scheduled starting times.

"No problem at all...easily done. Just talk to our goalie. All he has to do is to tell the referee that he needs an adjustment on his equipment. The ref will let him skate over to the bench and he can pretend to fix his straps or laces and you will have your time."

So I went in search of Dennis DeJordy, the team's backup goalie who was working that night to give a rest to regular Glen Hall. I found Dennis in the locker room and in a very quiet voice so that no one else, especially the coach, could hear, I explained the situation to him. If he would cooperate I would send him an interview fee of $25 (that was the going rate in those days) plus I would take him to dinner after the game at a restaurant of his choice. I could offer this because I was on an expense account and could justify playing the big spender.

He cautiously looked around to make sure no one had overheard us, and agreed to do it. Relieved, I headed up to the broadcast booth to join our announcer, Lloyd Pettit.

The teams skated out on the ice. At 8:00:15 p.m., the referee blew his whistle to start the game. I was watching DeJordy and saw him raise his hand and shout something to the referee. The official nodded and Dennis skated over to the Blackhawk bench.

I had previously warned our people in master control in Chicago that we might have a problem regarding our opening commercials, but now I grabbed the phone which connected to the open line between us and triumphantly told them to go ahead and roll the commercials...all was well.

But then I noticed that DeJordy was leaving the ice and heading down the ramp toward the dressing room. "What the hell is going on?" I wondered as I saw the referee skate over and talk to the Blackhawks' coach. Had they found out about my scheme with Dennis and thrown him out of the game? On my headset I heard Chicago informing me the commercials were over and I acknowledged the message, but my mind was elsewhere. I could see Dennis and myself being banned from hockey for life.

After what seemed like an eternity, DeJordy appeared and skated back to his position in front of the Black Hawk net. The game started. The delay was much longer than the three minutes I had bargained for and I began to worry that we would be facing additional charges from the telephone company for using their lines longer than planned.

After the game I cornered Dennis in the locker room but he refused to talk until we were able to isolate ourselves in the back of the bus carrying the team back to the hotel. Sitting next to him, I whispered: "What the hell happened?"

"I'll tell you what happened," he said in a very low voice. "I got so nervous at what I was going to do that I began to think I could get penalized by the league and suspended if they or the coach found out I was intentionally delaying the start of the game for television commercials. So when I got to the bench, in order to make it look good I told the coach that I had broken a suspender strap." (All hockey players wear suspenders under their jersey to hold up their uniform pants.) "So I went into the locker room to make it look good and really changed suspenders. Don't ever ask me to do anything like that again. And don't forget you owe me $25 and dinner in a restaurant of my choice!"

That was the longest speech in English that I ever heard from this native French-speaker.

So we had been able to insert all our scheduled commercials into the telecast, but we also later got a bill from the telephone company for an additional $700 to cover the extended use of our video and audio lines because my "creative delay" had caused us to run overtime. And that was probably more money than WGN-TV earned from the commercials. Especially when you add in the $25 fee to DeJordy and the cost of the dinner which also included players Stan Mikita and Pat Stapleton because they threated blackmail if they weren't invited.

But it was only a short time later when the National Hockey League established a rule that no televised game could start sooner than 5 minutes after the hour or half hour. I wonder what young Mr. Selke thought about that.

We were in friendlier climes one night when we were in New York to televise a game between the Blackhawks and the New York Rangers. Announcer Lloyd Pettit and I invited players Stan Mikita and Kenny Wharram to join us for dinner after the game. Because we were on an expense account, money was no object so we selected one of New York's finest steak houses. The place was not only noted for its fine food, but its unique ceiling from which hung hundreds of briar pipes. The pipes were intended for free use by the customers who chose to smoke following their meal, with tobacco supplied with the compliments of the management. (Being New York, I'm sure this little bonus showed up in the check in some manner.)

The four of us arrived in jolly fashion and had a few beers along with some appetizers. Then a few more beers along with four very large steaks with all the trimmings, along with a few more beers. Then we had dessert and a few after dinner drinks, during which we decided to partake of the pipes and free tobacco so we could leisurely puff away while exchanging bad jokes and racy stories.

At one point in the conversation, Mikita, who was feeling quite mellow, remarked to the announcer: "You know Lloyd, all of this high living is making you and Jack into out-of-shape old men."

At that time we were not that much older than the two players and we took exception to that remark. Pettit had played varsity football at Northwestern University and with the Iowa Sea Hawks during a tour of duty in World War II. I had played Minor League Baseball and still participated in softball and park district basketball. Lloyd and I prided ourselves on still being athletic and in shape. And certainly not old.

A few more puffs on the pipe, another round of drinks and a challenge was thrown. We, these two out of shape old men, would challenge the two professional hockey players to an arm wrestling contest. We'd see who was old and out of shape.

We flipped coins for opponents, with Pettit drawing Mikita and me matched against Wharram. I don't remember how Pettit's match with Mikita came out, but I do know that mine was a draw, despite Wharram's claim that I cheated by holding onto the leg of a table. (Which I of course denied, but actually did.)

I also remember the maitre d' asking us to pay the check and please leave before we were thrown out. And he added: "Please never come back." He was so glad to see us leave that he even hailed a cab for us.

During the ride to the hotel, the bragging and accusations continued and it was decided that we should resolve the issue in the hotel bar. But as we entered the lobby we encountered the last person we wanted to see: Blackhawk coach Rudy Pilous. To say that he was not delighted with the condition of two of his star players would be an understatement. Needless to say, the match did not continue. The coach ordered his players to go to their rooms and told Pettit and me that as long as we were traveling with the club, the hotel bar was not only off limits to his team, but to us as well.

In the elevator going to our rooms, Mikita said: "He's seen you two so much he thinks you're part of the team. If you think that's funny, see how you feel when he has the two of you out on the ice tomorrow morning taking laps!"

It did strike me funny. Me out on the ice. I wondered if they had double runner skates.

Fridays With Art

TV Time in LaLa Land
by John Vrba

I went to work at KTTV in Los Angeles when there were only 78,000 TV sets in the vast area reached by our signal. My first title was Promotion Manager, and I relied a lot on my fellow employee and college pal, Pete Robeck, for guidance. He told me it was important that we attend the Western States Chain Grocer's convention at the *Hotel del Coronado* in San Diego. We made plans to spend three days there, meeting and entertaining the people from various grocery companies, so upon arrival at the hotel I ordered and signed for liquor and supplies. This was new to me, but Pete said this was the way CBS would do it. Upon checking out days later, there were more papers for me to sign.

Norman Chandler was nationally known and widely respected as the owner and publisher of the *Los Angeles Times* and also, 51% owner of KTTV. He was temporarily maintaining an office at the station since our first General Manager had recently been terminated. A few weeks after the grocer's convention I was summoned to see Mr. Chandler. When I entered he looked up at me with a smile and said, "When do you think we will get title to the properties you bought in San Diego?" I didn't understand. Then he said, "I've seen copies of your expense report from that convention, so you must have bought something." I mumbled something lame.

He went on. "We had representatives there from the '*Times*' and they apparently were at a different convention."

I backed out of his office, wondering if the sales guys had sandbagged me.

At one point the '*Times*' asked a select group of younger employees to qualify for possible promotion by visiting an industrial psychologist in downtown L.A. My encounter began with being ushered into an office where behind the desk sat a stern man with glasses, poised with five fingers of one hand pressed against the five fingers of the other hand. He explained that there were a few tests that would be given, and that the first one consisted of a document with some fifty questions, each of which required a "yes" or "no" answer. He then exited the room, leaving me with the feeling there were probably some tricky questions.

After ten minutes or so, the good doctor (PhD) returned asking, "Did you complete the test?" I said I had trouble with question number five and have written in an answer. He replied that he didn't know the question by number...what was the question? I said the question asks, "Do you ever worry about sex?" and I have written "Constantly."

His reaction confirmed that PhD's have a limited sense of humor.

Despite such minor rebellions, I was eventually appointed Sales Manager.

When first-run programs began to be produced for syndication, one of the big hits was *Highway Patrol*, starring Broderick Crawford who, as a lantern-jawed crime buster was frequently shown in hot automobile pursuit of the bad guys. The show was especially important to KTTV in our effort to attract viewers. National advertisers were willing to buy spots in the show because they knew it would deliver an audience, and we soon sold all the legally available six minutes of commercial time within the program.

But our national sales representatives insisted that other stations which also carried *Highway Patrol* were taking more than six minutes, and that we were foolish in restricting the commercial content. We needed every dollar we could bring in, so I felt it prudent to try to discover what other stations carrying the show were really doing. I called my friend, Fred Ebener at WOW-TV in Omaha, as his station was one of those our reps had cited as carrying more than six minutes. "Sure," Fred replied to my question. "All we do is cut out all those driving scenes."

Just the essence of the show, that's all! Maybe he could get away with that in Omaha, but with the producers and cast living in our backyard, we couldn't even consider that from either a creative or contractual standpoint.

Shortly after KTTV had moved into new quarters in what was formerly the Nassour Studios, located at Sunset Boulevard and Van Ness, I was surprised one day to be told that three representatives from Procter & Gamble were in the lobby. People from the big soap works in Cincinnati...the country's largest advertiser!

I hastened downstairs and greeted the guests, suggesting we take a tour of our vast sound stages. Our live daily cooking show was just starting its telecast and I thought the timing was fortuitous. As we approached the set, I heard chef Freida Nelson say, "This morning girls, we are going to show you how to make *soap* at home."

197

The rest of the tour is a blur.

I was calling on ad agencies during a one-day trip to San Francisco and when I entered the offices of BBD&O, their Betty Share told me a man named Vince Francis had been calling and wanted to talk to me. I thanked her for the message, wondering why he had bothered to call me there. Vince was West Coast Sales VP for the ABC-TV network, officed in San Francisco. When I got to the next agency there was another message from him and I managed to return his call just before time for my lunch appointment. He said he must meet with me. Urgent. I explained to him that I was tightly scheduled right up to my 6 p.m. flight back to Los Angeles. His reply was that he would meet me at the airport.

As I arrived, there was Vince. What was so important that he would drive all the way out to the airport? He started expressing both his excitement and his frustration. He told me about a very talented man who Vince was certain would be a great hit on TV, but that he couldn't get his ABC associates in either San Francisco or Los Angeles to even talk to him. The man's name was Jack Lalanne and he wants to do a daily exercise show on TV. I told Vince to have the man call me and I would be happy to talk to him, but Vince said that the man would rather meet in person and that he would come to Los Angeles if I would promise to meet with him. I said, "O.K."

The next week Jack Lalanne did come to my office and I was impressed with his personality. I told him we could put his show on the air early in the morning, but he would have to buy the time and it would be fairly expensive as we would have to schedule cameramen and a stage crew at an earlier time than usual. I cleared the project with Program Director, Bob Breckner, and Jack signed a 13 week contract. Once the show started both the mail and telephone response began to gradually grow, proving that Vince had been right in his appraisal of Lalanne...he truly had a "TV personality." Our program department scheduled some cartoons just prior to Jack's time period. The kids discovered the cartoons, watched them, and momma stayed tuned in to watch Jack.

In an attempt to express his gratitude, Jack came into my office during his first weeks on the air and proposed giving me 10% of his company for helping him. I quickly declined, knowing the '*Times*' would have a policy against any such participation. But for many years, Jack proved to be phenomenally popular...far more so than anyone would have projected for a simple "exercise show." He also became comfortably wealthy through the sale of vitamins and gym franchises, but I was never bitter about not being a shareholder.

A major KTTV project I was involved in was the selling and production of the annual *Bing Crosby Pebble Beach Golf Tournament*. I first was approached by a man named Wally Gould. Everybody in their lifetime should know a colorful character like Wally Gould. His habits included hustling marks at the putting green at *Roxbury Park*, but he somehow had ready access to a lot of different people. He showed up one day to tell me the news that the ABC Network had not picked up its option to televise this premier golf event, information he had gleaned from someone in the office of Larry Crosby, brother of Bing. So KTTV did step in and managed to secure the rights to this celebrity-laden (and top pro golfers as well) two day event. We were even able to line up an ad hoc network of 123 stations to air the shows.

It became my assignment to sell commercials so we could cover the cost of rights fees for the event and one of my deals was for an insurance company to sponsor one-third. One week before the start of the tournament, I was approached by my contact at their ad agency. "We have to make a serious request of your announcers," he said. "What would that be?" "One of the performers who always participates in this event is Phil Harris. Under no circumstances will your people interview him on the air!" Naturally, I asked him why this edict? He said, "Last year an ABC announcer asked Harris to comment on the amateur/pro pairings and Harris said he was impressed with several young pros, including Gay Brewer. The ABC man countered that Brewer had scored well and was a new name on the tour, at which point Harris said, "Yeah, he sounds like a fag winemaker from Modesto!"

In connection with the '*Crosby Golf Tournament*' I had asked to have access to the President of the insurance company, to personally thank him for his sponsorship, and it was arranged that I should meet him at the clubhouse for lunch. When I arrived at the table it was obvious that he had been there for some time, as evidenced by the several emptied beverage glasses on the table. After introductions and a little small talk I indulged in a moment of shameless flattery by asking, "Your company is one of the most successful insurance companies in the country. Is there any one thing that you feel has been the secret of your success?"

Expecting some inspirational answer, I waited while Mr. President eventually looked up from his Tom Collins to say, "Hire enough lawyers so you don't pay claims."

I guess that was a "distilled" insider's summation of the insurance business!

When Ampex first introduced videotape to the television industry, this revolutionary new product created a sensation. Now stations could pre-record their local shows with a clarity and brilliance that equaled the look of live television. And advertisers could do the same with their commercials. KTTV was among the first stations to acquire these machines and so it was decided that we should demonstrate this magical new equipment by using it in the production of our annual pre-Fall buying season presentation to the major New York advertising agency buyers. But to do this we would have to find some facility in New York to play the tape for us.

I remembered that WOR-TV in New York had Ampex machines and I knew the General Manager, Gordon Gray, because we were both board members of the Television Bureau of Advertising (TVB). Even though his station was owned by General Tire, which also owned a station in Los Angeles, he agreed to air the tape for us as a special feed to our planned luncheon group. He rationalized that it wouldn't interfere with the operation of his station, as they didn't normally sign on with programming until 3 p.m.

We had reserved one of the large meeting rooms at the *Waldorf Astoria*, expecting some 1200 to attend this all-important presentation. It was mid-July and this particular day seemed more humid than usual. I arrived at the '*Waldorf*' about 11 a.m. and went to our meeting room, expecting to find a cool, comfortable venue. The place was warm! I frantically tried to find someone in charge to get improved air quality. Finally I located the famous Maitre d,' Pierre (who was later convicted of tax fraud, probably for failing to report all the "green inducements" he collected). After getting his attention with some green paper currency, he took me aside to explain a very delicate situation.

He confided that there was also a luncheon reception for the Prime Minister of Ghana, and that he had directed all available air conditioning into that room. "You understand, I am sure, Monsieur."

By applying some more green we were able to get some of the air diverted our way. A day later when the *New York Times* ran a story about our novel presentation, mentioning the fact that WOR-TV had transmitted it, Gordon Gray deflected his boss's complaint about him helping the competition by saying, "If we're so smart, why didn't we think of it?"

When the Dodgers made their historic move from Brooklyn to Los Angeles, one of those also transferring was a man from the program department of advertising agency Young & Rubicam named Wick Crider. Wick was a bulky man with a sardonic sense of humor. He also brought with him some big city habits, such as a printed card carrying the recipe for vodka stingers, which he would hand to waiters near the conclusion of a multi-martini lunch, in order to assure proper preparation of his concluding libation. While his size enabled him to tolerate lots of alcohol, I soon learned that lunch dates with him incapacitated me through the following day. Wick worked closely with Walter O'Malley, owner of the Dodgers, and had told me that O'Malley was convinced that Pay-TV was the future for the Dodgers, not free television.

So one day when my secretary told me that Wick had called, I told her to put him off and that I would talk to him later. The next day she said Crider had called again and was very upset that I had not called him back. I explained that I couldn't handle having lunch with Wick right now, as our General Manager, Dick Moore, was out of town at a convention and I needed to remain alert and at my desk.

But the next morning Wick caught me and said, "Dammit, I need you over here right now. All the other stations have submitted bids to carry nine Dodger games from San Francisco. One of your competitors, KCOP, through co-owner Bing Crosby, has even agreed to do it for nothing."

I enlisted Ed Benham, our Chief Engineer, to have him detail technical coverage while I scrambled to think how we could snag this highly desirable event and still make some money. Ed and I went to see Wick at his Y&R office in the Taft Building at Hollywood and Vine. Benham gave a thorough outline of camera placements and all technical details. The Dodgers were not asking any rights fee but they retained the sales rights to all the commercial positions within the games themselves. I proposed that KTTV carry the nine games on Friday nights, and daytime on Saturdays and Sundays, with 15 minute pre-game and 15 minute post-game shows where we could position our commercials, guaranteeing that the advertisers would not be competitive to the Dodger's sponsors, Union Oil and Carnation. I figured that we could sell the spots for at least double our normal rate, which should cover most of our line and technical costs.

Wick called early the next day and said, "You've got the deal. And I liked that engineering guy." No one else had thought about bringing their engineer to reassure that the technical aspect would be executed properly. The next day the *Los Angeles Times* had a headline the size of a war-declaration, reading: DODGERS ON TV. Huge news impact.

When I explained the coup to our traveling General Manager, Dick Moore, on the phone he said, "Get out of the deal! We'll lose our shirts." But fortunately for me, by the time he returned to his office he had recognized all the benefits of the deal, aided by the realization that we had sold all the commercial positions for even more than I had projected.

Moore led us to a Sunday meeting with O'Malley, who had just returned from Mass. O'Malley proposed a toast to our new relationship, and turning to me he said, "I know you'll have a J & B and water," and then proceeded to identify and order each person's preference. What a presence! KTTV's relationship with the Dodgers continued for many years, but the station no longer carries the games since both the station and the team have been purchased by Rupert Murdoch's News Corporation and telecasts are now mostly seen on that company's cable outlets. Sadly, it is generally agreed that the team's performance has suffered since the baseball-wise O'Malley family sold the team.

Selling media to the auto makers in Detroit in the 1960's was an adventure. The Japanese imports had not yet become such strong competitors to the U.S. makers, so the reception to media was relatively cold, especially to anyone from the West Coast. The KTTV sales message was that the U.S. companies needed to supplement their network TV schedules with local spots in Los Angeles, both because it was the best automobile market in the nation and because network programs here were delivering smaller audiences than in other markets.

Jack O'Mara prepared a detailed presentation for us to use with the car companies which detailed this under-performance. The study was enhanced by showing the marketing shares of various car models, using research from the respected '*Times Home Audit*.' The most popular brand was Ford, followed by Chevrolet, then Plymouth, on down to the 11th brand which was a category lumping together all Japanese brands, plus Volkswagen. This category had ranked only 29th the previous year. O'Mara had also included a separate area map showing dealer locations...one for Ford, one for General Motors, and one for Chrysler-Plymouth. Our plan was to thus tailor each presentation for the particular manufacturer we were pitching.

When I arrived in Detroit I was greeted by our Blair TV man stationed in Detroit, Gabe Dype. He was (either bravely or foolishly, depending on your point of view) driving a foreign-made Kharman Ghia car in U.S.A.'s Motor City! Regardless, our first two meetings with Ford and Chevrolet went well, with inquiries for further data. Our next meeting was with the Ad Director at Chrysler. He interrupted our pitch so many times it bordered on rudeness, and it was clear that his reaction to the content of our presentation was negative. The capper came when I pointed out to him the remarkable sales rise of the Volkswagen/Japanese cars in Southern California. His response epitomized Detroit's attitude at that time:

"Oh, that's nothing but a passing fad!"

One of the activities which made TV exciting in Los Angeles in the 1950's was the competing station KTLA's frequent use of live, on-the-spot remote telecasts. And when Dick Moore (by then, my third General Manager) arrived at KTTV he determined to match and hopefully even surpass KTLA in such endeavors, particularly in covering breaking news stories. We aired many live events, including the *Rose Bowl Parade*, Hollywood's *Santa Clause Lane Parade*, the *Golden Globe Awards*, the *Miss Universe Pageant*, and a host of sports and news events.

Dick conceived the idea of selling sponsorship of all these events, both planned and unplanned, to a single sponsor, and Mobil Oil agreed to be the automatic sponsor of any such event we decided to air. The commercial plan was a low key "Brought to you by Mobil," delivered live by the talent at the site. This was usually Bill Welsh, who was such a reliable and versatile performer we dubbed him "All Purpose Welsh."

However, a refinery fire started in Wilmington, and when the remote truck rolled, Welsh was far away in the West Valley, so Roy Maypole was pressed into service as the on-the-scene commentator. Roy was a high-energy personality with a rapid-fire delivery. Roy was describing the refinery fire and how the firemen were working to bring it under control, when he looked off camera, apparently for a cue. Then he said, "Oh yes, ladies and gentlemen, Mobil Oil Corporation is very pleased to bring you this Standard Oil refinery fire."

Fridays With Art

206

Just Don't Schedule it on Sunday Afternoon... Everybody's Playing Polo!
by Dick Feiner

When the financial backers of Universal Pictures decided it was time for new management to take over the struggling studio, they hired my uncle, Nate Blumberg, to be President and he brought along with him another of my uncles, Matty Fox. Matty, who was then in his early twenties, soon earned the label of "boy wonderkind," having lured into the studio's fold such popular performers as Olsen & Johnson, W.C. Fields, and the comedy team of Abbott & Costello.

Uncle Nate hired my father to run the studio's physical plant, so we settled into a community near the studio called Toluca Lake. Our next door neighbor was movie star and singer, Deanna Durbin, our best friend was Jack Oakie, the estates of Bing Crosby and Bob Hope were a couple of blocks away, and at North Hollywood High School, some of my classmates were "*Our Gang*" members Spanky MacFarland and Scotty Becket, Farley Granger, Marty Melner,

Bobby Haldeman, and a girl named Norma Jean Baker (Marilyn Monroe).

In the early 1940's World War II was raging and while I was still in school I had signed up in advance for the Army Air Corps. After graduation my unit was headed first to Europe, and when that phase of the war ended we were diverted toward the Pacific when the A-Bomb caused the surrender of Japan. Suddenly the war was over and I was free! The G.I. Bill enabled me to attend USC but I soon gravitated back to "the moovies" when I was offered a job of being manager of seven Fox West Coast theatres, and was paid $55 a week for a six day workweek.

But I left that dead-end job in 1950 to work for $50 a week when I learned my uncle Matty had formed a new company called Motion Pictures For Television (MPTV). Initially, the company created a library of about six hundred features and serials by combining titles controlled by Matty with those from Joe Harris's Flamingo Films and Elliot Hyman's Associated Artists Films. Our Sunset Boulevard office was opened by David Wolper, later to be famous as one of TV's most honored producers of documentaries. In addition to having sales rights to such familiar feature film titles as *Stagecoach* and *It's A Wonderful Life*, MPTV produced for syndication a half-hour series titled *The Adventures of Superman*, starring George Reeves. I acquired some useful production experience while acting as liaison between our producers and the Leo Burnett Advertising Agency, who represented Kellogg's, the sponsor of the program. Today it is hard to believe that because Kellogg paid us a license fee of just $16,000 an episode, that was enough to cover the entire cost of production!

One of the earliest, if not the first, barter deals for TV programming was made by MPTV in 1951 with the stations owned by NBC in New York and Los Angeles. Because MPTV retained the

208

right to sell commercial time in the group of movies we licensed to them, I worked out of an office at the Hollywood NBC station alongside other members of their sales staff. During the 18 month term of that deal, MPTV managed to generate $230,000 in revenue from selling time on the two stations which was a whopping amount in those days.

This is especially ironic in view of the great resistance to the deal initially expressed by Ted Cott, General Manager of NBC's New York station. He resisted the idea of scheduling movies late at night, claiming his audience was either asleep or out of the house attending such then-current Broadway shows as *Guys and Dolls, The King and I*, or *A Tree Grows In Brooklyn*. His attitude is reminiscent of the classic remark by some elite programmer who said, "Just don't schedule it on Sunday afternoon...everybody's playing polo!"

At the expiration of the term for the NBC deal, the films were licensed to the CBS owned stations in New York, Los Angeles and Chicago. But that deal nearly came unstuck over the issue of who would pay for the cost of shipping the heavy film prints. Movie theatres had always paid the cost of shipping both ways but CBS objected to the practice as being too expensive. Matty Fox solved the impasse by granting the stations the right to make a second telecast of each feature within a two week window, but they would have to pay shipping charges. He suggested they title the afternoon showing *The Early Show* and the nighttime showing *The Late Show*, formats which proved to be highly successful for many years, and the revenue from which made the shipping costs seem trivial. Sometimes great ideas appear overly simple.

I was briefly transferred to our New York office in 1953 where I would frequently visit uncle Matty who worked primarily out of his penthouse at 445 Park Avenue in the heart of Manhattan. It was there I witnessed a fascinating bit of movie history.

I was lounging around in the penthouse when there was a knock on the door and I opened it to find an agitated John Huston who said he urgently needed to see Matty. This was shortly after my uncle had helped reconstitute United Artists by arranging for their head man, Arthur Krim, to have access to a bank credit line for that studio. On that day I could see that the famous director, Huston, was a wreck. I started to leave the room so the two men could have privacy but was stopped by Matty and told to "sit."

Huston launched into an anguished litany of how he and James Agee had just spent weeks of toil, tears, booze and cigarettes -- and not much sleep -- creating a screenplay version of H. M. Forester's classic novel, *The African Queen*. He revealed that Katherine Hepburn and Humphrey Bogart ("Kate" and "Bogey" to him) were set and ready to pack their bags to go to Africa for the shoot. "Everything is set. But I don't have the money!"

Matty told John Huston, "Just sit there a minute." He went to the phone and called Arthur Krim, who acknowledged he had just received an eight million dollar production loan but had no pictures ready which needed financing, so Matty told Huston to go see Krim and pick up a check. The now ecstatic Huston ran out the door. God only knows when they actually signed the contracts, but they shook hands on the deal, and in those days, that was a blood pact. The whole thing had taken less than half an hour. Oh yes, the total cost of making *The African Queen*? Less than a million dollars!

Later in 1953 I found myself again working out of the Los Angeles office as a territory salesman. My boss, David Wolper, dispatched me on a tour of West Coast markets stretching from Los Angeles all the way north to Tacoma, Washington. It was a time when the FCC had just granted licenses to a number of new TV stations. Obviously they were going to be hungry to acquire programming and lots of it.

210

I had been trained in a sales technique known as "The Palmer Method," sometimes referred to by the acronym AIDA: A=get the prospect's *Attention;* I=stimulate an *Interest;* D=create a *Demand;* and A=move the prospect to *Action.*

I knew that some of my newly-licensed prospects had not even constructed their facilities yet and probably had no knowledge of what they would need to properly handle the films they would be airing. So I softened up the owners of the stations by telling them I had started in television for MPTV by inspecting, cleaning, and editing 16mm film, servicing two dozen stations. I carried along with me a blueprint, which I unfurled with great flourish, and which demonstrated how I set up my film room, including film racks, film benches, editing and splicing equipment, and information as to where my prospect could order the same for his station. Additionally, I carried samples of letterheads from existing TV stations so the new owner could get ideas of how to design his own. All in all, it was an impressive kit.

Maybe it was because I was the first "film person" these prospects had ever seen, but in my eight week trip I closed deals in 14 markets and generated contracts worth nearly a million dollars. Our National Sales Manager, Erwin Ezzes, was ecstatic and impressed about the number of sales I had made in such a short time. In fact, he soon met with a rep of "The Palmer Method" himself, and then set up a commission plan for the salesmen. He told all our other salesmen what I had done and sent them out to "beat the bushes," armed with a new sales technique.

In 1954 I was relocated to Chicago, and even though Frank Sinatra wouldn't popularize Chicago as *My Kind Of Town* until three years later, I reveled in the joys of such places as *The Gaslight Club*, *The Pump Room, Fritzels, The Stockyards Inn, The Red Lion, London House, The Soda Bar*, and the Chicago Theater. I saw Lena Horne at

Chez Paree and Barbra Streisand at *Mr. Kelly's*.

Conventional wisdom had it that people in the midwest wouldn't watch a foreign-made film on TV, but a local car dealer, Jim Moran, thought otherwise. He purchased the telecast rights to films, appeared in his own commercials, and ran a heavy schedule of spots during movies on station WGN-TV. So when he decided to purchase and sponsor the Italian-made *Bicycle Thief*, he started promoting it six weeks in advance and was rewarded with an astounding 54 rating! Jim Moran also had the courage to play *The Medium*, by Giancarlo Menotti, as performed by Anna Marie Alberghetti.

The opposite of Moran's positive attitude was displayed by the Program Director of the NBC station in Chicago who was resisting my efforts to sell him the Walter Lantz cartoons. I whittled away at him, but only to the point where he offered to buy just one telecast of each cartoon, with a correspondingly low license fee. I'll never forget his rationale: "A child won't watch a cartoon a second time...he will simply tune it out. A child has a memory like an elephant!" Fortunately, his management superiors at the station had a different view. They pointed out to him how many times a parent can read the same story to their child, how kids save comic books, reading them again and again until they literally fall apart, and even how they would watch and re-watch the same cartoon in a theater. Their view prevailed and after weeks of negotiations I finally closed the deal on Christmas eve.

In 1955, MPTV was merged into Guild Films, a company which proved to be a rudderless ship which soon sank like the Titanic, and took MPTV into obscurity with it.

But Erwin Ezzes resurfaced again as a sales manager when Matty acquired the TV distribution rights to 742 RKO features from Howard Hughes. Matty loved to tell the story of how he had been scheduled to fly back to New York from Los Angeles and Hughes had volunteered to personally drive him to the airport. Hughes was doing so in his battered Chevy when Matty told him he could raise all the money to buy the pictures via the First National Bank of Boston. Hearing this, Hughes pulled a U-turn on busy Sepulveda Boulevard and then pulled over to make a phone call. (Obviously this was before cell phones.) A terrified Matty said to Hughes, "What the hell was so important that you damn near killed us?" Hughes replied, "I canceled your TWA flight. Now we're talking real money!" And they returned to Hollywood to structure an option for the films.

After the demise of Guild, I had taken an interim job as a "producer's rep" for Gross-Krasne Films which produced such series as *Mayor of the Town*, with Thomas Mitchell, *Big Town*, starring Mark Stevens, and *The Lone Wolf*, with Louis Hayword. The distribution rights to these series had been granted to MCA, so my job was to keep an eye on the deals they were making so as to be sure they were good for the producers. But it was sort of a frustrating role for me, so when Ezzes called to invite me to work as a film salesman again, I was ready.

The company was called C & C Television Corp., and its mission was to "barter" the 742 RKO pictures which Matty had acquired from Hughes. Despite an offer to pay the travel expenses for a trip to Atlantic City for any station executive who would agree to barter time to C & C in exchange for telecast rights to the library, there were no takers. Not a single deal. "Ez" wanted me to set up an operation in Los Angeles which would cover the territory from the West Coast to the Mississippi, and he had already hired a sales staff for me to supervise. On my way back to the coast I stopped over in Denver to call on Bill Grant at KOA-TV, a station which I knew was partially owned (42.5%) by Bob Hope. I reasoned that if anybody would understand movies, it was Hope. (I knew Hope slightly, for we both lived in Toluca Lake and I saw him frequently at the drugstore. "Hiya, kid. Do you like my Pepsodent smile?" I had often played touch football at the bottom of Forman Avenue, adjacent to Lakeside Golf Club, and I would pass the ball to Hope and he would toss it back to me.) I sold the library to KOA-TV for $400,000 and C & C bought the needed barter time for its client, International Latex, on a different Denver station, KBTV, for $250,000. That deal started the ball rolling and so many other library deals were made that pretty soon I realized I had sold myself out of a job!

Then I became peripherally and briefly involved in one of Matty's boldest schemes. The Brooklyn Dodgers had recently left Flatbush and moved to Los Angeles and the New York Giants were now the San Francisco Giants. Matty envisioned building a Pay-TV operation which he labeled "Skiatron" which would offer television coverage of both team's games for a nominal fee to the viewers. In one of his fund-raising efforts to cover the cost of building Skiatron, Matty flew up to San Francisco to meet with a man named Lew Lurie, who, according to what Matty told me, was so wealthy that if one caught the cable car from the St. Francis Hotel (which Lurie owned), then looked both left and right from the car, he owned most of the property you could see, stretching all the way to Fisherman's Wharf! When Matty started describing his plan to Lurie, he was only a few minutes into his pitch when Lurie stopped him and asked him to wait there in his office. As he waited, a tray offering tea and coffee was sent in. When Lurie returned he handed Matty a document which showed that Lurie had ordered a deposit be made to Matty's New York bank for $2,500,000 as his guarantee of participation. Shortly after that, Stats and Company had raised $55 million in underwriting for Skiatron. But the California theater owners became panicked. They feared that the telecasts of seventy-seven home games and an equal number of away games would keep people out of the streets in droves, so they bankrolled a state ballot referendum which slowed

Skiatron down. Eventually the California courts ruled the ballot measure an illegal referendum, but by that time it was too late for Skiatron.

I'll never forget the kindness shown me by Len Firestone when he was Sales Manager of Four Star's distribution division. When he hired me he was aware that I had recently been through a horrible divorce and had been awarded sole custody of my son. So instead of assigning me to the usual salesman's beat of constant out-of-town travel, he arranged for me to focus on the Manhattan based station rep firms and to also provide research material to our men in the field. Years later, whenever I would encounter Len, I'd thank him for my son.

He even tolerated a breach of corporate protocol on my part when my enthusiasm caused me to overstep my authority. WNEW-TV was a major independent station in New York and I was having lunch with Jack Lynn, the station's Program Director. He was raving about the excellence of a one-hour musical special he had just bought, starring Lena Horne. He said he would gladly buy ten more such programs and when he told me how much he would pay for New York telecast rights, I said Four Star would produce ten such programs if we could handle sales rights in the rest of the country. When I told Firestone what I had done, he wasn't too happy. But to my relief, the company backed me up and Four Star commenced production with our first entry starring the sultry singing star, Julie London, produced by my pal John Bradford who had written 'Lena' for the BBC.

I left Four Star in 1966 and have since operated as an independent, making a living through my partial ownership of the *Hopalong Cassidy* movies, the *Laurel and Hardy* films, various remake rights to such classics as *The Bicycle Thief*, *Of Mice and Men*, and the remake rights to *Marjorie Morningstar*. I even dabble in producing some things, such as the remake in 1999 of *Three Secrets* for

CBS.

It's sort of like the fellow who was walking across Seventh Avenue in New York's garment district, when he was hit by a truck. A woman rushed over to tend to him and when she saw he was conscious she worriedly asked, "Are you comfortable?"

He replied, "I make a living."

*"The film starts out rather slowly, but about half way
along it stops completely."*

...Art Greenfield

Collective Infinite Wisdom
by Alan Silverbach

I started in the business so long ago I think it was then called
"19th Century Fox." About 20 of us, all ex-service (I, Air Force),
were to be the future of 20th Century Fox, replacing those employees who left during the war. World War II, not the Civil.

It was 1946 and television was more or less a dirty word if you
were in the theatrical business. After a couple of months indoctrina-
tion in Buffalo, NY, where the snow was piled higher than the train,
and a few weeks in a theatre in Hackensack, New Jersey, where I
watched Rita Hayworth sing *Put the Blame on Mame, Boys* at least
twenty times, I ended up, by choice, in New York, believing you were
better off in HQ giving orders rather than taking them in the field. A
lesson learned the hard way in the Air Force.

Somewhere about 1949-50 I talked Spyros Skouras, who was
President of the company, into letting me switch to the TV depart-

217

ment, which he assured me was making a major career mistake.

The TV department consisted of Peter Levathes, an ex-FBI agent, who at various times was President of the TV company and head of the studio, together with Irving Kahn, who later went to jail for some hanky-panky. Kahn had previously recommended to Skouras that the company take out an application to buy stations in New York, Los Angeles and Washington - which Skouras rejected, saying TV wouldn't work. (Kahn, each year for many years after, included a copy of his written recommendation to Skouras along with his Christmas wishes.)

Early in the 1950's I sent a questionnaire to all of our international theatrical offices asking for sensible information; i.e., number of TV stations in the cities, country, sets in use, type of programs, etc., etc. I should have saved the replies...some of them unprintable - the least offensive, "are you kidding?"

One of the unheralded benefits of traveling around the country or internationally in the early days of television was that you got to visit all the new stations that were on, or going on the air. First it was mandatory to take a tour of the studios, the sound booth, the storage rooms, the new lavatories, and not to be left out, the new tower which was undoubtedly designed as punishment for trying to sell a program. I handled most of the tours with a pained smile, but being hauled up in an elevator to the top of a rickety looking tower left a lot to be desired. The expression, "if you've seen one you've seen them all" was probably coined for some other equally unimportant event, but it fit nicely when it was tower-tour time.

Fox was going through the usual management changes in the 60's, 70's and 80's. Bill Self was President of television and in charge of production, and I headed both domestic and foreign syndication, based in New York. Seymour Poe came in as the Executive Vice President of the parent company, but hadn't a clue as to what television was or was not.

He sent memos in blue envelopes to make certain you knew who it was from. Among the many I received was a pointed one referring to the fact there had not been much sales activity in June which said simply, "Pretty punk." Following that encouraging message I had a meeting in his office and tried to explain that schedules were set, that new programming would have to wait for the November books, with any changes probably not until January. He suggested and instructed me that, since none or only a few programs would be sold between June and November, that I fire the whole domestic sales department and rehire them in January. (Come to think of it - he may have had an idea!)

About the time that *M*A*S*H* became available for syndication, the FCC decreed that adult programming could not be shown before 8 p.m. That blew the *prime time access* time period, i.e. 7:00-8:00 p.m.(ET), that was so vital for this type of programming. We hesitatingly sent out invitations to bid to the five major markets, and did not get one offer - but did get a call from Dick Woollen (yes, our Dick Woollen), the buyer for Metromedia. Dick made an offer of $30,000 per episode for all 5 stations - total, not each. I don't recall the actual number of episodes in the first go round, but a couple of million dollars excited the company, which was having problems in other areas. I tried to withdraw the offering, believing the timing and offer could not have been worse. But money overruled common sense (surprise) and Dick Woollen probably made the best deals for his stations in the history of the business.

Metromedia should have stuck a statue of him at the entrance to their building, since some years later he was also first in line to buy the very successful Carol Burnett Show which I had edited to half-hours. This did not start out to be a testimonial to Mr. Woollen, but he saw things a lot of other buyers didn't.

I won't go into the hits and misses at NATPE, except to mention that around 1980 we financed, together with the NBC O&O's (owned and operated stations), a talk show pilot with Robin Williams as the main guest, hosted by David Letterman. Letterman was under contract to NBC and they were trying to find a format for him. The pilot we produced was terrific, but needed an NBC O&O commitment to get it off the ground, and as it so often happens, in their collective infinite wisdom, they turned it down!

Our foreign department was a different game altogether. Herb Lazarus had previously joined Fox as Vice President International Television. (He had been selling weather spots or something for station breaks when we first met, but had paid his dues at TPA...Television Programs of America...and the Wrather Co.) We hired Bill Saunders, who had been working with the Motion Picture Association in North Africa, as head of the European operation. He was a logical choice since he had no television experience, but at that time, not many of us had, and what experience we did have was by trial and error. We opened offices in England, Europe and Latin America, selling some groundbreaking programs like *Adventures In Paradise, Hong Kong, Peyton Place* and *Daniel Boone,* which we could not sell to the Arab countries, since the little blond, blue-eyed son of Daniel Boone was named "Israel." The money involved was not worth changing his name.

Although product had something to do with making a deal internationally, personal relationships with the buyers were even more important - certainly in the early days. One well-known buyer for British commercial stations, Leslie Halliwell, always attended the spring screenings in Los Angeles, with a mandatory trip to Death Valley, requiring the accompaniment of the foreign sales heads for a three or four day stay in the desert. Halliwell wrote a number of books titled *The Filmgoer's Companion*, which he continually updated, and was also undoubtedly one of the great authorities on the flora and fauna of Death Valley. The year after he died, a number of us took the trip back and planted a tree in his name at the *Furnace Creek Motel*. Temperature about 110.

Traveling internationally sounds better than it actually was - certainly the envy of the company treasurer when he got our expense accounts - six or eight cities and countries in as many days, working weekends and playing nights. I can't remember how many clubs and pubs we closed, with Bill Saunders at the piano and Herb Lazarus and I selling our little hearts out.

Fox was eventually run by Dennis Stanfill as Chairman and Gordon Stulberg as President, both living in Los Angeles. It didn't take long for the decision to move all the departments from New York to L.A., and with many of us kicking and screaming, we moved to the studio about 1972.

Stanfill's experience was primarily in banking and accounting, which added nothing to his creative juices. His primary concern was his wife's passion to 'Save Venice' from sinking into the canals. Venice, Italy, not Venice, California.

In 1974, politics was the name of the game. Bill Self, President of Television for 15 years, and who made Fox Television a major player, was replaced by Jack Haley, Jr., who happened to be married to Liza Minelli. The thought was that with Jack in charge of television, Liza would love to do a TV series. She had better sense and that never happened.

After over thirty years at the company, Stanfill decided I wasn't playing his game, and in 1976 I was out. Someone asked me how many Presidents I had survived in thirty years at Fox, and I replied, "all but one." A year or so later, Stanfill was out. He didn't survive "one," Marvin Davis, owner.

Herb Lazarus, by this time, was the Vice President International at Columbia Television. I talked him into leaving a good paying job and joining me as an independent. We knew how the big distribution companies took advantage of the independent producers they represented. So we developed an alternative whereby we would handle their programs, in the name of each producer, with revenues flowing directly to them. It worked well, representing programs and producers including Carol Burnett, Lorimar, Fries, among many others. We had several names for the company, including Television Representatives International, Silverbach-Lazarus (or Lazarus-Silverbach when he talked to his mother), and at various times in the 1980's the company was bought by Metromedia, and later, London Weekend Television.

We closed the company several years ago as the mergers and consolidations started among the bigger companies, which made it much more difficult and costly to acquire programs as an independent.

If anyone really wants to hear all the funny stuff, we're available for hire.

No children's parties, please.

Timing is Everything!
by Herb Lazarus

How did I get into the business of distributing television programs? By accident.

It was 1954 when my brother was designing an "end credit" for a television company called Television Programs of America (TPA). This company was owned by a film producer named Eddie Small and a financier from Chicago, Milton Gordon. Their business was distributing first run programs to television stations around the country and selling those programs to regional advertisers.

Salesmen would go to a city and contact the television stations to get a time period they could offer the advertisers. Next, the sales guy would contact an advertiser and offer him a 52 weeks sponsorship of whatever program we were pushing at that time...*New York Confidential, Tugboat Annie, Ramar of the Jungle, Last of the Mohicans*, etc. The program would run in the time period the station gave us to sell. If the advertiser said he could only handle a 26 week deal, the salesman would then go to another advertiser and offer him the 52 week deal, but if he also said he could only handle 26 weeks, the two clients were put together and we took the advertiser contracts to the station where one of their staff salesmen would handle negotiations for the cost of the station's air time and everybody was happy.

My first job with TPA was as a gofer...go for the coffee, lunch, fill up the postage machine at the post office...whatever. I graduated from that job to being in "operations," making sure the 16mm film prints got to the television stations in time for their play dates.

TPA was a large company in the late 1950's, and at times we had 60 salesmen handling our shows. Some designated territories were as small as a single city...those where there was a concentration of major advertising agencies. TPA was bought by Independent Television Corporation (ITC), an English company run by Lew Grade (later "Sir" and eventually "Lord Grade"), whose headquarters were in London and who appointed Abe Mandel to run the U.S. branch.

I, however, left before that happened and joined Twentieth Century Fox, working for Alan Silverbach. It was at Fox that I stumbled into the international side, a step I never regretted.

In 1976, Silverbach left Fox to join Columbia Pictures Television, and I assumed the role of Manager of International Sales, reporting to Seymour Poe. Poe was the company's Executive Vice President and basically the Chief Operating Officer under Darryl Zanuck.

Poe was making a trip to Latin America and prior to leaving, asked me to give him a report detailing what the television landscape looked like in each of the countries...the number of television stations, the prices we get for our series and our movies, etc. His first stop was Mexico City where he met with the Theatrical Manager and our Television Manager, Alvaro Real. Poe returned to New York after 10 days. A couple of days later, Alvaro sent Poe a report, with a copy to me.

The report was a disaster. But Alvaro had felt he must send it, because he wanted to make up for his lack of mastery of spoken English which had been so evident during his meeting with Poe. Alvaro spoke seven languages, but English was not really one of them, as evidenced by the number of inaccuracies in his written report. The man was a poet and a novelist and one of the most educated and sophisticated men you'd ever meet and we all loved him, but he was not the ideal film peddler. As soon as I read the report I called Silverbach at Columbia and asked if he could meet me for a drink after work, and so we met at the St. Regis bar. As soon as Alan read the report he said, "Alvaro is in trouble!" which was my thought as well.

Sure enough, about two days later, Poe calls and tells me Alvaro is not the guy for us and I was to "get rid of him."

I do nothing for a week and Poe calls to ask if I took care of the problem. "Not yet," I tell him. "I'm trying to find someone else first." Poe tells me to call so-and-so in the Caracas office because he might suggest someone to hire. So I call him a few days later but he doesn't have any good ideas for me. Another week passes and another call from Poe. I tell him I still haven't gotten rid of Alvaro. Poe tells me if I don't do this NOW he will find someone to get rid of me *and* Alvaro. I tell Poe the best thing would be for me to go to Mexico City and take care of the dastardly deed on a face to face basis. He agrees.

I call Alvaro and tell him I'm coming down to see him and I'm arriving on Sunday. Alvaro insists on picking me up at the airport and I insist he doesn't. I win. Alvaro insists on picking me up on Monday morning at my hotel and I insist he doesn't. I win.

Monday morning I show up in the office at 9 a.m. and Alvaro

225

starts telling me of the appointments he's set for us. I tell him we need to talk. We go into his office and he makes me sit in his chair and he sits in the chair in front of the desk. I am just about to say something to him when his secretary comes in and tells me that my secretary, Barbara, is calling me.

Thankful for this delay, I pick up the phone to hear Barbara say, "Mr. Lazarus, Mr. Poe is out." "Out?" I say. "Where is he going? Is he coming to Mexico?" "No," she says. "He's out. He's been fired by Mr. Zanuck and locked out of his office!" With that, I turn to Alvaro and asked, "What time is our first appointment?" It was 10 years before I told Alvaro the truth about that day. Timing is everything!

Game playing is a good way to kill time and maybe have some laughs while "schlepping" around the world. One day Alan Silverbach and I were flying to Paris to start a European tour of network clients. Paris was our European headquarters and the manager of that office was Bill Saunders. On the way to the airport in New York for our departure, Alan and I were talking and at one point I couldn't come up with a name I was trying to recall, and sometime later, the same thing happened to Alan.

Finally, we landed in Paris and were met by Saunders and Jacques Porteret who worked with Bill, and as things happen, I blurted out the name I was trying to recall and within an instant Alan was able to do the same. Not to be left out of what he thought was fun, Bill blurts out a third name. Alan looks at me, I look at Alan and we both say, "Schmuck, you can't say Frieda Jones after an Irving Schwartz and a Leo Gurney. You lose. Give us both 20 francs."

That was the beginning of a wonderful setup that went on for several years. Alan and I only played the game when Bill was around because he made it fun. We developed twists like the time we were in London and Alan, Bill, Ray Lewis and myself were having a drink and I say, "Roger Hornsby." Alan says, "Francis Scott Key." Bill says, "Peter Frank," and Ray jumps in and says "Hugo Smith!" Alan and I look at each other and then back at Ray. At the same time we blurt out, "That's a winner, Ray," and Alan and I fork over 5 pounds each to Ray and we make Bill pay up as well. Once in a very blue sky we let Bill win, but over the years he must have given Alan and me a couple hundred bucks. There's one born every minute.

Fridays With Art

Stranger Than Fiction
by Sandy Frank

The life of a salesman is such that there are many memories that are highs and of course moments of great discouragement.

And in one's life, in one's professional career, there is a moment that supersedes all moments when you have done something or experienced something that overrides everything in your prior experience, or even, perhaps, future experiences. I will detail that later on.

In the meantime, let me say that as a hard-selling syndication salesman, I have been earmarked with or tagged with many stories regarding things that I have allegedly done over the years in selling our company's shows. I can assure you that these stories are more legend than truth, and are a collection of mostly untruths of mythical proportion. Some humorous, some even envious of sales accomplished.

The most circulated story of all is one that I want to relate now, and offer the actual facts, thus finally putting the myth to rest.

The story concerns my so-called heart attack on a plane, and my subsequently having the plane land in order for me to make a sale. Of course, this entire story is preposterous. It never happened. The truth of what actually did happen is as follows.

It was probably 1974, and I was on my way from New York to L.A. for a meeting with Ralph Edwards and Lynn Bohlen who was VP of Daytime Programming for NBC, and with whom we had done a deal for a show titled, *Name That Tune*. It was before the beginning of the wave of expansion of once-per-week nighttime game shows into additional exposure as five-per-week strip shows on the networks in the daytime and such usage of '*Tune*' was to be the topic of our meeting. For example, it was about then they were also shooting the pilot episode of what was to be the daytime version of *Wheel Of Fortune*.

I was on a TWA flight and also on board was a syndication executive of many years, Pierre Weiss, then a V.P. for Metromedia Program Sales, and previously, for a number of years the V.P of Sales at Ziv and ITC. I greeted Pierre in a comradely fashion and proceeded to enjoy the flight, when suddenly it was announced that the plane had to land in Kansas City because there was a passenger aboard who had a heart attack. The plane landed, the passenger was discharged from the plane, the plane then resumed its flight and we landed in L.A. I kept my '*Tune*' meeting with Ralph Edwards and Lynn Bohlen, and that was the end of it.

Then, for a number of years people kept saying and asking me, "Did you have a heart attack on a plane and get the plane to land so you could make a sale to a TV station?" After hearing this a number of times and asking myself, "Where did this story come from? Where did this kind of nonsense, this rumor, this tale start?" It eventually dawned on me that in fact it was Pierre who conjured up this version of our flight together.*

Over the years there have been numerous other mythical stories as well.

My very first job out of college was with Paramount Pictures. In my search for a job as a TV salesman I had sent out a hundred or more resumes to companies and had no luck with any, except for one. A letter came back from Hugh Owen, the Executive Vice President of Domestic Sales at Paramount Pictures in New York, requesting I come in for an interview. I did, and met him in his sumptuously ornate office befitting one of the handful of top executives at Paramount Pictures. He hired me to work as a booker trainee. A booker trainee puts hash marks in a book all day long, tracking the various movies that are sent to the theatres in a territory.

I reported to work on West 44th Street, between 9th and 10th Avenues in New York City, in an old run-down two story building. Needless to say, my illusion of glamorous Hollywood abruptly ended. This was the building where they shipped out the films to various theatres in the NYC area. Beyond the office situation, putting hash marks in a book was not what I had envisioned as a salesman and six months later I moved on.

The initial experience I had in my first TV job was quite surprising. It was with a company called West Hooker TV. West Hooker had just left MCA and started a new company to package television programs. It had several on the air, but there was one particular show

*(Editor's note: As an example of the widespread distortion of this story, by the time the rumor reached me, it had Sandy stuck in Miami, unable to get a flight to his target of New Orleans, and booking himself on a nonstop flight to L.A. and faking his heart attack with perfect timing so the plane would land in New Orleans, where he disembarked and made his sales call. DW.)

that it had no luck in selling. I had joined the company with the idea of agenting talent, not selling shows. After West tried unsuccessfully for a number of months to sell a show titled *Mike Stokey's Pantomime Quiz*, I mustered up my nerve and said to West, "Let me take a try at it." He had nothing to lose so he said, "Okay, go ahead," never imagining I'd be successful. In a combination of sales persistence and good timing, I called on Tom MacAvity, the new head of program procurement at the NBC-TV Network, who had just arrived from California.

I pitched '*Pantomime Quiz*,' and to my surprise he said that it would be an excellent show for NBC. He said, "It just so happens that my wife, Helen Mack, an actress, had been on '*Pantomime Quiz*' in L.A., where it had been a local show, and I love the show." He said that NBC had a 10 o'clock Thursday night slot where the canceled *Freddie Martin Show* had been airing. "We need a replacement," he said. But in order to close the deal I would have to go over to see Tom Luckinbill, the Senior Vice President of the William Esty Advertising Agency, and Account Supervisor on the *Camel* cigarettes account. I made my pitch and to my surprise *Camel* immediately agreed to sponsor the program, and it went on the air shortly thereafter. Here I was, just starting in TV with my first job, and before I turned around I'm making an NBC Network sale, when in fact I should have been sweeping floors somewhere in Ottumwa, Iowa! Beginner's luck!

This was also my first lesson in TV sales income. I never collected a dime on the sale, even after taking my case to court and winning. Hooker took the money out of the corporation, leaving no money to settle the $50,000 claim. Wow! What a bonanza it would have been. Instead it was a valuable life lesson that paid off later on.

I later went to work at NBC in the network's sales department, selling advertising time in '*Today*,' '*Home*' and '*Tonight*.' Dave Garroway was the host of *The Today Show*, Steve Allen was the host of *The Tonight Show*, and Arlene Francis and Hugh Downs were the hosts of *The Home Show*. My job was to sell participating advertising time in these shows.

At the time, network shows were being sold for full or half sponsorship. There was no such thing as selling 30 second spots or minutes as is done today. Our "T.H.T." sales unit at NBC Network pioneered in the selling of spots. I might add that one of the salesmen I worked closely with was Jim Rosenfield who later became President of the CBS Network under Bill Paley.

I subsequently worked as a salesman for the Wrather Corporation selling series such as *Lassie, The Lone Ranger* and *Sgt. Preston of the Yukon* in syndication. One of my '*Lone Ranger*' customers at the time was a Program Director in Raleigh, N.C., who later became a U.S. Senator by the name of Jessie Helms, of all people! I ended up as Senior Vice President after 3 years with Wrather. As it is for every salesman, I measured my success against that of other salesmen. I ended my Wrather stint having sold more than the other 13 salesmen combined. I was finally feeling successful and ready to go off on my own.

It was my success that led to my being fired. I had pressed my case hard to become President of Wrather's syndication division. I felt entitled to the President's job based on the high income I was generating for the company. Needless to say, I didn't get the job.

So I decided that the way to really become successful was to start my own company. The fact that I had been fired helped. Again, lessons learned helped me to vow to never work for someone else's company again.

I launched my company, Sandy Frank Program Sales, and my very first program to syndicate was a show called *Buckaroo 500*. It was on KNTV in San Jose as a local program. I ended up selling that program in national syndication to the makers of *Cocoa Marsh* chocolate syrup, the Taylor Reed Corporation. The program was cleared on a barter basis throughout the country.

Subsequently I made a deal to become the syndicator for *You Asked For It* by calling cold on Marcus Lipsky, the owner of the show and also owner of *Redi-Whip* whipped cream. I successfully sold the black and white *"YAFI"* throughout the country in many, many markets despite its prior limited sales in a small number of markets. Little did I dream at the time that I would one day own *"YAFI"* and finance and produce 300 *"YAFI"* half-hours in color.

Competition in the world of syndication sales was very tough in those days. With the exception of two strong independent distributors, Ziv and ITC, it was the majors which dominated and controlled the market. In those days survival alone was a feat. You had to scrounge to obtain sales rights to even marginal product and then go from market to market loaded down with heavy 16mm film prints to try to sell your show. It really was tough.

In the early 1970's, I got the rights to *Name That Tune* from its creator, Harry Salter, who I also called cold. This was a few years after the *prime time access* Rule came into being...a federal rule which required stations to broadcast original programming (as opposed to off-network repeats) in the hour preceding *prime time*. The first such series I sold was *The Parent Game,* produced by Chuck Barris. It sold in over 150 markets, which up to that point was probably the most widely sold first-run series in syndicated distribution, with the possible exception of shows placed by Ziv, with its army of salesmen. I personally sold *49* of the top *50* markets, but despite making a half dozen trips there, I couldn't sell Baltimore. It really gnawed at me that I couldn't get 50 out of the top 50 markets.

After getting the rights to '*Tune,*' I made a co-production deal with Ralph Edwards Productions. '*Tune*' was subsequently sold to the NBC network as a daytime strip, and soon after was launched by our company in syndication with the NBC O&O's, where it continued for seven years as one of the top 5 shows in *prime access.*

As I said earlier, there comes a time in one's life when opportunity presents itself to do something that goes beyond what you would normally be doing...where you achieve something or experience something that is of a mind-boggling and highly unique nature. That happened to me in 1977 when I read Menachem Begin's autobiography, *The Revolt.* I decided I wanted to get the rights to this book for a television mini-series or TV movie. I made the deal for Menachem Begin's book shortly after he had been elected Prime Minister of Israel, optioning the book for $100,000. This was but the beginning of many new and memorable experiences in the Middle East that I never dreamed I would have.

After the deal was made I was in Cairo, Egypt, on my way to Jerusalem to meet Menachem Begin for the first time. I had several days to kill before my appointment with him so I decided to go to Amman, Jordan, the nearest destination. I spent several days in Amman until the day of my appointment with Begin, which was on a Friday in November, 1977.

I had to leave Amman in the morning and ride on an old bus loaded with Arabs who were going into Israel over the Jordan River via the Allenby Bridge. The bus had many clothes bundles on top of it that served as suitcases for the passengers, and all of us were packed in like sardines. It was a rare and memorable experience in 1977; crossing over the Jordan River, then through the Allenby Bridge between Jordan and Israel, for there was no peace between the two countries.

Finally, I did get to Begin's office that afternoon and had the pleasure of meeting him. He was quite delighted that a movie was going to be made of his life story based on *The Revolt.* For one reason or another, the following week I had to go back to see Menachem

Begin virtually every day in his office around lunchtime. I ended up with him as he was taking his lunch break. The reason I was in his office was to meet various officials of the government that he wanted me to speak to and whose offices were right near his. So at lunchtime I would walk out with him to his car waiting in front of the Prime Minister's building and bid him farewell.

During that week I received a press pass from his office. He wanted me to go to London as one of the press on his plane. He was to meet with Prime Minister Callahan of the United Kingdom in London. I was all set to go when, the next day, as I'm walking out with him, something startling happened.

On this particular day, as I was standing outside the Prime Minister's office, standing right next to him, he made the dramatic announcement to the world that President Sadat of Egypt was coming to Israel to speak to the Knesset. Of course this was a very bold move on the part of Sadat. As a result, the trip to the U.K. was abruptly canceled.

Garrick Utley was the NBC correspondent in Israel at the time, and when Menachem Begin exited the building, Utley interviewed him with me standing right next to Begin. In all the excitement of this dramatic moment I didn't think to ask the cameraman to arrange for a copy of the tape. Starting several days afterward, I offered $10,000 to anyone in the NBC News department who would deliver a copy of this historic moment to me, but after a year of searching, no one was able to locate this particular interview, much to my considerable disappointment.

A day after that announcement I was walking down the corridor with Prime Minister Begin and the subject of Barbara Walters came up. I asked him if he would be interested in an interview with her. He said, "Absolutely. I would be delighted." Based on that information, I called ABC News in New York and got Barbara Walters on the phone with a cold call. I had never met her. I told her I had just been with Prime Minister Begin and he indicated he would be willing to meet with her and be interviewed by her in Israel when President Sadat came, which would be several days later. Her reaction to this news was like that of a child jumping up and down. She let out a loud whoop, yelling "Begin wants me to interview him with Sadat!" I told her that the one thing I ask in return for getting her this interview was to bring me a copy of *Weekly Variety, Broadcasting Magazine*, and a bottle of *Eau de Portugal* hair tonic. Over the years, whenever I have seen Barbara Walters she kids me about having "schlepped" this stuff all the way to Israel.

As this is written, there is much talk of war with Iraq which brings to mind a visit with Menachem Begin in 1991 at his home, quite some time after he left office. It was the anniversary of his ordering the bombing of Iraq's nuclear reactor in Osirak. I told him that I was sure Barbara Walters would very much love to do a 10th anniversary story on this historic attack which we now know destroyed Iraq's ability to produce a nuclear bomb. While Begin took pride in this daring and momentous attack for which he garnered worldwide scorn, his answer to me was, "I'll think about it." Those words from Begin, his aide later told me, really meant a "NO."

As a humorous aside, in a story told to me by Jim Coppersmith, there was a delegation of top broadcast officials who went to Israel in October, 1978. Ave Butensky, who was at Viacom at that time, put this group together - and when Begin's name came up, discussion shifted as to whether or not Sandy Frank really knew Begin, or was this just smoke from Sandy. While standing in the Knesset waiting for the next meeting, Ave noticed Prime Minister Begin walking down the corridor all by himself. He called out to him: "Mr. Prime Minister, I have regards for you." Begin walks over to the group, and as the broadcasters are eyeing Ave, not knowing what he is going to say,

Begin asks, "From whom?" Ave says, "From Sandy Frank." Begin then, without skipping a beat, excitedly says to the group, "Vere is Sandy? Vy doesn't he call? When will the film be ready?" After some picture taking and a brief chat, the Prime Minister leaves. Ave is now surrounded by all the broadcasters, arms folded, who tell Ave, "If you ever tell Sandy what just happened, we'll break your arm!"

Going back to the Sadat visit, Begin wanted me to attend the Knesset when Sadat spoke. As Sadat made his historic speech, I sat in the gallery of the Knesset with a relative of mine from England, Lord Barnett Janner. It was an incredible experience. After Sadat spoke I was waiting to leave the Knesset and within five feet of me, there he was. President Sadat and his entourage were standing and talking for about 5 minutes as I stood by, waiting for my ride. Little did I realize that I would personally be meeting him in a relatively short time.

I want to preface one thing: at that time, in 1977, the fact that an Egyptian leader, or any Arab for that matter, would come to Israel was unthinkable. It had never happened before and it was a moment of profound historical significance, and there I was right in the center of it.

Subsequent to Sadat's visit to the Knesset, an historic moment occurred on the lawn of the White House in 1978, when President Carter announced to the world that, after having met at Camp David for about a week of intense negotiations, both Prime Minister Begin and President Sadat had reached an agreement and made peace. As I previously stated, this was an historic breakthrough of profound significance, as Egypt became the first Arab country ever to make peace with Israel. It made headlines around the world. President Sadat and Prime Minister Begin at this particular moment in history were probably among the two or three leading figures in the world in terms of newsworthiness and significance.

238

I had previously commenced work with my co-production partner, Roger Gimbel, on producing the Begin film, and prior to Begin's departure for Camp David to meet President Sadat, a script was submitted to him. Lo and behold, at this moment of great history, while he was at Camp David, I got a letter from him approving the script! I couldn't believe that at this moment, while he was negotiating for peace with Egypt, that he would have actually taken the time to read the script and give me a letter with detailed script comments on it.

Moving ahead, after the historic meeting on the White House lawn in March, 1979 between Begin and Sadat, I made another decision: to get the rights to President Sadat's life as well. He had written a book entitled *In Search of Identity*, which was his autobiography. I read the book and felt it would be excellent as a mini-series or movie.

At that time our company was represented by the William Morris Agency and the person responsible for representing our company was Sam Weisbord, who was the President of the Morris Agency. When I attained the rights to Begin's autobiography, Sammy promised me that he would get it made into a movie, which unfortunately never happened. As it turned out, Lou Weiss, who had been Senior V.P. at the Morris office in charge of television, made a deal with Fred Pierce, then the president of ABC Television, to do a *Movie of the Week* on the life of Begin. After that deal was made, and before contracts could be drawn up, Fred Silverman, President of ABC Entertainment, said, "Let's go to script rather than go straight into production."

As many in the business know, that usually puts a project into the "deep freeze." That's what happened and no movie was ever made.

Right after the White House ceremony between Sadat and Begin, I told Sammy Weisbord of my desire to get the rights to Sadat's autobiography in tandem with Begin's because these were two world leaders and their life stories on television would be a tremendous event. Sammy said, "Sandy, go ahead and do it, for it will lead you to experiences and adventures in the Middle East that you have never dreamed of. You will remember it for a lifetime as among your most valuable memories.

I then proceeded with my attorney to work through the Egyptian Embassy in Washington which led to meetings in Cairo with President Sadat's representatives to negotiate the deal. President Sadat's attorney was Ted Sorenson, who had been President Kennedy's senior advisor when he was in the White House. During an afternoon in Cairo we sat with Colonel Assem Abbas who was representing Sadat and negotiated the deal with a commitment for $100,000 for the rights to the autobiography. Sadat was obviously not going to settle for anything less than I paid Begin for the rights to Begin's book. Sadat did not want to be left out or be one-upped after I made a deal for the rights to Begin's book for TV.

During my stay in Egypt I met with President Sadat at his country house, *The Barrage*, outside of Cairo. I spent an incredibly exciting hour and a half with him recounting the fact that my father lived in Alexandria in Egypt at one point when he was a young man, and that I had been raised listening to Egyptian music from childhood. This was the truth, and when I mentioned it, Sadat was elated. We really hit it off and he was incredibly warm towards me. Things couldn't have gone better in this meeting.

As I left Sadat's home I commented to the Minister of Culture who was with me, after seeing only three soldiers guarding his home, "Shouldn't the President have more security? Isn't Sadat apprehensive with so little security to protect him?" The Minister's reply still vividly remains in my mind, for he said, "The President is not worried for his life. He believes Allah will protect him."

During my stay in Cairo, at President Sadat's request, and

through his representative and liaison, Col. Assem Abbas, I was asked to make an announcement on TV to the Egyptian nation of the plans for a movie of Sadat's life. Specifically, I was asked to tape a speech at a certain day and time to go out over Egyptian television. I immediately got on the phone to Hollywood with David Levy, my TV producer, who had been involved with me on *Name That Tune* and my other programs over the years. David was formerly the President of the Entertainment Division of the NBC TV Network. David and I carefully crafted an 8 minute speech over the long distance phone. I subsequently videotaped my remarks but had no idea when the speech would be telecast.

A few days later I'm in my room at the *Mena House Hotel* in Giza, located outside of Cairo and right at the foot of the pyramids. It's 9 o'clock on a Saturday night and I'm watching television when suddenly my speech announcing my plans to make a TV movie of Sadat's life, preceded by a short announcement in Egyptian, comes up on the screen, and there I am addressing the Egyptian nation. I couldn't believe it. I was absolutely dumbfounded. It was such an incredible thing to see my speech actually being televised to the Egyptian nation at 9 o'clock on a Saturday night. It boggled my mind.

The significance of this speech is an interesting one, in that as it turned out, I had become the only person, other than Sadat's predecessor, President Gamel Abdel Nasser, Sadat himself, and subsequently President Mubarak, who ever addressed the Egyptian nation. Here I was, a foreigner and a Jew besides, addressing tens of millions of Egyptians. Through a very strange set of circumstances, President Sadat, for whatever reason, wanted me to announce in a talk to his nation that his autobiography would be made into a movie. In Egypt, which was a dictatorship under Nasser and Sadat and remains so under Mubarak, it would just be unthinkable for any foreigner or any outside foreign political leader to address the nation. So to this day, I am left with the unique distinction of being the only foreigner to ever address the Egyptian nation.

During my meeting with President Sadat I said that I understood there was going to be a very special military ceremony at El Arish in the Sinai Peninsula (which Israel had won in the 1973 *Yom Kippur War* with Egypt). Begin and Sadat had agreed during their historic meeting at the White House in 1978 that Israel would withdraw entirely from the Sinai Peninsula, and the portion of the Sinai that they would initially withdraw from was the military base at El Arish. So, during my meeting with President Sadat I said, "That sounds like a very important event, and I sure wish I could attend." He said he would be delighted to have me as his guest. Sure enough, two weeks later I got an invitation in the mail from Egypt to be Sadat's guest for the weekend in Cairo to attend the military flag-raising event at El Arish. On Saturday I boarded a military plane in Cairo along with Mrs. Sadat and leaders of the Egyptian government. Among them was Colonel Abbas and the Minister of Culture. We headed for El Arish. I remember flying over the beautiful Nile and over Port Said on to El Arish in the Sinai. It was an historic moment, this El Arish ceremony, for it was Israel's initial withdrawal from what eventually was the entire Sinai Peninsula bordering Egypt and Israel.

It turned out that no other foreigners were invited to this ceremony. It was just the press from around the world, and Egyptian politicians and Army officers. Upon my return to Cairo I left the next day for the *Cannes Film Festival.*

Regrettably, as it turned out, Prime Minister Begin's autobiography was never made into a movie. Sadat's book was subsequently made into a mini-series through our company's production deal with Columbia Pictures. It was a mini-series entitled *Sadat.* Incidentally, in the making of the mini-series Columbia Pictures chose to cast the outstanding Academy Award winning actor, Louis Gosset, Jr., to play Sadat. Unfortunately, this selection was greeted unfavorably in Egypt by the then existing government and leadership who took exception to the dark-skinned actor playing the light-skinned Sadat. This resulted in a ban in Egypt, for a term, of sales of *Coca Cola*, the parent company of Columbia Pictures at the time.

While I've spent many years working in TV syndication and producing, my Middle East experiences - meeting President Sadat and Prime Minister Begin, getting the rights to their autobiographies, and addressing the Egyptian nation - those events stand as my crowning moments. So, as I said, there sometimes comes a moment in one's life when one has an experience that transcends every other experience in importance that you have previously had, or probably ever will have. Such is what I experienced in Egypt and Israel.

With many TV sales and non-TV experiences behind me, the business is still fun, as I continue to bring classic shows like *Name That Tune, You Asked For It* and *Battle of the Planets*, plus brand new series like *Past Lives* and *The Great Date Fake* to the TV marketplace.

In retrospect, as I look back on my various experiences as a TV syndicator and producer, some of which I have recounted, I guess all too few in this business have been fortunate enough to have had as much fun as I have had and continue to have.

Fridays With Art

"I'm more sorry for the things I haven't
done than the things I have."
...Art Greenfield

Redwings, Rascals, and Robert E. Lee
to the Rescue
by John Serrao

I suppose I could properly be labeled a "nomad" in the television industry. I've worked in 10 different markets in my 47 year career until retirement in 1998 when we settled into a home in the desert area not far from Los Angeles. Oh, we also have a summer retreat in Victoria, B.C. just so we don't abandon travel totally.

For me it all began in 1947 when I landed a job at KNX (CBS) in Hollywood where my duties were a combination of being a lobby guard and a stage hand. By 1950, I had achieved the white-collar post of Sales Service Manager, where my primary job involved serving the needs of the personnel at the ad agencies and their clients who sponsored our network's radio shows and gradually, also the TV shows which were just beginning to blossom at that time.

It was hot and smoggy that summer when I found myself left nearly alone up on the fifth floor of our building because most of the

245

management team were either on vacation or out of town on business. That included my boss, Bill Brennan, who was West Coast VP of CBS Network Programming; Station Manager, Austin Joscelyn; and KNX's General Manager, Merle Jones.

I had arrived early that memorable Monday morning, had my coffee, read the trade papers and then looked around for something to do. I telephoned the office which stored our television program films and kinescopes and inquired as to whether anything new had arrived. As luck would have it, I was told they had just received a new pilot film of a show titled *The George Burns and Gracie Allen Show.*

I decided to see if I could lure an authentic advertising agency person to have lunch with me and then screen the show, secure in the knowledge that I was allowed to use my expense account to entertain such clients. So I called Charley Lowe, who was the Program Coordinator in the Los Angeles office of Erwin Wasey Advertising. I had worked with him on some of their accounts such as Carnation and Albers Milling. He agreed to meet me for lunch and was nice enough not to snicker when I suggested we meet at DuPars on Wilshire Boulevard, a decidedly mid-scale coffee shop, but which had the advantage of being near his office where we later went to screen the program. We ran the film in the agency screening room and he loved it. He wanted Norm Best, the Account Executive for *Carnation's Evaporated Milk* to see it, but he was out of town so I returned the next morning at 10 a.m. and ran it for him. After seeing just the first 10 minutes, Best was on board. He recruited other agency personnel to also screen the film and we ran it several times during that day, until it was time to visit a neighborhood bar for a drink or two. Charley Lowe asked me how much it would cost to sponsor the show, and I answered him honestly by telling him I didn't know. But I promised to get back to him.

My next step was to telephone Jack Van Volkenburg who headed up sales for the CBS Network in New York. He accepted my call, but wanted to know who the hell I was and, "How did you pronounce that name again?" I explained that all my bosses were out of town and I was trying to cover until they returned. Once he was satisfied that I really worked for CBS, he gave me the bottom line. The price for the program itself would be $28,000 per broadcast, plus the air time and the commitment was to be for 26 programs to be aired over a 52 week period, firm, alternating with *The Robert Q. Lewis Show*, which was sponsored by American Safety Razor. I typed up an offer for our show and made a date with Charley to have a real lunch the next day at the Brown Derby on Vine Street in Hollywood. After sipping the ritual (at the time) dry martini and indulging in a Cobb Salad I gave him the offering letter and he said he would get back to me.

The Monday of the following week began with a call from the agency for me to get down to their office as fast as I could and to bring the print of the '*Burns & Allen Show*' with me. My screening was for the President of the agency and fortunately, he also loved the show. I was then turned over to Lowe and their Media Director, Glen Bohannan, to discuss station clearances and other distribution matters. At this point in television's history, interconnection between the East Coast and the West Coast was still 18 months in the future, and CBS could only deliver 32 markets for live clearance, with the rest of the country receiving a sort of film (kinescope) coverage. Heading up these details for the agency was a very excitable executive manager type (think Don Knotts) who was the most nervous person I had ever met. He seemed distressed and under extreme pressure. I was told that his wife suspected him of pursuing a young woman and had detectives following him around. (Great script material for one of the shows.)

Now it was time to call New York and let Van Valkenburg know where we stood. I carefully laid it all out, trying not to reveal my excitement or any special enthusiasm. His response was not to me but to someone else in his office. "Take the show off the street!" he shouted. When I asked what that meant he simply said, "Talk to you later."

Now things were rolling. Charley Lowe told me Mr. Stewart, President of Carnation, was flying down from their Seattle headquarters to see the show and they would be meeting after to make a decision on this show and a lot of other buys.

I decided the place for me to be the next morning was at the agency, so I went over there and sat with Lowe and Bohannan as we nervously waited for news and consumed lots of coffee. About noon, Bohannan was summoned to a meeting and returned with their office executive in tow and both were smiling. They said they couldn't confirm it yet, but it looked like a deal. He followed them into the executive's office where he seated himself, then exulted: "Hot damn. We've got that show for 26 weeks!" I glanced at Lowe but he said nothing. I had my offer letter in my breast pocket and started to reach for it, but decided it would be better if I just verbalized the terms of the deal. So I told the executive the deal would have to be for 26 programs over a 52 week term.

He exploded like nothing I had ever experienced. His howls bounced off the walls and down the agency halls. His secretary rushed in with a glass of water and a bottle of aspirin. A few minutes later he cooled down and did an Edgar Kennedy routine (rubbing his hand slowly down his forehead and over his nose) and said, "God damn it, you got us into this mess, now what do we do?" I was so scared that the only thing I could think of was, "Why don't you go back upstairs and tell them it's 26 shows over 52 weeks?" He sat there looking at me and finally turned his chair around and looked out the window for about a minute. He then got up and walked out of the office to the elevators. I didn't really know what happened upstairs until the next day.

Meantime, my CBS bosses began to return to their offices that morning, and when General Manager Merle Jones heard about my adventures he decided I needed a small lecture. He reminded me that my job was sales service and that my job function did not include network sales. I related the whole story to him and brought him up to date on where things then stood. We called Van Volkenburg in New York to let him know of the problems. You guessed it. He said, "OK, we'll put it back on the street." By now I could understand the commands.

I drove Merle Jones to the agency that afternoon to see what could be salvaged. Mr. Stewart and his agency people were still in meetings. Jones couldn't wait and had to get back to his office but I remained behind. This is when I finally found out what had happened the previous day when the executive headed upstairs to discuss contract length. Seems he stuck his head in the conference room door and waited. Mr. Stewart finally turned around and said "Yes?" The executive said, "It seems the deal is for 26 shows over 52 weeks, not 13 over 26." Mr. Stewart said, "So!" And that was it. The executive was so relieved he walked down the street to a famous watering hole at LaBrea and Wilshire and didn't return for a couple of hours. Now, whoops were heard around the office and Lowe confirmed we had a deal. I called Jones and he hurriedly returned to the agency. We called Van Volkenburg, and he said, "It's off the street!"

Jones wanted to call Burns & Allen at their home and tell them the good news, but we didn't want the agency people overhearing the conversation so we crossed the street to a gas station. Merle called Anne Nelson, a bright and rising star in our business office, and she had the number. Merle dialed and Gracie answered. When she heard the news she exploded with far more colorful language than the agency executive had used the day before. In a tone more worthy of a longshoreman than a demure comedienne she asked what the hell

249

right did we have committing them to Carnation without first getting her approval! She then passed the phone to George who seemed lighter of heart and said they 'would be in touch.'

Now, this was Friday, the ninth day of this story, but the tumult was far from over. Since it was already after 6 p.m., Merle and I drove direct to the *Hollywood Roosevelt Hotel* to attend the farewell cocktail party for Wayne Steffner who had just resigned from West Coast Sales Manager for CBS Radio. He was leaving to join with Frank Oxarart to produce and market the new TV series *You Asked For It*, hosted by Art Baker and sponsored by *Skippy Peanut Butter*. Wayne's efforts for CBS Radio had been much appreciated and there was a big turnout to wish him well.

I am told that Merle Jones was never averse to enjoying a cocktail, but to my knowledge he seldom drank. I have to assume that on this evening, after the successful network program sale, he felt like any salesman would feel. Anyhow, as the evening moved along he became a bit grouchy. He began to needle a young woman who ran our transcription department (they fed network radio shows to different time zones). She was also a shop steward for the local union. After a few challenging remarks by both of them, Jones pulled out a piece of paper and said she had been out to coffee 15 times that week. By this time a number of people were listening and it got quiet. Just then, one of our radio news anchors who did the 10 o'clock news feed to the West Coast for *Bell Brand Potato Chips* ("If it's *Bell,* it's Swell"), moved into the circle. He was quiet, unassuming, dressed in a sport shirt with no tie. His name: Chet Huntley. He put his arm around Merle and said, "Oh, come on Merle, this is a party for Wayne," and Merle said, "Take your arm off me, you communist SOB!" and Huntley said, "Do you want my resignation tonight or tomorrow?" Jones replied, "Tomorrow would be fine."

A laid back man from Montana, Chet Huntley wasn't a spotlight seeker. Most people who knew him well said he would have remained in his radio anchor spot for many years to come. Yet this event changed his life and career forever. Sometime later, Elton Rule, General Sales Manager at KABC-TV, the ABC owned and operated station in Los Angeles, smoothed the way for Huntley to come with KABC-TV for his first job as a television news anchor. Later he moved to New York where Robert Kintner, then president of NBC, put together the famous team of Huntley & Brinkley.

I let it be known to management that I wanted to leave sales service behind me and move into the ranks of local sales, but grew restless when nothing seemed to be happening. So when one of radio's premier rep firms announced they were expanding into the television rep business I gladly accepted the offer from Peters, Griffin and Woodward to join their Hollywood sales staff.

I first visited all of my CBS management team to thank them for their friendship and association over the last five years. I visited with Howard Meighan and he said I was making a big mistake; that they had plans for me. Unfortunately, they had not shared them with me. And while it left a bitter taste, it did nothing to diminish my total respect for this amazing organization. I was there when Bill Paley, Chairman of CBS, secretly worked out of a railroad car in downtown Los Angeles at the Union Station. He met with and sold big stars on the use of capital gains and how they could own their own shows. He won over Jack Benny, '*Amos & Andy*' and Edgar Bergan from NBC and Bing Crosby from ABC. There were others, but these broke the NBC control of radio, and soon to be, television.

I was there when Harry Ackerman and his network television program team began to successfully develop program series that would be owned by CBS. This was a huge breakthrough that finally gave CBS independence from ad agencies and clients that felt better schmoozed by NBC.

My tenure with CBS was the greatest five year college course anyone could have, and it did much for my future career. To be there during the transition from radio to television (both local and network) was breathtaking. It taught me a formula that worked rather well with the TV stations that I later built and managed, as well as handling two turnarounds during my labors in 10 different markets over a span of 51 years. Assuming you had technical parity with your competitors, programming was 1st, promotion was 2nd, and sales 3rd. If you don't pull them off in that order, you can never really maximize a TV station's potential. Do all three well, and you win...*big*!

Most of my working life was with independent TV stations, mostly UHF. Kaiser's Dick Block inspired me in this adventurous crusade and it was exciting to help pioneer this new expanding spectrum into most markets where viewers had been limited to only a few choices from the 1940's up to the early 1960's.

Little did I know that as General Manager of Block's first UHF station, WKBD-TV in Detroit, we would be involved in a major test of whether or not UHF would survive. I call it, "Finger In The Dike."

Dick Block expertly zeroed in (see Block's chapter in this book) on the revolutionary changes from limited television frequencies of VHF channels 2-13 to the advent of the all-channel law broadening the spectrum to channels 2 to 83 (later reduced to 69) in the mid 1960's. Block's plan to file applications to operate UHF stations in major markets was revealed to me in Honolulu in the summer of 1961 where I was General Manager of Kaiser's KHVH-TV (Channel 4, ABC). Dick knew the all-channel law would be up before Congress in 1962. It passed the Congress in late 1962 behind the aggressive lobbying efforts of FCC Commissioner, Robert E. Lee. The all-channel law became effective on May 1, 1964, mandating all TV set manufacturers to produce TV sets capable of receiving channels 2 through 83. Of the six major markets Kaiser filed for, Block picked Detroit as the first market to build. I was sent to Detroit in the summer of 1962 to study the advisability of a startup in 1964. Three months of study convinced us that the gamble made sense and it would represent the first major market UHF independent after the all-channel law.

As Block pointed out, even though our Honolulu station was profitable and the number one ABC affiliate in the country with a 54 audience share over four years, the Kaiser Company and family didn't exactly react with explosions of talcum powder. Conservative, and highly successful in heavy industry, the idea of building a division of TV stations, especially UHF stations, went over like a cut in salary. Nevertheless, Block was patient, applied gentle pressure, and I transferred to Detroit in the summer of 1963. WKBD-TV signed on January 10, 1964.

While other broadcasters around the country seriously considered a similar effort in a major market, the television set manufacturers were beginning to grumble. The public was now paying about $24 more for each TV set and there were still only a few UHF stations operating around the country, except in markets designated "UHF only" by the FCC back in the late 1940's and early 1950's. The manufacturers turned up the heat and the pressure was on as their lobbyist and ranking industry executives poured into Washington with personal visits and lots of money to demand that this UHF nonsense stop. They wanted the all-channel law REPEALED! It was a very dangerous time for UHF and, if the manufacturers had won, you could kiss off UHF, at least for the next decade, maybe forever.

As Block points out, we did generate some ratings with Detroit Red Wing hockey and the '*Little Rascals*' for the kids. We accomplished this with only 20% estimated UHF penetration in the Detroit market. And who rode into our battle of UHF survival? None other than our patron saint, FCC Commissioner, Robert E. Lee. He made powerful and compelling speeches to Congress (in session and in the cloak room) and pointed out that Red Wing hockey was getting a 5.0 household rating in both ARB and Nielsen, and the '*Little Rascals*' were generating 2's and 3's, and that this was not the time to scrap the law of spectrum growth. Give it time. He made such a fuss that the manufacturers looked like an anti-public industry which was furthering a VHF monopoly and restricting the choices for the starved viewing public. Lee knocked them dead and the manufacturers went home to concentrate on color. Good news for everyone.

Those early days were dark and lonely and a lot of people (ad agencies and clients) wished Kaiser had stayed in Hawaii. Some days we didn't know if we were air conditioning or FM. To illustrate how new the UHF industry was, and how unfamiliar people were with its jargon and meaning, Mr. Kaiser would often ask, "How's that '*FUH*' station coming along?"

Bless his heart and money. This takes nothing away from the people who labored in smaller UHF markets around the country. But remember, the test and pressure would always come in the first major markets. Look bad there and the TV set manufacturers will be on you like the black plague.

The early survival of UHF, and its subsequent success, is due mostly to the courage of Dick Block, the support of Henry Kaiser, and the unshakable confidence of FCC Commissioner, Robert E. Lee. They all put their fingers in the dike...and it held.

My, How Time Flies!
by Don Dahlman

While driving to lunch in Dayton, Ohio in 1967 I heard a talk show host on my car radio whose ability to relate to his audience fascinated me. I later would be able to lure him to work at my television station. A chap you may have heard of: Phil Donahue.

But more about that later.

Even back in the 1930's, the cost of a college education posed a challenge to my family and to me, and also to most young people of my age. Fortunately, there was a program called "Co-oping." It meant I was allowed to switch back and forth, every 13 weeks, between going to school and working. I thus earned enough to cover tuition and books, and because I was still living at home and eating at the family table, I was even able to have a little pocket money.

But war clouds were on the horizon. The events in Europe had caught the world's attention and by the summer of 1941 it seemed

255

inevitable that I would be drafted into the service, so I decided to enlist. When I tried to get into the Navy, they rejected me as being too small. Then the Air Force refused to accept me when they discovered I was color blind. But the doctor for the Army didn't seem to care about those things, and I was accepted for service in June of 1941.

During training I had been assigned to what was called the "Counterintelligence Corps." America was not officially at war yet, but the Army was concerned about the activities of civilian Nazi sympathizers who were trying to popularize a movement among potential draftees to evade military service. It was given the acronym of OHIO, standing for the slogan "Over The Hill In October" and was being spread by the German fifth column. The Army was concerned this activity might infect the troops and our mission was to identify and recruit one soldier in each company who would monitor his group and report to us if there was any subversive activity in the unit.

We were based at Camp Wheelor, Georgia, and it happened that several of us were on leave in Atlanta on the weekend which turned out to include the terrible events at Pearl Harbor on December 7, 1941. I remember we were in Atlanta's *Ainsley Hotel*, and I awakened with a terrible hangover just in time to hear President FDR's famous radio speech which included the phrase "a day that will live in infamy."

Naturally the news prompted us to scramble back to camp as soon as possible, fearful that our company might be moving and leave us behind. It was about this time the Army discovered I had a college degree in Business Administration, so they transferred me to the Finance Department at Fort McPherson in Atlanta where I was trained for finance work before being transferred overseas.

Soon they moved us for a 30 day stay at Indiantown Gap in Pennsylvania and then to Brooklyn to board the *SS Argentina*. We were melded in with many other troops and they tried to squeeze all of us into the bottom deck of the ship. But we couldn't all fit and the smell of latrines and cooking was overpowering, so our company spread our blankets on the ship's top deck, moving only for the daily hose-down. It was cold and wet, but livable. Ours was the largest convoy that had ever left these shores, and while sailing across the Atlantic we heard many loud explosions but did not actually see any sinking of ships by submarines.

Eventually we landed in Scotland, at Edinburgh's Firth of Forth. We then boarded a camouflaged train and went directly to an old British Army camp in Cheltenham, in England's Cotswalds area. We were then attached to the "Service of Supply," the major service HQ for the European theater of operations.

Work in the Finance Office was interesting. After my training in Cheltenham, the Army would send me to other bases to train their personnel in the handling of my specialty which was "per diem" payments.

Eventually I earned a ten day furlough and eagerly looked forward to my first visit to London. Some of the medical workers at the base suggested I call a girl they had worked with who was employed in London by the British Ministry of Health. Her name was Phyllis "Babs" O'Connor and to my relief, she agreed to meet me for dinner in London. That blind date dinner in a Picadilly restaurant called *The Queen's Brasserie* led to our marriage on March 27, 1944 and, to date, 59 years of marriage and three kids.

But it was only years later that she revealed to me that her job at the Ministry of Health was only a cover for her real job. She was a spy for Britain, including such derring-do activities as making secret landings in occupied France and Belgium as part of the group labeled "Special Operations Executives."

The SOE had been created by Winston Churchill and a Canadian named Stevenson. It conducted secret operations the world over, similar to the United States espionage group, the OSS. Babs said nothing about this organization, religiously honoring for 40 years her oath of secrecy.

Shortly after the D-Day invasion I was sent to France; first to Cherbourg, then Paris where our office controlled the currency being used in Europe. At times it became quite confusing, as our Paris Finance Office had basement vaults which were knee-deep in foreign money of all kinds and denominations.

When the European phase of the war finally ended, I had sufficient "points" to be transferred back to the U.S., but instead I transferred to United Base Command in London so that I could see about getting my British bride back to the states with me.

I soon found that traveling home together was not possible, but the base commander said if I could straighten out his personal finances he would see what he could do about arranging transport for Babs. Early in 1946, he handed me a ticket for a War Shipping Administration boat called the *Francis D. Calkin*, a small Liberty Ship. So, on only two day's notice, Babs said her farewells, packed and then boarded the small vessel which resembled a fishing boat more than an ocean liner, and sailed from the port of Fowey, Wales. It took nineteen and a half days before she finally landed in Portland, Maine. I left England later for my eighteen day crossing and we had a joyous reunion at my aunt and uncle's apartment in New York before deciding to make our permanent home in Cincinnati.

Then it was time for the challenge of earning a living.

I had a brief fling with an effort to sell half-gallon jugs of detergent to housewives, but soon dropped that when Babs and I created "The United States Bottling Corporation." Why bottling? Because as a veteran I was entitled to a federal license which gave me access to a limited amount of scarce sugar. Ours was truly a "Mom & Pop" operation, as I would go out and call on customers to sell the product and when I'd get an order I would call Babs at the plant and she would make whatever the customer had ordered. We sold half gallon bottles of orange and grapefruit drink and fancy small containers of maple syrup and grenadine mix. Eventually, we sold the bottling plant to a local food broker.

I then tried another job, that of being advertising manager of the Adler Co., selling their new *shrink-controlled* white wool socks. The wool had been dipped in a solution that prevented the little wool nodes from becoming twisted with the rest of the material, thus...no shrinking. We were using a very clever advertising agency from Chicago called Ruthrauff & Ryan, and we worked well together. After two years, Tom Adler, President of the company, told me that the tax situation did not permit him to reinvest in new knitting machines, but I had a job there as long as I wanted.

I began to look around for a position which might offer more of a future, and after 125 interviews I decided I wanted to be part of the exciting new industry called "television." I created a hypothetical role for myself as being a person selling advertising time on behalf of a TV station and worked with our Chicago ad agency in preparing an imaginary sales pitch to a department store. I used this pitch as a demonstration at the two TV stations in Cincinnati that would see me. I should explain that WCPO would not consider me because it was owned by the Scripps Howard newspaper chain and my father worked at their local paper as Racing Editor and they had a policy that father and son could not work at the same company. But the other two stations each offered me a position and I went to work for the one that wanted me to start the next day: that was WLWT, the Crosley Broadcasting Company, owned by AVCO. I was excited at the prospect of introducing advertisers to this powerful new medium of television. And I soon found that most of my clients were pleased with the results TV generated for them.

By my second year, my track record of sales was going so well I even received a personal letter of congratulations from Victor Emmanuel, Chairman of the Board of our parent company, AVCO. He was especially pleased with my efforts in capturing the regional business of a brewer who bought time in all four of our AVCO markets for his new beer which was named *WonderBrau* (not to be confused with a later era's *Wonder Bra*). I had also brought in a new client who was selling men's suits for the Palm Beach Company.

I was winning all the sales prizes and was very pleased with my progress. But then WLWT got a new sales manager who spent each morning's sales meeting telling the staff how to sell from the vision he saw on his bedroom wall that morning. I found his method of leadership to be a little strange and my discomfort led me to look around for something in the television field which could expand my boundaries. I wanted to stay in Cincinnati, so I decided to apply for a sales job with a new company located there which was rapidly becoming very well known in the TV syndication business, the Frederick W. Ziv Co., known throughout the industry simply as Ziv.

Their specialty was producing new half hour shows, most of which were not offered to the networks, but instead were sold to individual markets...a method called syndication. Each series would feature at least one well-known star. The series titles included *Cisco Kid, Harbor Command, Sea Hunt, I Led Three Lives, Everglades,* and *Highway Patrol*, to name a few.

They hired me as a salesman, but before I was allowed to start calling on stations and clients in my territory, I was put through three weeks of intensive training directly under a wonderful sales manager named Edward Broman. He was in charge of the Cincinnati division and was one of the major reasons why I went to work at Ziv. He was a strong Mormon from Salt Lake City with a wonderful ability to sell product. Broman was also the leader in the setting up and building of

260

a new Mormon congregation and church in Cincinnati.

My first experience of actually doing the selling was the next three weeks of going to Louisville, Kentucky, trying to sell *The Eddie Cantor Comedy Theater*, leaving every Monday at 9 a.m. and not coming home until the weekends, and doing this back and forth and back again until a sale was finally made...a Ziv principle. The entire three weeks were very rough, but I met new and different people, from the executives of Brown & Williamson to the General Managers and sales managers of the three TV stations in Louisville, to almost every advertising agency representing clients big enough to afford the cost of TV time. Eventually my territory was increased to include southern Ohio and Indianapolis. Then I was promoted to the job of Spot Sales Manager under the new Division Manager, Mike Kievman.

For the next two years I traveled weekly, often not returning home until Saturday and leaving again on Sunday in order to get to appointments in Cleveland, or Minneapolis or Omaha in order to help our local salesman there who had not yet sold one of those important markets.

It paid well, but my family was missing me, so I discussed my concern with Fred Ziv, and he moved me and my family to Detroit, from which I covered a much more manageable geographic territory.

We lived in the attractive Detroit suburb of Bloomfield Hills and spent a year there, but because of the problems that the kids were facing in school, it was decided we should return to Cincinnati. I resigned from Ziv and returned to the station management side of the industry by rejoining AVCO where John Murphy and Walt Bartlett offered me the job of Station Manager at their station in Dayton, Ohio: WLWD.

This was an exciting time because my ambition was to be manager of a large station, and this was my first. The management gave me free rein, and it was then up to me to represent the station in all interests in the community.

Babs and I joined the Symphony Board and the Opera Board and the Library Board, to name just a few. In this manner we were soon able to get WLWD better known by the involved people in the community and became some competition to the Cox-owned station, WHIO, which had a transmitter tower twice as big as ours. The FCC would not allow us to increase the size of our transmitter in Dayton because AVCO also owned stations in relatively nearby cities such as Cincinnati, Columbus and Indianapolis which aired signal patterns we might have clashed with if we increased our power.

While driving to lunch one day in Dayton, a person in the car tuned my radio to a station airing a talk show hosted by a chap named Phil Donahue. The subject the audience was talking about was "ironing their husband's underpants" and I was intrigued to learn that he was able to spread this single topic over his entire ninety minute show and continue with the same topic the next day. Three hours on ironing underpants? Was anybody listening? Oh, yes! In fact he was broadcasting his radio show opposite our popular TV show *The Ruth Lyons Show* and was actually keeping our ratings lower than they used to be. Phil was an extremely busy man as he also appeared on WHIO television where he co-anchored the 6 p.m. and 11 p.m. news shows, and also did a five minute interview show each night from 5:55 to 6:00 p.m.

As the saying goes, I "set my cap for him." But it took months of conversations before I could convince him to leave WHIO and join us at WLWD. But he finally did, after I offered him a two year contract where he did not have to do live personal commercials and did not have to do the 11 p.m. news, so he could be home with his family. Unfortunately, this did not prevent his wife from leaving him a few years later when the show changed its base of origination to Chicago.

She did not want such a public husband, and soon Phil Donahue was one of the most well-known talk show hosts in the country.

The Phil Donahue Show started in Dayton, Ohio, on WLWD-TV in 1967 and presented a new type of television talk show, with Phil roaming through the audience to get them involved in the subject being discussed. Oprah Winfrey freely and frequently admits that she copied much of the format of her talk show from watching Phil in those early years.

Phil is a wonderful guy to work with; we had very few problems. He did want to control most of the show, and as I think of it, the only show I sat through with much trepidation and a finger on the control button which would cut him off the air, was one done with Jerry Rubin and his pot-smoking audience. We had the audience augmented with undercover policemen in case anything untoward happened, but it didn't. Our confidence in Phil and his producer, Dick Mincer, later Pat MacMillan, continued to grow.

Actually it was Phil's very first broadcast on our station which demonstrated to us how strong his audience was. Here, in Bible Belt Dayton, he booked as his guest, Madelyn Murray O'Hare, the famous atheist. Madelyn was responsible for the Supreme Court decision barring prayers in school, and the audience had some strong feelings. The phone system was clogged and our very building seemed to rock. But this was nothing compared to the reaction to his show later in the week called *Little Brother Doll*.

Phil's studio audience was violently divided on their reaction to a male doll, complete with penis and scrotum. The arguments went back and forth, and finally Phil held the doll up to the cameras and suggested that the audience use the WLWD voting lines, some 100 of them. Those that thought the doll should be available for their children to play with were told to use one set of fifty lines and those who wanted to register negatively were told to call the other fifty lines.

263

At this point I was working quietly in my office and I was surprised by the ringing of my private line. As only my wife knew this number, I answered with "Hello, Darling." A male voice on the other end, identifying himself as the President of the Ohio Bell Company, was furious. Something we were doing had wiped out all the dial tones in Dayton. The jails, hospitals, and all personal and business calls were impossible to dial. I asked him to wait while I went into the studio to find out what was happening. I talked to Phil, and he then told the audience that the voting was over.

I then explained this to the head of Ohio Bell, and as the dial tones were beginning to return to the lines, he told me he would be in my office at 9:00 a.m. the next day. He then hung up, a very angry man. The next day my office was bulging with executives from Ohio Bell, all making me swear that we would not do that again.

I don't remember the final tally on the "Doll" vote but I do remember that we nearly caused the same problem in Cleveland. We fed the show "live" to Cleveland and were discussing some topic which was sensitive to that city's viewers and the telephone response was heavy.

It was our belief at the time that being "live" was essential to the success of the show, so as we expanded our coverage to additional markets, we were buying lines for the feed from the telephone company. But when summer's Daylight Savings Time came and Detroit changed time but Dayton didn't, we had to send them tapes. Soon we realized our Detroit ratings were even better than before, and so we canceled those expensive telco lines and serviced all of our customer stations with videotapes. And our list of customer stations continued to grow as word spread throughout the broadcast industry of Donahue's success. We even expanded into the international market with sales being handled by Tony Morris in London who headed a fine staff. Phil did especially well in England. And as all sales were under my jurisdiction, it "necessitated" Babs and I going to France and Monaco at least twice a year...trips which Babs loved.

On his vacations, Donahue used to take 150 of his closest friends on trips to places such as Hawaii and Bermuda. Or to Paris to commence a trip down France's canals, staying at gorgeous chateaux along the way, followed by a trip around the Mediterranean on the *Sea Goddess*. Or a wonderful around the world trip on a private jet, including ten days on the China Seas aboard the luxury yacht, *Seabourne*. They were great trips, and he not only paid for everything, but in addition, his accountant was one of the guests, so if anyone got into money problems he was there to bail them out.

Phil was also a good talent scout as demonstrated by his recommendation to us that we take a look at an aspiring talk show hostess named Sally Jesse Raphael. We first gave her an on-camera test in our WLWT studios and then assigned her to do a daily half hour show on our station in St. Louis, Missouri. Soon she was enjoying great success and we were able to sell her show in syndication throughout the U.S. And, to even further expand our syndication efforts, we assigned our own Tom Robinson to produce a series called *Young People's Specials*, which proved to be salable everywhere, from as near as Virginia to as far as Africa.

Donahue continued to win Emmys and trophies of all sorts because of the uniqueness of his show, the outstanding methods of his handling of the audience, and the fascinating guests he presented on the air. The '*Donahue Show*' lasted an incredible 29 years, going off the air in 1996, and Phil had done over 6,000 shows in that period. It was a thrill for me and my family to be part of this meritorious ride.

As for me, I retired at the age of 70 as President of Multimedia Program Syndication. The General Manager at WLWT in Cincinnati was kind enough to let me use an office there for several years until the company was sold to the Gannett Corporation. I then retired to a very comfortable office in my home where I have my own computer, telephone, fax, and my own playback machines.

Walt Bartlett and I are still good friends. So are Jim Lynagh, Peter Lund, Bruce Johansen, Dick Mincer, Chuck McFadden, Joe Ciffarelli, Dick Thrall, and many other *"Crosley-ites"* that I see at the yearly Cincy reunions.

I am still called on once in awhile to develop another Donahue, and I sometimes am impressed enough with the individual to try. To date I have not been successful, but I remain hopeful.

My name is Mel Smith. I started my career in the TV business at WCSC-TV in Charleston, S.C. on August 19, 1953 at 3 p.m. ET. Now, fifty years later, I still enjoy dabbling in the program production business, but I've forsaken the corporate towers for a home office. My wife, Seiko, is a location producer for several Japanese networks. I'd like to dedicate this chapter to all the men and women who pitched their hearts out to make a sale, and I'm sorry I couldn't buy all of your programs! For fourteen years I was with the Tribune Company and enjoyed that association with what became my favorite company. I was variously a Program Manager, Station Operations and Program Manager, Director of Programming and eventually, Vice President of Programming with offices in Chicago's lofty Tribune Tower for 11 years. To you syndicators who sold me hundreds of millions of dollars worth of programming, I send my thanks and this chapter.

Pardon Me While I Drop a Few Names
by Mel Smith

Even before I started working in TV, I often found myself unexpectedly in the company of the great, near great and the infamous.

I suppose we are all in awe of the greats of any business. But it seems that when the movie stars come down off the silver screen and you find yourself talking to them, it's especially special!

As a nine year old, I was walking along the lovely Rosarita Beach in Baja California, Mexico. My mother, whose father owned eight movie theaters in Kentucky and Indiana, stopped me and said, "There's Wayne Morris and Melvyn Douglas!" In the late forties both were well-known stars and of course my star-struck mom recognized them. She began chatting with them and told Mr. Douglas that I was, in fact, named after him. (The truth is that I was named after a family friend, Melvin Schweinhardt, a bartender!) But at least she had taken the 'MelvYn' spelling from Douglas. When she acquainted the distinguished actor with that fact he bent over to tell me, "Well then, my condolences, Melvyn! And when they misspell your name M-e-l-v-i-n you can blame me *and* your mother!"

Just a few years later I was going into my school friend's family restaurant on the Isle of Palms, South Carolina, and I was startled to see the late Gregory Peck and his wife Greta having lunch. He was in the area making a movie (*View From Pompey's Head*) and was enjoying a break by touring just up the coast from his location work. I immediately called my mom who arrived fifteen minutes later, autograph book and camera in hand. We let them finish their luncheon and as they came outside we asked them if we could take their picture. "Why certainly," smiled Peck. They held hands and posed in front of the beach front eatery. The fellow who was with them asked us, as we were getting an autograph, if we could send them a copy of the picture of the twosome. He gave us a business card which carried Mr. Peck's address.

We often wondered if that day had been some sort of special occasion for them...like an anniversary. The Pecks seemed to be very nice folks, and even as an eleven year old, I decided it would be nice to look and sound like Mr. Peck.

When I was a teenager we produced a local TV program on WCSC-TV. We called the program (what else!) *Teenage Beat*. Like every station in America, we copied Dick Clark's *Bandstand* and our show became very popular with the local teens and our sponsor, Pepsi Cola. We also did a radio program for Coca Cola which had a teen format. The radio show had nationally-furnished elements from Coke, and when celebrities came to town we would haul the station's 50 pound "portable" tape machine out to the venue to interview them.

One day at the station two fellows named Bill and Scotty showed up to promote a single record which, as I recall it, was titled *Milk Cow Boogie*. It was a strange sounding mixture of country, rhythm and blues, and rock and roll all blended into one disc. The lead singer was a fellow named "Elvis." I went to see and interview this young star, along with the local newspaper Entertainment Reporter, an attractive young lady. After a very nice joint interview, Elvis shook hands with me and then took the reporter lady's hand and bit her playfully. She jerked back her hand and said, "What did you do that for?" "Ma'am," Elvis smiled, "Ah jes wanted you to remember me." I'll bet she still tells that story to her grandchildren. I remember Elvis as a friendly young fellow with a whole lot of pomade on his black hair.

About the same time, I also interviewed a handsome, clean-cut young lad in white shoes, Pat Boone. Unlike Elvis, he was the guy American parents wanted their daughters to date. He told me that he just finished his Master's Degree at Columbia University. This was in the mid-fifties, but let's fast-forward to 1971 when I was working in St. Louis at KMOX-TV as their public relations guy. I was waiting at the elevator to welcome no less than the CBS Network's Chairman, William Paley, and it's President, Dr. Frank Stanton, who were arriving for one of their occasional station visits. As the elevator neared I could hear someone who sounded just like Pat Boone singing one of his big hit songs, *April Love*. Then the elevator doors opened and the volume of the song increased and there was Pat Boone, white bucks and all, honoring a Paley request to sing that song, which Paley enjoyed so much. As I ushered Paley and Stanton into the station, Boone said his goodbyes and continued his trip up to the building's next level where he was scheduled to do an interview for radio station KMOX. Paley told Stanton, "Frank, we ought to do a variety show with Pat." But ABC beat them to it.

As a major-market CBS affiliate, we were one of the stops many of the network stars made on their annual tours to promote the new fall season. One of the most memorable of those stars was

269

Lucille Ball, who proved to be a real "pro" and terrific to work with. I always had my ducks lined up and made sure she had her little list of wants and desires fulfilled. I even made sure her hotel room had a nice view of the famous St. Louis Arch.

Lucy was not a prima donna. One thing she did not like was to be questioned about her divorced husband, Desi Arnaz. All she would say was something nice about his talent and business expertise helping to make their show a hit. Lucy was heartbroken about the breakup and I always cautioned newspaper writers to let it lay. Once, when the *Cleveland Plain Dealer* TV Editor, a favorite of Lucy's, and a new lady editor from the *Columbus Dispatch* were interviewing her, the young lady editor began asking "Desi questions." Bill, of the '*Plain Dealer*' began giving little negative head shakes to cue the lady to "cease and desist" from this fatal line of questioning. This took place during a quiet dinner the three were sharing. Despite Bill's best efforts, the lady editor plowed ahead. Finally, with a healthy swig and a bite of steak, Lucy said to '*Ms. Columbus Dispatch*,' "You want a quote about Desi for your column? How about this: "the only thing good about that Cuban pr**k was his Cuban pr**k!" That's one reason why *I* love Lucy!

I also liked Desi Arnaz very much. He was a charming and friendly guy, and even as a tough businessman, he was well respected in Hollywood. He once told me he titled his autobiography *A BOOK* by Desi Arnaz because everyone told him, "You ought to write *a book*!" I met him in Cleveland at WUAB-TV where he was appearing on a talk show to promote his book.

Several years before, when I was in St. Louis, I had met Lucy's daughter and had gotten her to get her mother to pick out her 20 favorite episodes for a May "sweeps" promotion which we titled *Lucy's Favorite Lucy's*. I had in my file, one-minute clips of each of the twenty episodes that Lucy had chosen. During my lunch with

Desi I found out that he didn't even have access to Desilu stills, much less any video. I gave him a reel of the clips to take on his promotion tour and he was very grateful.

Sort of a sad ending for a great couple.

Many of my syndication colleagues don't know (and rightly so, don't care) that I spent a lot of my so-called career in television news. I am proud of my association with some of the top journalists in the business. I've had the pleasure of meeting and talking with the "Dean" of American journalists, Walter Cronkite. One of his competitors, NBC anchorman John Chancellor (who preferred his name be pronounced "Chan-sa-lore") always enjoyed regaling his crew when we were 'standing by' endlessly to contribute a Washington point of view to some big news event.

My favorite story that he told us was that when he had taken a leave of absence from NBC to head up the Voice of America for a couple of years, FBI Director J. Edgar Hoover played him some surveillance audio tapes of a very famous civil rights leader in a motel room tryst with a woman who was *not* his wife. The hysterically funny part was John's reenactment of the pillow talk and passionate moments of the unsuspecting civil rights leader. We also heard stories about Hoover's penchant for backless evening gowns and high heels, but we never reported it. Ah, them were the good old days! (For the politician.) When I left NBC to go to CBS, Chancellor gave me his NBC News-issued stopwatch, saying, "Since you won't be around to get one at retirement, take this one." I told him I couldn't take his watch. He said, "Mel, for crissakes, take it. I'm an anchorman. They'll get me another one!" I still use it to time tape bits.

Although I was technically assigned to be a member of the production crew for NBC News, there was a fluke in the union contract which allowed me to be required to often serve as a make-up man for the people appearing on news programs.

After a White House press conference one day, Dick Showers and I were summoned from the NBC News van by a Secret Service man to "come with him to the oval office immediately." With trepidation, we were hustled into the presence of Lyndon Baines Johnson (POTUS, the Secret Service called him), President of the United States.

"Ya'll boys trying to f*** me?" he scowled. "Mr. Kintner here, says my make-up looks like s***!" Bob Kintner, then recent, but no longer President of NBC-TV, was "consulting" to improve LBJ's poor TV performance skills. Dick sent for his make-up case and we used a darker "more masculine" shade of pancake as Kintner said. Satisfied, probably relieved of the indignity of what he called "sissifying make-up," Johnson turned to us two scared young NBC guys and said, "Ya'll boys want a *Fresca?*" We both had a *Fresca* on the Prez. He told us that it was his favorite soft drink but the "no good s.o.b.'s have changed the formula and it wasn't half as tasty as it used to be."

At NBC News in Washington we often did "insert interviews" for *The Today Show*. One early morning, technical director Bob Van Sothen and I were tweaking up the interview set and the lighting for General Westmoreland, just in from Viet Nam. "General, would you please scoot your chair about two inches to the right," boomed Bob over the studio P.A. The general obliged. "Fine General. Now edge it back about two inches." The General slid back his chair. "Good, good, now edge just an inch or so to the left." This went on for another minute and I asked, "Bobby, what the hell was that all about?" Newly returned Army vet Bob replied, "That son of a bitch ran my ass all over Viet Nam and now we're even!"

NBC had hired a young reporter fellow from South Dakota by the name of Tom Brokaw. One night he stumbled a bit through a shaky recital of his Washington insert for the network's evening news show, *The Huntley-Brinkly Report.* The tense young reporter was very upset at his tiny bobble and walked quickly out of the studio as soon as the program was over. My crew and I headed for the *Hot Shoppe* to eat and as George Light was discussing what we might order for dinner, we passed Tom Brokaw retching his guts out in the bushes in front of our studio. When we were seated I told George, "That guy'll never make it. He's too intense." I have always been an expert on the subject of TV talent. I can prove it. When they told me that Roseanne was going to do a sitcom, I said, "That ought to be a short order of six shows!" See, I am a genius at recognizing talent!

In some make-up room banter before a *Meet The Press*, I asked King Hussein of Jordan what the difference was between being King and the President of the United States, whom he was to visit. "Well, you are only President for four, maybe eight years," he said. "Then you get your life back." He sighed and went on. "When you are King, you are King for all of your life and your life belongs always to your people." Gee! And I had thought that, as Mel Brooks once famously said, "It's *good* to be King!" Apparently, in reality it is not. His wife, Queen Noor, is the daughter of U.S. Air Force General Pete Quesada, and an American. She has a lovely presence and the King was obviously very close to her. You could see it. We miss his evenhanded counsel in the Middle East turmoil of today.

Years later, after I had left *Meet The Press*, the producer told me that she was always afraid I'd say something that would offend one of the guests on the show. Many of them told her that they enjoyed the chap in the make-up room...a chore that most world leaders hate to have performed on them. One Sunday I had British Prime Minister Ted Heath. He was obviously tickled when I brought in my album of music by bandleader Ted Heath for him to autograph, and which he dutifully did. He signed it, "To Mel Smith from the *other* Ted Heath."

One of my chores on *Meet The Press* was to do a "just before

273

air time" make-up touchup on the panel of newspersons and the guest. News still photographers would often be on the set and would take that opportunity to snap a picture of the guest with me dabbing on their foreheads. I made the front pages of the *New York Times, Los Angeles Times, Chicago Tribune* and *Washington Post* on various occasions. This always seemed to amuse my college classmates who always dutifully clipped the photos out of their local paper and sent them to me. My father was surprised by a photo on the front page of the *Post and Courier* in Charleston captioned "Unidentified make-up man socks it to Senator Thurmond." The picture looked like I was planting a left cross to the eye! "Are you really a make-up man?" my father wrote.

Years later, when I was a CBS promotion maven, I was unsuccessfully trying to convince the aloof and erudite Eric Severeid to stoop to do a very simple on-camera promotion announcement. My late son, Phillip, then about 12 years old, was with me as I was taking him on a "day at work with Dad" day. Severeid, a news editorialist the likes of which we have not seen since his retirement from CBS, seemed pleased to see my young boy and spoke to him in a friendly manner. "Son, do you watch the *CBS Evening News?*" Phillip replied, "No, sir." "Ah," Severeid said to me, "an honest lad!" He turned to Phillip and said, "I hope you grow up to be President!" No, Severeid didn't do the promo, but at least he did give my son a wonderful comment to grow on!

Some irreverent members of the press privately referred to President Richard Nixon as "Tricky Dick." He was on the run from Watergate and speaking before the *Radio & Television News Directors Association* (RTNDA) in conclave at Houston. I had volunteered to serve as an usher, helping to seat the reporters who were going to query the President about Watergate developments. Since I had "White House Clearance" I was allowed to sit with the group on stage.

As it would happen, I was right behind CBS's peppery Texan, Dan Rather. During the news conference Rather asked him, "Are you running from something, Mr. President?" "No," retorted the sweating Nixon. "Are you?" Rather ended up on the CBS carpet for his aggressive questioning. I ended up with the back of my head showing behind Rather in the archive tape of the incident.

As a young WCSC-TV news photographer I was once assigned to film President Eisenhower on his visit to Columbia, South Carolina. When I got within about three feet of him (try *that* today), I began filming a nice Eisenhower grin. "Isn't that an old Bell and Howell combat camera?" he asked. "Yes, Mr. President." "Good. That camera and I are both World War II surplus!" You'd be surprised at how often Presidents say the darndest things. I'm just old enough to have met every President since Herbert Hoover, except FDR. And, oops, George W. Well, I hope there's still time to meet "Dubya."

Of them all, probably the one I most enjoyed talking to was Gerald Ford. Not a pretentious bone in his body! Jimmy Carter is southern-friendly but actually sort of a nerd. When I met Ronald Reagan at Wrigley Field in the last few weeks of his presidency, he seemed to know and enjoy he was at a ball park, but I felt he really didn't know which one. I'm not making fun of Mr. Reagan. He was a very good President, but he seemed like he was "not there." Having done several of President Kennedy's press conferences, I was taken by his sense of humor and smile. Only Magic Johnson has a better smile. Bill Clinton is the ultimate 'in person' Presidential experience. What other President could you expect to meet at MacDonalds?

At the NATPE convention a few years ago in New Orleans, along with my son Phillip, we were 'Rollin' Down The River' on a sternwheeler and enjoying the buffet as guests of Dick Clark Productions. While we listened to a live rendition of *Blueberry Hill* by Fats Domino and his orchestra, Dick Clark came up to us and said, "Well Phil, how do you like this New Orleans food?" Phillip told him he liked it a lot! When Dick went on to greet other guests, Phillip turned to me and said, "Dad, I used to tell everyone that I know Dick Clark...now I can tell them that Dick Clark knows me!" Dick is still one of the best guys at PR I've ever seen.

All of us have marveled for decades about the youthful appearance of the now "pushing seventy-five" Dick Clark. One day, and I'm not sure what I had said to have Dick launch into a spirited revelation, he told me his secret. He was taking an acre of vitamins every day! I got the list and have been taking them since 1990, and I haven't aged a bit. Not!

In the forties and fifties, MGM liked to say they had "more stars than there were in the heavens." I once had lunch with two of their very biggest at *Carrie Cerinno's* Italian restaurant in Parma, Ohio! After a WUAB-TV talk show we took our two stars to lunch. Van Johnson, as nice a star as you'll ever meet, was charming and friendly at lunch. He was quite taken with the other star and couldn't seem to stop petting her on the head as she snuggled up to him. He told us, "I never got to make a movie with Lassie, but I always loved seeing her on the MGM lot." I guess Lassie and her trainer, Rudd Weatherwax, were accustomed to being able to eat together at a restaurant. And yes, Van was wearing his trademark red socks. Lassie was very well-mannered and ate only treats from Rudd. I was the only one who 'wolfed down' my food.

Like most of you, I enjoyed *Hogan's Heroes*. A comedy based around a Nazi prison camp would certainly sound like a questionable premise, but I thought it would be great, probably because one of my favorite movies, *Stalag 17*, had used a similar locale. When I was working in Chicago, I was one day 'reading my lunch' at my favorite Michigan Avenue bookstore. As I worked my way down one of their narrow aisles I found I had to stop because my pathway was blocked by a tall, thinnish, balding man. I instantly recognized Werner Klemperer, who had played the monocled, inept Colonel Klink on the *Hogan's Heroes* series. "Pardon me, mien commandant!" I said. Klemperer responded with a smile and, clicking his heels together, said "Of course, mien herren!" I went on my way, satisfied that I had been able to escape from Colonel Klink!

When I was at Tribune Entertainment we made numerous mini-series. One was *The Achille Lauro Affair,* a true story of a terrorist group 'seajacking' a cruise liner, and starring Burt Lancaster. When it came time to do the premiere party, we wondered if he would show up as he was contracted to do. So when he showed up on time and ready to go we were relieved. George Paris, the Tribune's West Coast guy, asked him, "How are you, Burt?" He replied sharply, "I'm 74 years old and I feel like s***!" But, old pro that he was, he schmoozed the press.

As an astronaut, Neil Armstrong once made a magnificent emergency landing with the Lunar Lander on the moon. He later became a member of the Board of Directors of Taft Broadcasting. He may have been a great pilot, but one icy and snowy day while arriving at Taft's Cincinnati headquarters for a meeting, he slid his car into the passenger-side front fender of my car. He didn't even notice it and the company President, realizing it was a company car, just paid to have it fixed because he didn't want any police or insurance reports. I tried several times to chat with Neil at various Taft functions, but his social skills never made it back from the moon. "One great fender bender for mankind..." Buzz Aldrin, on the other hand, is a gas to talk to. Jim Lovell, "Houston, we have a problem" Apollo 13 commander, has a great restaurant in Chicago and his son is the head chef.

Note that I seem to have a lot of stories that involve eating. Well, I want you to know that since I had a 'cardiopulmonary event' of some kind three years ago, I am down from 264 pounds to 205. This 'event' happened during NATPE several years ago, and at the urging of Joe Goldfarb, I immediately was examined by a doctor. He didn't really help me much because a month later I ended up in intensive care. But at least that examination legally established a start date for my insurance and Medicare claims that followed. Jim Dowdle, Chairman of Tribune Broadcasting and Entertainment, now retired, was fond of saying, "Nobody gets a free lunch around here except Mel." Hey, Jim, I found out that all those free lunches can almost kill you!

Jim was a great guy to work for. He told me when I was tapped as his "program guy" that he wanted me to "go to lunch with or see in the office any syndicator that wanted access to Tribune." He also said, "You only have to go to dinner with the guys you really like." I'm not blaming my colleagues in syndication for nearly killing me with cuisine. I enjoyed every meal and you will please note that I also went to dinner with almost all of you!

"The Irish Independent" is my nickname for Joe Loughlin who was a longtime manager of independent stations. While we worked together at KWGN in Denver, he invited me to attend a charity ball given by billionaire Marvin Davis. Davis, then moguling his way through a Hollywood studio, flew in a lot of top stars for the event. The group included the truly legendary Cary Grant. While chatting with the Metropolitan Opera's Beverly Sills (I thought she'd make a great wife for me but she was already married), none other than Cary Grant wandered over to say hello to his friend, Ms. Sills. She introduced him to me and we shook hands as one of the ditzy Denver society matrons edged into the group. "I recognize you," she said to Mr. Grant. "Thank you, my dear. We all love being recognized whether we admit it or not," he said. "I just can't seem to say your name..." she said. "It's Archie Leach," Grant said, much to Beverly Sills' amusement. He gave his real name to the lady and she was PLEASED to meet him.

Over the years, as programming chief of our Tribune-owned group of TV stations, I probably dealt with nearly every syndication company in the business, and as a group I found them to be superior people who earned my respect for their intelligence, their wit and their persistence. But I can't refrain from telling you about one major screw-up which lingers in my memory because it is so hilariously untypical of the way these businessmen usually operate.

I had received an urgent sales call from the General Sales Manager of one of the major distribution companies whose sales offices were in New York. He told me his company was about to offer in syndication the first off-network broadcast rights to a highly popular comedy series with a long track record of high network ratings. He wanted me to set up an appointment and to marshal all of Tribune's top executives for a major presentation to us, and he underscored the importance of the session by telling me that even the famous President of his company was arranging to fly in to Chicago from his production offices in Hollywood to attend this meeting.

I agreed to his request and watched in fascination as first the New York guy arrived in a white stretch limo, followed shortly later by a black stretch limo delivering his boss. I escorted the two of them to our screening room on the 18th floor of our Tribune Tower facilities and introduced them to my associates. After a few minutes of the usual pleasantries, the Big West Coast guy said to the Big East Coast guy, "Show them the tape." Mr. East Coast guy said, "I thought YOU had it." Neither of them did. So we all just went to lunch instead. In stretch limos!

Years earlier, when I had been Program Manager of Tribune's Denver station, KWGN-TV, I was looking at a program being offered by the intense and hard-charging independent syndicator, Pete

Rodgers. (Whose son, Steve, has a chapter in this book.) As the credits started to roll and then the music faded I could hear Pete across the screening room saying over and over under his breath..."Please buy it. Please buy it!" To this day I can't decide if it was just his well-known intensity or a clever way to get me to subliminally buy it. I bought it. I couldn't resist that all out effort to close the deal. I miss him peering over his glasses with that "Well?" look, as he asked for the order. Peter was a PRO!

If you don't have a personal and unique story about the legendary Sandy Frank (another contributor to these pages), you are nobody in the program acquisition business.

Once, while I was heading up programming for our Tribune group, Sandy persuaded me to arrange for him a "pitch session" at our Chicago Superstation, WGN-TV. He had an hour western of not much fame and fewer episodes, but, as created by master pitchman Frank, his case for its success was impressive.

In addition to my presence at WGN, whose studios are located some distance from our corporate headquarters, he also asked for and I enlisted the station's General Manager, the General Sales Manager, the Program Manager and the Promotion Director. I told Sandy that, due to a previously scheduled meeting at the Tribune Tower, I would have to leave midway through his pitch. Now, as all his customers know, if for any reason Sandy is interrupted in his pitch, he simply starts it over again from the beginning. But when I explained my scheduled departure, he accepted and agreed not to again "go back to the top."

As the time came for me to leave and I reached for my briefcase, I noticed that Sandy had nervously kicked off his shined-to-the hilt Gucci shoes, so I surreptitiously scooped them up and put them in my briefcase just before saying my "goodbyes." Sandy was so totally focused on his message he didn't even notice what I had done.

True to his word, Sandy picked up his pitch at the point where he had stopped. As I left the studio I gave the Gucci's to the security guard and said I had found them in the hallway. I'm told that when Sandy came back to the lobby in his stocking feet to call a cab, he was told by the security guard, "These must be yours, sir."

To add insult to injury, WGN did not clear his western hour show. I saw Sandy at the most recent NATPE convention and he looked fit, and ready to pitch, but didn't answer when I said hello. It must have been the Gucci's!

When a controversial show comes out and you agree to buy it and it becomes a big hit, of course at renewal time you get a break on the price...right? Wrong! You end up at the end of your contract term with the threat of having your little Naughty Hit moved by the distributor to a competing station because they offered more money. At the time I was working at WKRC-TV in Cincinnati, Chuck Barris produced a somewhat risqué game show, hosted by the charming Bob Eubanks, titled *The Newlywed Game*. Questions were on the order of "Where is the strangest place you and your husband have ever made whoopee?" Sometimes the answers were wild, sometimes bland. My Program Assistant got a great idea. When the answers weren't naughty enough to be funny, she would "bleep" part of the answer out and leave it up to the audience's "filthy imagination" as to what was said. The syndicator liked this idea so much, he dubbed copies off our version of the tapes and sent them around to his other customer stations.

One of our WKRC-TV stage managers at the time must have been paying close attention to these telecasts, because George Clooney has recently directed and starred in a feature film based on Chuck Barris' life which, among other things, portrays Barris' claim that while masterminding this and other TV series, he was also allegedly assassinating bad guys for the CIA!

We were getting huge ratings with the show but when it came time to renew our contract, the distributor demanded a five fold increase in our license fee. I offered double. The negotiation dragged out over five days and my boss, Bob Wiegand, suggested I do something "dramatic" to get the negotiations "off the dime." Next day I tried raising my voice, making wild gestures and even getting up and yelling a bit in the salesman's face. But he wouldn't budge. Sitting back down, I finally turned and tossed a glass Coke bottle at him, which smashed into the wall behind him. He took off like a shot. (If your reading this, John Barrett, I did aim to miss you!)

Next day we made a deal with distributor Group W to acquire *PM Magazine* to air in that time period and *Newlywed Game* never aired again in the Cincinnati market. So much for outrageous demands!

The prime access time period of 7 to 8 p.m. is a critical area for a network affiliated station and a major source of revenue. So we were all excited when our acquisition of *PM Magazine* resulted in our earning an astounding 47 share of the available audience in the 7:30 p.m. time period. There were many candidate programs available for the 7 p.m. half of this hour to act as lead-in to '*PM*,' but the most impressive pitch came from syndicator Dick Colbert. He knew more about my station, my market, and my time period problems than I did. He had spent the time and the money to create a type of research I had never seen before, called a flow chart. It was designed to prove to me that his program, *Tic Tac Dough* would be the perfect series to lead into '*PM*.' I remember my astute boss questioned me closely about whether a game show could be compatible with a quasi-news magazine show, but I had been convinced by Colbert, who had done his job so cleverly, almost so lovingly, that I actually thought I knew what I was doing. So I bought *Tic Tac Dough*. But it didn't do as well as '*PM*'...it only generated a 45 share! And Colbert's work made ME a hero!

Art Greenfield was a catalyst and a mentor to many of us. Art was all the things I love about this business. Independent, helpful, friendly, knowledgeable, and never a hard-boiled sales guy. When we toast Art at these Friday luncheons, we're glad to have been in the business with him. Having spent most of my career in the Midwest and East and South, and with Art primarily operating out of the West, I didn't get to spend as much time with Art as I would have liked. But I find *his* circle of friends and colleagues to be *my* circle of friends and colleagues. May *Fridays with Art* go on forever!

Fridays With Art

Not Dirty, Just a Little Sandy
by Rob Word

It's an old syndicator's joke. What do you get when you make love on the beach? I had already found out one answer to that question on Clearwater Beach, Florida, long before I started working for the legendary television syndicator, and the answer to that question, Sandy Frank.

I had just left a whirlwind career as an ABC News cinematographer, producer, programmer and on-air celebrity interviewer/movie host in Orlando, and as a movie programmer and a Monday through Friday late night host in Tampa, Florida. I packed up my trusty Betamax VCR, my boxes and boxes of video tapes, my Leonard Maltin reference books and headed west...to Hollywood. It was 1979.

After just a couple months of eating tuna fish in my apartment and 79-cent breakfast specials at *Norm's Coffee Shop*, Phil Oldham, a friend, and one of the brightest executives at the station rep firm, Katz, phoned to say that he thought there might be a job opportunity for me in LA.

"Hmm. That's why I moved," I told him. "Doing what?"

"I know a man who's interested in putting together packages of movies to syndicate," said Phil. "He's looking for someone to send to film festivals, meet with independent producers and acquire the domestic distribution rights of those movies for television. Then he'll license broadcast rights to independent stations and network affiliates across the country."

Gee. That sounded fantastic! I had selected and hosted lots of movies back in Florida and seemed to have a knack for knowing what types of films worked and got big ratings on local stations. The newspapers hadn't labeled me "The Movie King" for nothing! I didn't know what I was in for, but I leapt at the chance for a new adventure...and better food.

Phil told me to expect a New York call that evening from Sandy Frank. SANDY FRANK. Well, I'd heard stories about Sandy. Who hadn't? He was a living legend. Going from market to market, station to station, selling re-run rights to such off-network fare as *My Little Margie* and *Lassie*, he'd begun in 1956 as a sales executive at NBC, moved to Senior VP of the Wrather Corporation TV sales division, and formed his own company, Sandy Frank Film Syndication, in 1964. He had made a fortune as one of the first, and best, television syndicators.

In 1975, the "Frank Organization" was the most successful independent distributor of *prime time access* shows in the United States, becoming the first distributor to simultaneously syndicate three top shows in the 7-8 p.m. time period during the same season: *Name That Tune*, *Treasure Hunt* and *The Bobby Vinton Show*. His company was small; almost a one-man show, but he had placed more shows in *prime access* that year than any other of the major distributors. Each series had been sold in 45 of the Top 50 markets, a critical benchmark for advertisers looking to place commercials in *prime access* shows. Syndication was, and still is, hard work!

The original kings of syndication used to drive up to the front of a television station in a flashy rented convertible, or their own car, usually a beat-up station wagon (on it's third go-round on the odometer), and unload about 40 pounds of "selling tools." It was back-breaking.

In those days, the 1950's-60's, there were no lightweight video tape "screeners" and "presentation reels" to carry in your briefcase. First to come out of the trunk would be a pushcart, empty. Next would come a Bell & Howell 16mm film projector with an empty take-up reel. A spare take-up reel. A portable screen. A box of spare bulbs. Then cans and cans, heavy, of whatever shows were being offered. If you were lucky, you'd be selling only half-hours. They were lighter than the cans of hour-long shows.

These salesmen would drag their equipment into the Program Director's office. Just setting up was grueling work. If they were lucky, the General Manager would be in the meeting. Most good syndicators demanded the GM be there. Sandy Frank did! He wasn't there to have a meeting. He was there to make a deal!

Everyone in local television either knew him or knew someone who did. And, they all had stories. Bob Doty, former Station Manager at WTVT in Tampa, and that man who hired me right out of school at WFTV, the ABC affiliate in Orlando, told stories about Sandy wheeling into his office, a wagon loaded with a 16mm projector and heavy stacks of film cans. Plus, something new. Flip cards. Large boards with ratings data, graphics of new trends in the market that spelled out why these particular series would work. Sandy *always* had flip cards. He could really put on a show.

But, if you let Sandy through the door and into your office, he would *not leave* until he had made a sale. Unless he was interested in buying something, Bob Doty had a standing rule with his secretary. "If you see Sandy Frank walking in, tell him I'm not here." Then Doty would duck out the back door until Sandy was gone.

I thanked Phil for the recommendation and hung up. "Sandy Frank. Okay," I thought, waiting in my West Hollywood studio apartment on the block where Sal Mineo had been murdered. "This could be a BIG job. Don't get nervous."

Several days later, I was still waiting for the New York call.

After about a week, the phone finally rang and it was Sandy. I had had time by then to get a little nervous. Hey, I needed the work and felt qualified, but maybe getting this job wasn't going to be so easy. Grabbing the phone, a pad and a pencil, it was hard for me to stay calm as Sandy's rapid-fire speech filtered through the receiver. It sounded like Phil was on the phone, too. That was good.

Sandy was talking a mile a minute about a film festival the next week in Montreal, giving sketchy details about the event. I had read something about it in *Variety* and was scribbling notes as fast as I could. He was asking me a lot of questions. Mostly about movies. Nothing I couldn't answer, but it seemed that some of the questions weren't directed at either Phil or me. Was he talking to me? It sounded like other people might have been listening in on our conference call too.

I pushed the phone tighter against my ear. Yeah. I counted about eight different voices. There were also, at least, eight different opinions! Later, I learned that Sandy liked opinions from a diverse group of "mavens" that he kept on payroll. I would later become one of his mavens, on and off, for the next twenty years. Depending on your frame of mind at any given time, this was either a good thing, or not.

When I hung up the phone about three hours later, I had the job. For the next several months, I screened dozens and dozens of movies and wrote long, detailed evaluations of them. The films were mostly pretty bad, sometimes laughably so. It was hard to sit through *Werewolf of Washington* when my mantra was "Sandy Frank Syndication is interested in acquiring only the highest caliber of feature films." Hmmm. Maybe this wasn't going to be as easy as I thought. If I couldn't sit through them, how was Sandy going to sell them?

Going through some old files the other day, I came across a few of my early reports and was surprised at how much paper work we all faxed back and forth. Pages of detailed opinions. Thorough evaluations. About a dozen names were always cc'd on the top page with Sandy's scrawl. David Levy, Sol Schwartz, Irving Klein, Sam Sacks, Bob Cohen, Leonard Reeg, Jesse Vogel, Morrie Gelman, Albert Williams, Rob Word. They weren't all pseudonyms.

"Please give your opinion PRONTO! I don't feel it makes sense! SF"

"NOTE: This is urgent. Please reply ASAP in detail! SF"

"I don't understand your viewpoint. I need more information!"

A lot of things never made sense to Sandy. "Just think of me as a man from Mars," he was fond of saying. Sure, we thought. Of course, you are. Whatever makes you happy. Sandy always wanted multiple thoughts and angles to make that perfect decision.

He was in his mid-40s when I joined him. With his dark hair combed back, pre-Pat Riley, dressed in fancy white or navy blue suits, thin socks, polished black loafers, a light tan overcoat of expensive cashmere and topped with a pair of Lew Wassermann-style tortoise shell glasses, Sandy was handsome, continental. He was one of those people that always carried around a pad of paper to jot down anything and everything that he thought was important. It wasn't actually a note pad, but a wad of tiny yellow pages with ideas, phone numbers and dates wadded up with a twisted thick rubber band holding the paper together and stuffed in his pocket. They seemed illegible. I wondered how he could ever find anything on them. Sometimes he couldn't.

He also carried, or had carried, a large, well-worn brown leather briefcase that seemed to weigh 50 pounds. I know because I ended up carrying the damn thing for him wherever we went together. He moved at a constant lurch, bent a little forward like he was fighting against a powerful headwind.

"C'mon, Rob. C'mon. C'mon. C'mon," he'd command without looking back.

Lugging his overstuffed briefcase, it was hard to keep up. There was a certain rhythm to Sandy. Fast. Intense. A real pressure cooker. He screamed. He shouted. And (on rare occasions) he brought people to tears! I really had no idea what I was in for. None, none, none. It was a test. If I could live through this, I felt I would be ready for anything.

Sandy had honed his work ethic and survival skills while he clawed his way up. Now it was my turn to learn whatever I could from being near Sandy. Syndication is a cutthroat business. A business where people in slow motion got left behind or trampled on by more aggressive sellers. God, it was exciting! I was part of Sandy Frank's inner circle. The center of a walking tornado.

It was better than college. Sandy taught me a lot. How to never reveal what you were really thinking or expose your emotional state, because then you'd be human, weak, and lose all your negotiating leverage. He taught me it was all right to have an opinion, to say just about anything. My point of view mattered!

Not only was I learning from the best, I was having a great time. It was actually fun to hang out with him. We'd go places together and talk about film product I'd uncovered or what new trends we should be following. Sandy would arrive at LAX. I would pick him up in my yellow Audi 100LS and take him to whatever fancy hotel he had booked.

We'd go to the best restaurants together where the Matre d' would make a big thing about his arrival and make sure he was given the best table. Waiters would swarm around him, making sure he was well taken care of. Sandy was very generous with his tipping, so they all treated him like royalty. He came in dripping of twenty dollar bills. Paper money floated off him like rose petals at a coronation. I had never experienced anything like this! But I could quickly see how effective his entrance worked whenever and wherever we dined.

"Too dry. Is this chicken too dry for you? Try it. Take this back! It's too dry! Too dry, right?"

Between sending back orders of boiled, skinless, boneless, and to me, tasteless, chicken and steamed broccoli, industry big shots would drop by Sandy's table to pay their respects. Sammy Weisbord, the long time President of the William Morris talent agency, might sit briefly and chat. Weisborg was Sandy's "personal agent." He was handling Sandy's true passion of making a film biography of Israeli Prime Minister Menachem Begin and Egyptian leader Anwar Sadat. Sandy actually got it made, too.

When his West Coast trip was over and the meetings concluded, we'd pile back in my car and race to the airport.

"Which is the fastest way? Is this the fastest way? Which way are you going? Why? You're going to make me miss my flight!"

I drive fast anyway, but it didn't take me long to realize that Sandy had multiple reservations on a variety of airlines. It didn't really matter what time I got to the airport, there would always be a plane waiting for him. He always made it all soooo exciting!

Almost as quickly as I had flown to my first film festival in

Montreal, Sandy decided that producing his own new game show was the wise thing to do.

"I am talking about new television projects the company can do," he declared. "I am NOT talking about buying existing TV properties, be they series or specials, domestic or foreign. And I am not talking about buying theatrical features for syndication. I am talking about *new* programming we will collectively create, produce and own."

Cool! To insure continuity of product, Sandy would have to move into his own original productions.

Two years earlier, Sandy had already tested his ability with a "new" production. He had acquired the rights to a Japanese cartoon series entitled *Gatchaman*. The series had featured a group of kids fighting giant robots. Normal programming for the Far East at that time, but very radical for the American market. Coincidentally, a little science fiction film was premiering that spring and *Star Wars* mania was about to explode!

Sandy realized that by controlling the syndication rights to *Gatchaman*, he had a unique opportunity to create a new afternoon strip for kids…if he could successfully dub the series into English.

Setting up production in Los Angeles, Sandy registered the *Star Wars* friendly title, *Battle of the Planets*, and planned to re-cut, re-score, re-write and dub 105 episodes from the original version of *Gatchaman*. A new animated character was created and named *7-Zark-7*. Like *R2-D2* from *Star Wars*, *7-Zark-7* was a robot! The new robot could also act as a narrator and be inserted anywhere it seemed necessary to fill in continuity gaps in the re-edited English dubbed half-hours. Now all Sandy had to do was sell this idea to enough stations to cover his investment.

"TV stations in every city in the United States had to be convinced, one at a time, that this brand new show would do for their station what *Star Wars* did for movie theaters," Sandy recalls in *The Official Battle of the Planets Guidebook.*

Over 70 stations had to agree to buy *Battle of the Planets* for it to be given a production go ahead. The fact is, that while we could make it without Peoria, we had to have New York, Los Angeles and the other big markets. Unfortunately, the big markets were the hardest to convince that they were ready for something this new. Having already invested in the non-Asian rights and assembled a production team, I had a cutoff date to commit to go ahead into actual production, or to pull the plug and cut my losses. Literally at the eleventh hour, after consistent turndowns, I finally convinced WNEW (now Fox flagship station, WNYW), and the then Metromedia Group of major market stations, to buy the programs.

From an initial $5,000,000 investment, *Battle of the Planets* reported worldwide grosses of over $25,000,000. This wildly successful series gave Sandy the financial security to try and develop his own programs. He decided on an original game show compatible with the already established hit, *Name That Tune*, which he syndicated. Sandy had the distribution rights to '*Tune*,' but wanted to create and own a show of his own! That show was to be called *Bet the Music.*

With only a vague outline in place for the new show, we started run-throughs almost immediately, setting up at the cost-efficient old ABC building on Vine. Our team was fortunate to include David Levy. David was an elderly man with experience that spanned the ad agency business, networks (former head of programming at NBC), and independent production (*The Addams Family*). He drove a white 1967 Thunderbird. When the Audi was in the shop (which was often), David would pick up Sandy in Beverly Hills, then swing by for me, and cruise down Fountain Avenue with the top down on the way to the studio. He was a classy guy, a real gentleman, and became

Executive Vice President of Sandy Frank Film Productions, Inc.

Producers Ray Horl and Peggy Touchstone, and music arranger/conductor, Tommy Oliver, were brought in from *Name That Tune*. The director was another game show vet, Lou Tedesco. The associate director was a kid about my age from local television in San Francisco, Michael Dimich. He was an exceptional *Pac-Man* player who got his DGA card on the show and today is one of the top directors of live programs.

After weeks and weeks of exhausting 12 to 16 hour days, we had honed the concept *Bet the Music* to a traditional type game with lots of music. Contestants were to bid for notes and guess song titles. Tommy and his orchestra performed the notes, one at a time. The more notes played, the easier it was to guess the song title. The Bonus Round was a celebrity identification game. Eight large photos of a famous personality, showing them from infancy to maturity, were individually covered. The song titles were the clues to their identity. The contestants guessed the song and matched celebrity faces with musical themes associated with them. Revealed one at a time, the color photos showed celebrities in a way that they had rarely been seen before. The baby pictures were what viewers would talk about. It was clever, involving for the audience, and visually striking as well.

Like a lucky rabbit's foot, Sandy even added a mechanical *7-Zark-7* type robot to the game. It delivered musical clues, too, but was constantly breaking down.

Now we needed an emcee. A game show host. It's a tough gig. You have to be glib, handsome, quick-witted and smart. We met with the usual suspects. Hosts from the past. But, Sandy wanted a fresh face and what Sandy wanted, Sandy got!

One day, Ray Horl brought in a tennis buddy to try out for the job. It was Patrick Wayne, the Duke's son. This was a real surprise for me! Not only to see Patrick as emcee, but also to see how good he was. His perfect smile was flashing all the time. He was terrific at punctuating lines and pauses. He had it all. Charming wit, a startling smile, clear blue eyes and a great look.

"The homemakers will love him," I declared. "Their husbands will watch because of the Wayne heritage." At first glance, he seemed like a strange choice. But after watching him work, he was the perfect choice. The right package to become more popular with the ladies than any other daytime host. I could not believe his manager would encourage his participation in a *game* show.

"There is no question about Patrick's capabilities," I wrote in a memo. "Sign him and there is little chance of losing an audience. He has that little extra boost that will assure a general tune in. Before the run-through he chatted with the contestants. Literally, I could hear the girls' hearts flutter."

It was not to be. The timing probably was not right. John Wayne, Patrick's father had died only a few months before and his heart just wasn't in it. So, we kept looking. More auditions, more run-throughs, until we finally found a proper replacement. It was another tennis buddy of Ray's! Ex-TV *Tarzan*, Ron Ely,

Now we were ready to actually tape a pilot. We moved to the Metromedia lot on Sunset in Hollywood. Torn down now, you couldn't miss it at the time. The building had what looked like a weird metal *Erector Set* on the roof. Norman Lear had taped many of his Embassy sitcoms on the lot. I remembered watching a taping of *Fernwood 2Night* there with Ken Smith, General Manager of the Orlando NBC affiliate, WESH-TV, a couple of years earlier.

We set up shop and began work on the pilot. We got a new name, *Face the Music*, and staffed up. More attorneys. More researchers. More crew. We hired Lisa Donovan, a singer from Florida, as our vocalist. Ray Horl rounded up good, no--*great*, contestants. He had a real sense of who would make interesting and enthusiastic competitors.

The day of the pilot taping started early and went on and on. Just before midnight, Sandy called the crew together and pleaded with them to stay through to the bitter end. He was a great convincer, besides the crew would be getting "Golden Time." They all stayed. The robot continued to malfunction. An emergency vote by the producers to junk it passed unanimously. Even Sandy agreed we should turn it into scrap metal. God, he was funny sometimes. I liked him and loved to make him laugh. It always broke the tension.

Into the night we taped, finally ending up with two pilots. Both were good and both would work. It was a hard decision to pick which one to screen for the buyers.

When the Metromedia Group failed to pick up the show, we were demoralized. But, only momentarily. As "The Chief," veteran syndication legend Dick Colbert always said, "If you don't like this show, I'll take it to the other shit house across the street!" That's exactly what we did.

Independent Channel 5, KTLA-TV. It was literally across the street from Metromedia in Hollywood on what had once been the original Warner Brothers Studio lot. *The Jazz Singer* had been filmed there. A good musical omen. Even though Thanksgiving was only days away, Sandy mounted a full throttle assault to sell KTLA, Golden West Broadcasters. It was cowboy star and media baron Gene Autry's station and it was a powerhouse in Los Angeles.

Our pitch was scheduled for Thanksgiving eve. No one could believe it. Would anyone from the station be willing to work that day? Attending the sales pitch would be Tony Cassara, President of Golden West and Gregg Nathanson, General Manager and programming whiz for the station. They were begging to get out of it. Change the meeting until after the holiday.

"We've gotta close this before the weekend," Sandy declared.

"It's a must!"

Like magic, Sandy made it happen. We moved onto the lot and a call went out for "writers and researchers, secretaries and clerical help. Preferably people who like popular music, yesterday's and today's." Meanwhile, Sandy also cleared the show in over 90% of the United States. For the next two years, *Face the Music* was a staple around the country.

Working with Sandy had been the best of times for a new kid in the city. But, things were about to get even better!

After the first season of '*Face*,' I left Sandy to join Jamie Kellner as head of marketing for a new team he was building at Filmways Entertainment. Filmways (soon to become Orion) had just purchased American International Pictures from co-founder, Sam Arkoff. A.I.P.'s huge library was filled with Roger Corman "classics," the Frankie and Annette beach party titles, B and C grade drive-in movie fodder, and much, much more. It was just my type of fare.

Jamie had just left Viacom where he had been selling mostly CBS off-network sitcoms and dramas in syndication. He was looking for someone who knew movies and had remembered meeting me at NATPE a couple years earlier in New York. Yeah, count me in!

Scott Towle was already there. So was Roger Adams. We grew to include Rick Jacobson, Tom Cerio, Jimmy Ricks, Larry Hutchings, Ritch Colbert, Arthur Hasson and Jerry (J.J.) Jameson. What a group! The laughter, the camaraderie and the friendship. We helped build the company into something fine and all of us learned a lot along the way. Some of the greatest experiences of my life, with people and events I will never forget, happened there.

The 1980's turned out to be the Golden Age of Syndication. They were the boom years and we enjoyed them. We always knew how lucky we were to be working together during that time. When an offer to join another, rival company was made to one of us, Jamie would tilt his head, and look us in the eye.

"If all you want is more money, go ahead and leave," he'd say with a slight smile. "Or you can stay here and have fun."

We were all pretty much party boys, so stay we did. That is, until Kellner left for the new FOX network in February of '86. In the months before, Jamie had been quietly going around and extending everyone's contract with Orion. Luckily, I had already planned to leave the month before, in January, to become Sr. VP of Production and Marketing at Hal Roach Studios. Not long after, the rest of the team went their separate ways.

Starting with Sandy Frank had turned out to be a real blessing. He had prepared me for the hard work ahead. It had been a great ride, so far, and the first of many lucky breaks for me. Opportunities in Hollywood were plentiful and my life on the West Coast was really only just beginning. There are so many, many more stories to tell. But, I'll save them for another book because I was only asked to write one chapter for this anthology of media memories.

I remember Ricky Jacobson always saying, "Is this a great business or what?" It wasn't really a question. We all knew the answer. Then he'd do his trademark, high-pitched giggle, cracking us up.

Guys on the road selling, laughing, and sharing in a literal celebration of life. Through yarns exchanged and differences now forgotten, there was an intangible spirit of something great between us. I was lucky to have been a part of it. During those years, life in syndication was America at its best.

For Whom the Bell Toils
by Steve Bell

Up until ten years ago, one of the best jobs in the television business was running an independent television station. You were literally the CEO of your own local business, making decisions on a whole raft of issues from program purchases to program scheduling, from time sales to news, from promotion to the local community. You generated your own programming from sign-on to sign-off, whether it was syndicated or locally originated. That, in itself, set the job apart from running a network affiliate (where most of the programming was spoon-fed from New York) and demanded a measure of creativity that was unique.

You competed with the affiliates on a head-to-head basis, and with other indies in your market. You were part team leader, part entrepeneur and part paterfamilias to a close-knit team of department managers who, in my experience, always seemed to be 30 years old, while I seemed to get progressively older.

It was the ultimate "line" job in the business and if you were lucky with your corporate management, you could do it with a measure of local autonomy that I've never encountered before or since. It's hard to believe today that the job ever existed in this form when you consider that there aren't any "independent" stations left -- the proliferation of networks took care of that -- and from what I've observed, the autonomy and creativity has virtually gone, too, with the consolidation of large station groups and the spread of centralized decision-making.

I was lucky enough to be the General Manager of two independent television stations over a period of 17 years, from 1975 until 1992. And before the memories fade altogether, I'd like to share some of them with you.

There I was in 1975, Vice President of Programming for Petry Television in New York, a sales rep where I had happily spent the previous 5-1/2 years. What my title meant was that I was in charge of seeing that Petry's station clients maximized their rating potential so that Petry salesmen could sell those rating points at top dollar. At the time, that was rather forward-looking on the part of Marty Connolly and Bob Muth, the two sales guys who rescued Petry from certain bankruptcy and were desperately trying to turn it around. In those early days of their "occupation" it was a thrill a minute as client businesses tend to be.

For me it started right after I joined the firm in 1971. During my first week on the job, a tall southerner, whose unsuccessful independent station in Charlotte was repped by Petry, barged into my office uninvited, sat down on my couch, stretched out his long legs, and said in a loud southern accent, "Say something to me in programming!" I was at a loss for words. Who was this loser, I thought. I later learned that it was a then-unknown Ted Turner, pre-Superstation, pre-CNN, pre-mogul. It taught me once and for all that in the television business you can't tell a book by its cover.

My Petry job was my first in the TV business and I took it very seriously. I travelled more than 450,000 miles a year visiting station clients across the country. I advised them on what programs to buy, where to put them, how to promote them. My particular specialty was booking local movies, which I did on a regular basis for 15 of Petry's 35 clients. It was a great way to learn my craft and my clients generally seemed to appreciate what I did for them. In the early 70's the times were a-changing in television. Things were getting increasingly competitive and most of the old-line stations that Petry repped were having trouble coping with what was happening to them. And new clients which Petry was able to acquire were usually so down that even Petry seemed up to them.

I made many friends from among Petry clients who have passed in and out of my life over the years. Bob Muth sent me to an early NATPE in New Orleans, the first of 25 consecutive NATPE's for me. He correctly predicted that I would meet all the program distributors there and that they, too, would remain a constant factor throughout my career. I also went to early INTV (*Independant Television Association*) conventions where I met many of my fellow indie broadcasters. Eventually, I represented them on the national INTV board. Indies were coming into their own in the early 70's and they were becoming a force to reckon with. It was an exciting time to be in the broadcasting business and especially for independents.

I devoured rating books, holding my breath until each "sweep" report arrived. I geared up for the spread of overnight ratings which gave us our programming "report card" every morning, instead of only six times a year. The pace of the business was quickening and demographics were fast replacing household ratings as the audience measure of choice. And I was beginning to get a reputation in the business as a "Station Doctor."

Two Petry clients were a particular kick to work with: KTLA (Los Angeles) which eventually hired me to be its General Manager in 1981, and WTOG-TV in Tampa, run by Jim Dowdle, who would return to my life in 1986 as the best boss I ever had, when the Tribune Company bought KTLA for $510 million...more money than anyone had ever spent for a TV station.

KTLA came into Petry in 1971, "the eighth station in a seven station market." It was more dead than alive, but with a dial position on channel 5 in a rapidly changing LA market which had overnight ratings, it had great potential. John Serrao was my point of entry. He was essentially running the station at that time. He welcomed my programming input, and I was grateful to him for letting me in. He was the first of our Petry clients who did. In addition to being a thorough professional, he is one of the nicest people I've ever met. My advice became increasingly valuable to KTLA, I guess, and I was written into KTLA's first Petry renewal contract by Rich Frank, then General Sales Manager of the station. Given the state of rep programming advice in those days, this had to be something of a first. By contract, I was to visit KTLA at least four times a year and advise them on programming and promotion. These station rep trips to LA made up for Tulsa, Quad Cities, Lake Charles and other markets I hoped never to return to. I always thought Rich did it just to tweak Petry management. Whatever it was, I wasn't complaining. Neither was my wife who shopped in Beverly Hills while I slaved in Hollywood at KTLA.

Jim Dowdle was National Sales Manager at KSTP-TV in Minneapolis when I first met him. I visited his market one frigid January day in the early 70's to pitch his boss, Stan Hubbard, on some programming purchases that the station desperately needed. And I think Stan actually listened. I guess this endeared me to Jim. When he was about to be sent to Tampa to run Hubbard's unsuccessful UHF indie, WTOG-TV, he came to New York, took a pile of movie files from his briefcase which represented the Tampa station's inventory, laid them on my desk and asked if I could do anything with them.

I used every movie booking trick I had ever tried in my other markets: *thematic weeks* with Elvis Presley and John Wayne, *Creature Double Features* on Saturday afternoons, *Doris Day* and *Jerry Lewis Festivals* on Sundays. It worked. They got numbers for the first time, and Jim went on to put together a fabulously successful independent station.

I did have a couple of clients that didn't get it, and I couldn't do much with them. One was in Salt Lake City and I frequently was ready to kill them. One day I finished a heated phone conversation in which they told me they were cancelling a program that was getting a 40% share in favor of another one that I knew would fail. I slammed down the phone and was ready to quit.

The next call I received was from a former Petry salesman who was now in Boston as the General Sales Manager of a UHF independent station owned by Kaiser Broadcasting. He called from time to time for programming advice, which I was happy to give him I solved his problem, I guess, and he said, "I wish you could be with us all the time." I replied, "So why don't you ask me?" Stunned silence on the other end of the phone. "You mean you're touchable?" "Try me," I said.

That phone call and my response opened a Pandora's box for me. It led to a fateful meeting in Sausalito with Don Curran, newly running the Kaiser group, and an offer to run that very station in Boston. Don was definitely a benefactor in my life. He really stuck his neck out for me, considering that I had no hands-on TV station experience...just radio.

But Don did things like that. He was an ex-radio Promotion Manager and so was I. That's all he had to hear. He used to say, "UHF television is the radio of television." Running a "U" in those pre-cable, pre-FOX/WB/UPN days was a kamikaze job at best. And WLVI-TV (Channel 56 in Roman numerals) was the most God-for-saken television station I ever encountered. And I had encountered them all from my station travels. But I took the job anyway. What did I have to lose? I was free from the Salt Lake Cities of the world and I finally had my own station to run in the place where I was born.

The first six months were a horror. I was holed up in the *Howard Johnson "57" Hotel* in downtown Boston (a station recip deal), living on room service and watching how bad WLVI looked on the hotel TV system. It was pathetic. My wife was still in New York recuperating from the birth of our son, and wasn't about to move to Boston just yet. So I had 24/7 to worry about turning Channel 56 around. And I worried. Did I ever worry. Had I known at the time that Don was trying to sell the assets of WLVI to Boston's other UHF indie, WSBK, in exchange for going off the air, a gambit that he had successfully brought off in Cleveland, I would have been even more worried. But Storer Broadcasting, WSBK's parent company, wouldn't play ball, my family moved to Boston, and my profession-al life moved forward.

The first week I was in town, I attended an industry lunch hon-oring sportscasters in the city. That left WLVI out. We didn't have any sports franchises. The sports anchors of the affiliates were on the dais, as were the sports commentators from the Red Sox baseball fran-chise, recently acquired by WSBK. The sports anchor from the CBS affiliate got up and said, "I want to tell you folks that the Red Sox coverage on WSBK has made this a four-station market." My Local Sales Manager, Jerry Walsh, leaned over and whispered to me in his prominent Boston accent, "How does it feel to be the fifth station in a four station market?" On that day, not very well I can assure you.

Thankfully, I inherited a remarkable Program Director in Lucie

Salhany, then at the beginning of a great career. She had been "salvaged" from the ashes of Kaiser's now-dark Cleveland station and
wasn't very happy to be in Boston. Lucie was a lot more experienced
than I was, but she, like I, had never seen anything as screwed up as
WLVI. Lucie was somewhat wary of me at first. She came into my
office early on and told me she knew about my reputation as a programmer and didn't feel she could deal with it if I was going to program the station from the GM's slot. My former Petry colleague, now
my new General Sales Manager, didn't help matters by telling her
that she'd "learn a lot" from me. Ouch! Well, I sat her down and said
to her, "Lucie, you have nothing to worry about. You're the Program
Manager. I have a lot of other things to learn." And I meant it. And
ever after, I kept my word. It turned out to be one of the best working relationships I've ever had. And a friendship forged in the trench-
es of Boston which has endured for almost 30 years.

The station was located in a former supermarket on the border
of South Boston and Dorchester, respectively, Boston's leading blue
collar Irish and African-American neighborhoods. If a black person
crossed the borderline, a riot usually ensued. Talk about being close
to your community!

There was a certain logic to the way the station was organized:
where the supermarket used to cut meat, the station now cut film. I
had the only office with walls and a door. It was all pretty grim. The
only solace was visits from traveling syndicators who would come to
Boston to sell their shows and take Lucie and me to lunch. I've
always been grateful to people like Dick Colbert, Pierre Weiss, Joe
Indelli and so many others for coming to visit us in the provinces and
giving us the latest news and gossip from the outside world. And from
time to time, our corporate "overlords" would venture out from San
Francisco and come to visit. One thing we knew for certain: they
wouldn't come East during the winter, so from December through

April, we were safe.

The station eventually turned around. How? Through programming. All of the great sitcoms were sold and on the air when we arrived, so we bought what we could: *Mary Tyler Moore* and *That Girl*, and laid away *Happy Days* and *Laverne and Shirley* for future availability. In the meantime we bought movies, which were plentiful and cheap. Some distributors had never sold a picture in Boston. We delivered solid ratings and demos on the weekends and we started to get numbers in *prime time*. We were, after all, "Boston's Movie Station." We also turned ourselves into the highest-rated kid station in the market.

WSBK was famous in Boston for a local public affairs show they called *Ask The Manager*, scheduled Sundays at 10:30 p.m. It was a cheap, simple concept: The General Manager and a host answering viewer mail on the air. What better way to reach your viewers. Well, not in this case. WSBK's GM was gruff and unresponsive. He seemed as if he had too many cocktails before he taped the show each week, and would have been right at home in a *Saturday Night Live* routine. People watched it to see if he would fall under his desk on camera.

Lucie decided that we should do a competitive show, called *Meet The Manager,* and scheduled it opposite their show. She read the letters and I answered them. We were quite the pair! The two stations split the hash marks in the rating book. I salvaged a few tapes and when I now look at them, I write the whole thing off to youth and chutzpah. I did the show for several years and although it never got more than a "1" rating, I was recognized at every industry function I attended. I was a mini-celebrity. Such is the power of television. Or, as Lucie used to call us: "Mattel Television."

Lucie eventually moved on to bigger and better things, leaving me alone to face the public when I had the temerity to run *Benny Hill* at 7:30 p.m. It was the biggest hit we'd ever had in the time period, but the humor was thought too blue for Boston. An organized protest ensued and everyone, including *Action for Children's Television,* took sides (suprisingly, they approved). But when the *Boston Globe* ran an editorial supporting us and decrying the protest, the controversy ended and Boston settled down to enjoy the show.

I had a chance to move myself to San Francisco and run Cox's indie KTVU, but I wasn't quite ready. I wanted to finish the job in Boston and I didn't particularly like the man I would have been work- ing for. He locked himself out of his office, with me in it, while he was interviewing me in Atlanta. Not a good sign.

Happy Days eventually became available to us and the station began to do well in the critical 6-8 p.m. time period. We even outrat- ed one of the affiliate newscasts at 6 p.m.! The station became prof- itable for the first time in its 9 year history and then I was ready to move on.

In January of 1981, I got a call from Tony Cassara, whom I had known at Petry as a young salesman and who had been running KTLA in Los Angeles while I was in Boston running WLVI. Tony asked me to come out to L.A. and talk about replacing him as General Manager of KTLA. He was moving up to head Golden West's televi- sion division.

I jumped at the chance and several months later I began my new life in Los Angeles.

The difference between KTLA on channel 5 and WLVI on channel 56 should have been obvious to me, but it never seemed so pronounced as after my first May "sweep" in 1981. In Boston we pro- moted long and hard and, at best, only reached 50% of the market. I came to LA thinking I'd have to do the same thing. We poured on the on-the-air promotion and also bought tons of radio. The results were somewhat overwhelming. The *Prime Movie* broke all existing records as did most other key time periods, and our sign-on to sign-off share went up by a full share point.

Gene Autry owned the station. I was totally in awe of him. I'd grown up with the "Singing Cowboy" in the movies and on early network television. He had a reputation as an arch conservative, and I didn't know how he'd respond to me, an East Coast liberal. He was great. When he heard I came from Boston, he told me stories of touring with his rodeo and getting the best of corrupt Boston Mayor James Michael Curley (*The Last Hurrah*) by making a substantial contribution to the Mayor's re-election campaign. Gene really didn't understand television, though he was extremely supportive. His five years of weekly shows on CBS in the 50's were essentially short motion pictures. His medium was radio and his passion was baseball, but we did have in common a particular interest in William S. Paley and we frequently discussed what was going on at CBS in those days under Larry Tisch. Whenever Gene felt his prerogative wasn't being followed, he'd always say, "Bill Paley wouldn't have put up with that!" Clearly, he'd modeled his career as a mogul after his old boss at CBS.

KTLA gave me a unique opportunity to revive old Hollywood on the air. This was the early 80's and homevideo and cable movie channels hadn't hit big as yet. When we bought a package of pre-1948 Warner Bros. classics, they had only been seen in the market on KCBS's *The Late Show*. I'll never forget the thrill of acquiring a 35mm print of *Maltese Falcon* and running it in *prime time* and getting big ratings. Since we also had all of Bette Davis's classic movies, we invited her to host a week in *prime time*. She came to the station with five changes of costume and endless ideas about how to shoot her intro segments. David Simon, my Program Director, arranged for a lunch in Gene's private dining room during a break in the shooting. It was magic. She lived up to her reputation. We did the same with

Esther Williams, shot beside her swimming pool. And I remember a week called *Outlaws of the Movies*, put together by my friend Rob Word, with Roger Corman films and with wrap-arounds featuring everyone who was in them. What a time it was! There seemed to be no limits to what could be done.

Once we ran *One Flew Over The Cuckoo's Nest* complete and uncut in *prime time*. Remember, this was before cable stretched the envelope in terms of acceptable content. Frankly it was a "stunt" to draw attention to what we anticipated would be a low-rated film. But it worked beyond anyone's expectation. The numbers were huge and we were heroes. The *Writer's Guild* even took trade ads praising our courage for championing free speech! We tried it again with *Appocalypse Now!*, advertising it again as "complete and uncut." Visually, the content presented few problems. But the soundtrack was impossible, the language unbleepable. Using the latest in digital equipment, we covered each and every offending word with gunshot sounds lifted from the soundtrack (and there were literally hundreds of expletives to be covered). Though the sound track was anything but "complete," every scene from the theatrical version was there and we scored huge ratings once more.

KTLA wrote the book on "alternative programming." We ran hour action-adventure shows at 6 p.m. when the indie competition ran sitcoms. The affiliates ran their nightly news at 11 p.m., so we ran ours at 10 p.m.

We ran a *Twilight Zone* marathon on Thanksgiving Day, opposite football bowl games. The "marathon" concept was created by Greg Nathanson, one of the industry's most creative programmers and a friend since my Petry days. Greg also came up with the idea of reducing the commercial breaks in the *Prime Movie*, boosting the ratings and charging more for the spots remaining. Another thing that worked was the first-run sitcom "*checkerboard*" concept (a different show each weeknight) at 7:30 p.m. Like everything else, this concept was born of necessity -- no programming -- and worked for two seasons and got us tremendous national publicity.

KTLA also helped launch the first of many *prime time* barter movie showcases with Embassy Pictures and Gary Lieberthal. *Escape From New York* was the first attraction and it worked so well that Larry Gershman at MGM became the first major studio to follow suit. Don Menchel and Shelly Schwab at Universal were not far behind.

KTLA was now set with major theatrical movies for a few years, until cable started to buy everything in sight and it was all over for movies on the indies. The same thing happened to off-network hour shows which we had programmed so competitively and profitably at 6 p.m. Our steady stream of cheap hour product ended abruptly when basic cable discovered its audience value, forcing us to program more expensive half-hour sitcoms just like our competitors. It was getting tough to be truly "independent" in the indie television business.

There are so many unique things to be said about KTLA, not the least of which was its historical position as the first TV station on the air west of the Mississippi. KTLA's rich history influenced just about everything we did and our frequent anniversary specials with old kinescope footage were eagerly anticipated.

Our coverage of the *Rose Parade* was also unique. We had been the first to do it in 1947 and we continued to outrate our five competitors combined. Fifty plus years later, KTLA is still doing it each New Year's Day.

One year, when Greg Nathanson was running KTTV, he came up with the only stunt that has ever challenged KTLA's *Rose Parade* dominance. He dropped all commercials in the live coverage of the event. With KTTV's meager rating position, what did he have to lose? When the overnight ratings came in, KTLA was still far out in front, but KTTV had grown considerably at KTLA's expense. You can imagine the press impact in L.A.! And there was Greg, needling us in print. I was so angry, I didn't speak to him for a year. The next year I faced the inevitable and dropped commercials, too, making them up in the repeats throughout New Year's Day. The ratings stabilized and KTTV's one year advantage was forgotten.

When I left the station and went to FOX, and Greg had taken my place as General Manager of KTLA, I remember a conversation with my new boss at FOX, Rupert Murdoch, who had also been Greg's boss when he was at FOX, on the subject of the *Rose Parade*. Rupert wanted to give Greg and KTLA a run for its money. He was willing to spend anything it would take and he asked me what would work. He was really motivated. And as much as I would have liked to settle the score with Greg, I looked at Rupert and said, "Save your money, Rupert. There's only one 'given' in Los Angeles television and that's KTLA's dominance of the *Rose Parade*." I could tell he wasn't happy with what I said. But there was nothing else I could say. It was true then and will probably be true 50 years from now.

KTLA's news operation was also legendary in the L.A. market, with veteran newsmen like Hal Fishman and Stan Chambers well known and widely respected. Stan, particularly, never worked anywhere else and is currently in his 56th continuous year at KTLA! If that's not an all-time record, I'd be surprised. Whenever a big local story broke, KTLA would instantly drop regular programming and go with live continuous news coverage, much like the cable news networks do today. Through earthquakes, fires, floods, riots and visits from the Pope, KTLA excelled in this kind of breaking news coverage, and it was a thrill to encourage our News Director, Jeff Wald, and his staff to keep the live coverage coming. Before I finally left KTLA I also got to launch the much-imitated *KTLA Morning News*, the first one with the crazy anchors, which among other things, made KTLA a 24-hour news operation for the first time. Unquestionably, one of my proudest moments at KTLA was winning the *Peabody Award* for the station's news coverage of the Rodney King videotaped beating which led to the 1992 Los Angeles riot.

In 1983, KTLA was sold for over $200 million to the kings of leveraged buyouts, KK&R (Kolberg, Kravitz & Roberts). It was Tony Cassara's deal and he made me, my Station Manager, Mike Eigner, and a number of us, part of what turned out to be a very profitable investment, though at the time we had no idea of what we were getting into and where it would lead. Cash flow became king at the station and there were times when I had to cut into the jugular vein to boost a quarterly profit. Fortunately it only lasted for 3-1/2 years and KK&R sold it for double that amount to the Tribune Company.

That's when Jim Dowdle came back into my life as my boss and made the next six years with Tribune the most productive and happy of my entire career. What made Jim so unique is the fact that he had been a General Manager, but when he became President of a group of stations, he never forgot what it was like.

When Tribune took over the station, Jim asked me what I needed. He acknowledged that the preceding years had been tough and he wanted to restore KTLA to its former luster. I told him that one of the most difficult things to compete with was *Operation Prime Time* on indie KCOP. These high-budget, first-run mini-series got extraordinary ratings and increased KCOP's overall average *Prime Movie* numbers by an additional rating point or two. There was nothing that could compete with it, so I asked Jim to find a way to do mini-series for KTLA and the other Tribune stations. He not only did that, but arranged for '*OPT*'s New York and Chicago outlets to withdraw and, in effect, that was the end of '*OPT*,' which was riddled with internal bickering and was already on its last legs.

In addition to my General Manager duties at KTLA, I spent the next four years working part time on European co-productions with the Kirschgruppe in Munich, and RAI and Berlosconi in Italy. Shelly Cooper, Tribune's head of first-run program production, needed me to be the station's guy on the project and was extremely generous in opening the door for me, and George Paris, who was in charge of the day-to-day activities, needed someone to help out. I loved doing it, especially the many trips to Rome that I made for the company. Not all the mini-series properties were successful...far from it. But it was a fascinating new area for me to learn and when, in 1992, Lucie Salhany, now heading up 20th Television, gave me a chance to move out of station management and into network production, I was will-ing, though somewhat wary. But that's another story.

After eleven productive years at KTLA, I spent three years at FOX, first running network series production, and then creating a production company to produce TV movies for FOX and non-fiction programming for cable; two years running TCI's Starz/Encore cable networks (and running back and forth every week from L.A. to Denver!); and three final years running the *Museum of Television and Radio* in Beverly Hills before I retired to teach in 2000.

I had spent 38 years in the business and got to do more in those years than I had ever expected.

On reflection, I must say, that as interesting as many of these jobs were, nothing came even close to matching my experiences as an independent General Manager in Boston and Los Angeles. It was the ultimate job for me and, thankfully, I got to do it before the job and the business changed forever.

Fridays With Art

Where I Come From,
Dessert Means Dinner is Over
by Bob King

I began my broadcast career as a temporary fill-in radio announcer on KSOO Radio in my home town of Sioux Falls, South Dakota. I was still a high school teenager when, in about 1943, the demands of war caused the military draft to decimate the station's announcer staff by taking four of its five on-air personalities. The one left behind suffered from very bad eyesight and was declared *4-F*, a total exemption from service. As a result, two high school buddies and I got an early taste of the business at a very tender age and all three of us made radio, and later television, our life careers.

The fact that I was even in broadcasting surprised a number of my friends and relatives. I was born into a family of profoundly deaf parents. My mom and dad could not hear or speak. My communication skills at home began with sign language. There wasn't a radio in our home until I was twelve years of age. That wasn't insensitivity on

315

my parent's part. It was purely economic. My father made very little money as a teacher and athletic coach at the state *School For The Deaf*. He was paid for only 9 months of the year. In summers he worked as a house painter and later, at a local print shop as a vacation relief linotype operator. It was a terrific struggle in those depression-era years to support a family, and tough to come up with about $13 for our first radio...a red plastic one from Sears. Hard to fathom that only three years after that first radio, I was a fledgling part-time announcer at our home town station.

I enlisted in the Marine Corps in 1945 at age 17. I was trained as a tank crewman and went to the Pacific with the Fleet Marine Force, largely doing clean up on the islands where hundreds of Japanese were holed up in jungle caves, refusing to believe that Japan had surrendered and the war was over. Guam was our home base. Whenever I was off-duty, I'd hitch a ride to the Armed Forces Radio Station, and I began to take on some announcing chores -- music shows, news, et al. The Air Force fighter pilot assigned to the station as manager asked if I could arrange a transfer to become a full-time member of the staff. An approval by the USMC for this type of duty was nearly unheard of. Somehow, after weeks of campaigning, the transfer was approved and I spent a year at the station before coming back to the states for discharge. Now I was hooked!

When I returned home after my hitch in the Marines, I was fortunate to be hired as a full time staff announcer at radio station KSOO.

In the early days of radio, so much of which was live, it was common to "initiate" a newcomer to the business...the "rookie." Think of it not as a "hazing," but rather a frivolous "welcome" to the fraternity. The rookie knew it was bound to come. He just didn't know when.

Mine came on a day when I was scheduled in the large studio, rather than the announcer's booth. I was the emcee of a daily music show which began at 12:05 p.m. following a 5 minute news report at noon. The regular newscaster was ill and I was asked to do the news report immediately preceding the live *Western Music* show.

The veterans on the staff...the pranksters...knew I'd be delivering the news from my stand-up studio microphone, and that I'd be at it for a full 5 minutes without a break. About 20 seconds into the news, two of my colleagues tip-toed into the studio, having made sure my "cough button" had been disabled. (That's the device that would permit an announcer with a frog in his throat to "kill" his microphone long enough to cough and clear his throat.)

They proceeded to undress me. It was an acid test of one's power of concentration to keep going...eyes on the news copy...while the belt came off, the shoe laces were untied and shoes removed, the zipper zipped down, the trousers removed, the tie removed, the shirt unbuttoned. You get the picture. The final result was a mortified announcer, delivering the news in his skivvies. There were visitors to the radio station that day, standing in a hallway where they could view the studios and announce booths through double-plate sound-proof windows. Thank God for soundproofing! They were doubled up with laughter at a sight they never expected to see during their visit to the local radio station.

After four years at KSOO I accepted an announcer position at WNAX, a huge and powerful radio property in the very small town of Yankton, South Dakota. The name Yankton may ring a bell as the home town of NBC's Tom Brokaw.

WNAX was owned by the Cowles family, owners of *Look Magazine,* the *Des Moines Register*, and several other radio properties. No television station licenses were granted while the war was on, and Cowles had applied to the FCC for post-freeze TV licenses in Des Moines and Sioux City, Iowa. We were all stunned to learn in

1952 that it would be Sioux City which would be the first on the air in that part of the midwest. I begged for the chance to move into TV. The early indicators were negative -- no transfers from radio to TV. I kept pressing my case and ultimately won the job. I would be Channel 9's first, and for over a year, its only announcer.

KVTV, Channel 9, signed on in March, 1953 as a CBS-TV affiliate. There was no videotape then. National commercials were produced and aired on film and local ads were almost exclusively live. We expanded our local programming slowly until by the Christmas season we were on from early morning to late evening. As we gained experience, we produced lots of local variety programs -- kids, local interview shows, even a game show, plus the early and late news, weather and sports. At the peak of activity, I was delivering as many as 35 one-minute commercials a day.

Small businesses seeking to advertise via local television often could not afford regular *prime time* television. They bought ads in late night movies, or, if they wanted a presence around the regular news, weather and sports, they'd do so on weekends. We had such a sponsor...Jordan's Jewelers...on the Sunday night weather. I was the store's spokesman.

We were introducing a brand new type of wrist watch. You didn't have to wind it. The movement of the arm and wrist kept it running. It was probably a Bulova product. For purposes of displaying it on television, the watch was mounted on an electrically powered display device which swayed back & forth, left to right, and sat on the top of a typical jewelry counter in our studio.

As I came toward the conclusion of the commercial, for emphasis, I touched the top of the display and it shorted out with a black puff! It badly burned my hand. I was on "live," and I had to stifle any sound. I had to "grin and bear it" and finish the spot. When the camera's red light went out, I raised my voice, uttering an expletive beginning with *S* and ending in *T*. But the audio engineer wasn't as fast at shutting down the audio as the video engineer had been with the camera, and that scene made the morning papers.

Except for that incident, those were pretty heady times for those of us on-the-air. The folks within reach of our signal...watching TV for the very first time...took all of us into their homes and hearts as though we were real celebrities. You couldn't go anywhere - a restaurant, the drugstore, the grocery store - without being fawned over by the fans. We worked hard to stay humble.

My home town of Sioux Falls is 90 miles north of Yankton. My mom and dad bought an early Sylvania (remember the "halo light?") and erected an antenna on a pole about 30 feet high.

They watched a snowy picture, and since they couldn't hear, read the lips of their announcer son.

In August of 1954, my wife and I traveled to Texas to visit family. I arranged a tour of WFAA-TV in Dallas, a visit conducted by Program Director, Jay Watson. Before the day was over, Watson offered me a job. I accepted and a month later moved to Dallas as an on-air personality.

My 18 months in Iowa had been my "boot camp." The years in Dallas were my "advanced training" and provided a broad platform for everything which came later. My mentor and good friend was the later-to-be-legendary, Mike Shapiro. He was a patient teacher who always encouraged me to grow and reach higher. I was on-air a lot, and later began to write, direct and produce. Managers in those days came mostly from the sales side of the business and I asked for the opportunity to try that. I became a local salesman and my account list was the phone book's *Yellow Pages*. After about a year of that, I was asked to reorganize the program/production department and I became WFAA's Program Director. Later I returned to sales to function as Regional Sales Manager, with the state of Texas as my territory, but soon after that Mike Shapiro asked me to again take over the program department and serve as his Station Manager.

It's hard to believe now, but in the early to mid 1950's, the NBC affiliation was shared by two stations in the market: WFAA in Dallas and WBAP-TV in Fort Worth. It was a programmer's nightmare, and perhaps a syndicator's dream. WBAP had *The Today show* and we had *The Tonight show*. Blocks of daytime network feeds alternated between the stations and *prime time* also alternated by days and hours. As a consequence, lots of syndicated programs were given *prime time* exposure on both stations. *Highway Patrol*, fully sponsored by Conoco, ran on Wednesday night at 9:00 p.m., followed by a fully sponsored *I Led Three Lives*, leading into the late news on our station.

During one of Mike Shapiro's absences from Dallas, the station was being managed by Alex Keese, a fine musician who had gravitated to WFAA radio, but knew very little about television. He became obsessed with the notion that NBC would prefer to be a full-time resident of the station in the "big city" of Dallas rather than that "cow town" of Fort Worth. He decided on a power play with NBC.

What he failed to account for was a long-time debt NBC had with the owner of WBAP, Amon Carter. In the early days of building its radio network, General Sarnoff enlisted Amon Carter to help recruit radio affiliations throughout the Southwest. Everyone knew Amon Carter. His *Fort Worth Star Telegram* was the newspaper of choice for much of Texas west of Fort Worth, as well as New Mexico and Oklahoma. Carter helped NBC put down anchors in a wide area of the region, and the General's son, Robert, never forgot.

When Alex Keese made his "all or nothing" pitch, NBC stunned the industry by selecting WBAP as its primary affiliate. WFAA became an ABC affiliate. It continued to be a syndicator's dream, as there wasn't enough ABC programming to fill seven days and nights, and there was scant programming from DuMont to fill the voids. Many first-run syndicated shows found their way into *prime time* on WFAA-TV until ABC's better days arrived much later.

We did a lot of live programming in those days. We had full-time musicians and singers and other performers. We built a daily late-afternoon show around music and local and celebrity interviews. Trini Lopez's career began on WFAA on a locally produced music show.

One of our live productions was the launching pad to another, though lesser known, performer's career. A young local lad on our staff, named Allen Jones, was winning fans with his looks and his rich baritone voice. We decided to enter him into the competition for *Arthur Godfrey's Talent Scouts*, airing Monday nights on CBS. We knew of another somewhat famous Alan Jones (think *Donkey Serenade*) and decided to create an on-the-air contest to change his name. Our Allen's father owned a spiffy men's store in the Oak Cliff section of Dallas. One of our regular viewers knew that Allen's father's nickname was "Casey." She submitted the name of Allen Case. He liked it because it honored his father and we liked it. A few weeks later Allen Case won the '*Talent Scouts*' competition. You may recall that the winner was a guest on the morning Godfrey show for the remainder of the week.

Talk about the "accident" of good timing! The week that Allen Case performed on Godfrey's morning show was the week Arthur fired Julius LaRosa on the air. Allen became a regular for the next couple of seasons. Later he won a part in a new Broadway show called *Once Upon A Mattress,* and at *Sardi's* in New York, introduced me to his fellow cast member, a newcomer named Carol Burnett. Then Allen became the "Deputy" on the Henry Fonda series of the same name on NBC's Saturday night schedule.

In TV's infancy, network news was fed to the nation's affiliates as a 15-minute package. (Remember John Cameron Swayze and the *Camel News Caravan*?) The other 15 minutes consisted of musical variety; Nat King Cole once a week, Perry Como twice, and Dinah Shore on Tuesdays and Thursdays. After a few successful seasons, the networks began to think about musical performers on a larger scale.

NBC made a deal with Chevrolet to sponsor Dinah Shore for an hour each week. Dinah's Executive Producer, Bob Banner, decided to wrap up her 15 minute series on the road. Her final week originated in Texas and, because at that time we were still an NBC affiliate, we were asked to host the show in Dallas. A brand new country club, *RiverLake Country Club*, had recently opened in Dallas and in an effort to enhance their publicity, had given free memberships to a number of broadcast and print executives. Because I was one of them, I was able to make a deal with '*RiverLakes*' to turn their Grand Ballroom into a TV studio, including ample seating for an audience.

Dinah, along with her cast of singers/dancers, key orchestra members, set designer, the line producer and the director came from Hollywood, while the camera crew, floormen, boom, video and audio operators were WFAA employees. As the show was nearing its air date, Bob Banner left for Las Vegas to begin preparation for Dinah's forthcoming month-long engagement at the *Flamingo Hotel*. I was named the Associate Producer for the show from Dallas...the only network credit I have ever received. Dinah's new show opened in September to rave reviews and remained a Sunday night staple for many seasons.

There were other network feeds over the years. We did a live *Lawrence Welk Show* from Dallas. We provided all the manpower for the *Cotton Bowl Football* telecast for several years. My recollection of New Year's Eve remains today the memory of several quiet, and early, dinners with NBC's venerable play-by-play announcer,

Lindsay Nelson, the night before the big sports broadcast.

During his years in Dallas, Mike Shapiro earned the sobriquet of "head hunter of the Southwest." Whenever anyone, anywhere in the country was in search of new talent, be it sales, management or production, they'd call Mike. He'd know where the "stars" were. He was not reluctant to recommend his own people if he thought they would fit the bill for bigger things.

Two of our early production "whiz kids" went from Dallas to bigger things. Andy Sidaris became one of the original directors of ABC's Saturday network football games and earned a massive reputation. Andy was the first guy to call for a close-up of a beautiful girl in the stands. It was his "inside" trademark.

Another star was one of our production assistants and part time cameraman. He was John Alonzo, who became one of Hollywood's leading cinematographers and won an Oscar for his work on the classic film, *Chinatown*.

Mike knew that I was champing at the bit for a chance to be a General Manager. We both knew that opportunity would not come in Dallas, as Mike, now suffering heart trouble, was through chasing around the country. On his third go-round, he was determined to remain at the helm of WFAA until his retirement.

Mike got a phone call from a TV owner in Oklahoma who was looking for a new GM. Mike asked if I would like to be recommended. I thought it over for a day or two and decided that, yes, I had to start someplace, even if it was in the tiny market of Lawton, Oklahoma.

My brief stint as General Manager of KSWO-TV in Lawton was a great disappointment to me and unremarkable. The owner knew or cared little about quality television. He was, at heart, the owner of pawn shops, located near military bases in Oklahoma and Texas. That's where his soul rested...pawn shops.

    With help from ABC affiliate relations executives, who knew of my unhappiness in Lawton, a breakfast meeting was arranged at the *Ambassador East Hotel* in Chicago, so that I might meet George Bolas of Tatham-Laird Advertising and also a gentleman you might have heard of: John Kluge. Bolas was the lead man for a group of investors who owned WTVT, Channel 17 in Decatur, Illinois. He had just sold the station to Kluge's Metropolitan Broadcasting.

    Decatur and Springfield were UHF markets which competed with the powerful and mighty Channel 3, WCIA, in Champaign. When Kluge offered me the General Manager's job in Decatur I was thrilled to accept. I couldn't wait to exit Oklahoma.

    Somehow we rebuilt the Decatur property, strengthening the local news, making some good program purchases, and growing ratings sufficiently well to attract increased national spot advertising. As the station continued to grow, we reached the unheard-of level of $25,000 each month in national spot advertising and I threw a huge staff party to celebrate.

    The news of this success at this out-classed UHF property reached Tom Murphy through a mutual friend of ours. I had never met Murphy or anyone else in management of this fairly new company called Capital Cities Broadcasting. While on a business trip to New York I was called to the Capital Cities offices for a meeting. The meeting led to a discussion about whether I would like to be a candidate for the General Manager's position at a brand new Capital Cities acquisition, WKBW-TV in Buffalo, New York.

    Uncertain about the wisdom of leaving Metromedia, a company which seemed to have a pretty bright future, I agonized for nearly a week. But then I received a phone call from a friend who now worked for Murphy. "Murphy doesn't think you're interested," he said. I quickly called Tom to accept. It was time to *"Shuffle Off To Buffalo!"*

Capital Cities Broadcasting was a company which had sprung from humble beginnings, originally owning just a single UHF station in Albany, New York. But the founder of the company, Frank Smith, was an electric personality who gathered together early investors such as New York's ex-governer Thomas Dewey, and famed newscaster and explorer, Lowell Thomas. He also had lured Tom Murphy away from Lever Brothers to become his General Manager in Albany. I'm sure that Murphy's early experience in operating that UHF station which faced a powerful VHF competitor led to his appreciation for what I had achieved in Decatur. At the time I joined Cap Cities, the company consisted of three radio stations (New York City, Providence and Albany) and TV stations in Raleigh-Durham, Providence, Albany and, now, Buffalo.

In December of 1961, I became the General Manager of WKBW-TV. The call letters stood for "Well Known Bible Witness." The station was founded as a radio station by a colorful character, Dr. Clinton Churchill. Churchill, apparently a bit of a "rounder" in his early days, was said to have been "saved" by the legendary evangelist of the 1930's, Billy Sunday. Churchill put the radio station on the air to broadcast religious services on Sundays. He had no money to buy the equipment, but the folks at the manufacturing level, like RCA and G.E., were anxious to sell to this new medium called radio. They happily arranged a line of credit which Churchill pledged to repay weekly from "collections" from his listeners. It was said that listeners' contributions gushed in like the waters of Niagara Falls. The radio station flourished and grew its schedule to a seven day operation. He later had to battle fierce competition for a TV license, but Churchill won out over other local interests and the station became an ABC affiliate in 1958.

What Cap Cities inherited in 1961, however, was far from a winner. Our CBS and NBC competitors were miles ahead of us in every category you could imagine. We had to fix everything...our on-air look, our people, our department managers. We had a news department that was almost non-existent. And in a manner which was to become a hallmark in the industry, the Capital Cities approach was to leave us alone but to encourage us in every way possible.

They gave us the money we needed to buy syndicated product and movie packages. We knew we had to grow on a local level. There was little we could do about ABC. We'd just have to be patient and wait for the network to "arrive." For now, we'd cherry-pick the network schedule to run *prime time* movies. We were the first TV station to run *Psycho* in *prime time*. We promoted it for weeks and dominated the time period the night it ran. We scheduled a daily movie from 5:30 to 7:15 p.m., followed by a quarter hour of local news, weather and sports.

We had a huge Canadian audience because our signal bounced across Lake Ontario into Canadian homes as clear as a bell! Some may recall that Peter Jennings had an earlier incarnation as a network news anchor. It was in the mid-60's when the networks were scheduling a 15 minute package. But we didn't clear it. Peter called me from time to time to urge our carriage. He said (and I kid you not) "Please clear it for me. My grandmother lives in Toronto and she can't see me." Later Peter was assigned to London and years later returned to become ABC's long-time nightly news anchor.

We set out to staff our station in a professional way. We named six new department heads over the first year. We hired new on-air talent and found places for them to make great contributions to our local programming, whether in kids programming or in the news department. Nothing was spared our surgical tools. Every department was affected.

We learned how to exploit our Canadian delivery. We didn't get credit for those viewers in the rating books, nor were we getting credit for the network delivery north of the border. We set out to prove the Canadian market was a heavy purchaser of American goods we advertised. We traveled a "dog and pony" show to ad agencies in New York, Chicago and the West Coast markets. Our arsenal included two of every product...canned goods, cereal, toothpaste, soap, detergent, soft drinks, cigarettes, you-name-it. One of the products had been purchased at a Canadian outlet, and its exact twin had been purchased at local markets in New York City. We opened hundreds of eyes with this pitch, at the network level as well as most all of the national ad agencies. Our national spot advertising rate card began to reflect this vast total audience and for a number of years, while we ranked as the 27th U.S. market in size, we ranked 6th in total spot advertising revenue. We were also a profit powerhouse.

It took a couple of years to build our news operation. Our radio News Director, Irv Weinstein, was on vacation in Miami Beach in April of 1964 when I called him at his hotel and asked if he'd like to be in television. I thought he'd have the presence for it because of his interest in community theatre and his enjoyment of being on stage. He said yes and joined us as our on-camera anchor and News Director. A year later we stole Tom Jolls from our CBS competitor and he became our weather anchor, joining our long-time popular sports guy, Rick Azar. We had Jolls originate his weather report from outside the studio, which in frequently frigid Buffalo was tantamount to a suicide mission, but certainly created attention.

A handful of folks thought I'd lost my mind for selecting Weinstein as newscaster. He wasn't particularly good looking. He wasn't a big hunk. He name was Irv Weinstein, and we chose not to ask him to change it. But he had a powerful voice and a singular, commanding style of delivery. He was the News Director so he made the content decisions and wrote most of his own copy. He had a colorful vocabulary. That wasn't a policeman or a police officer, that was a "cop." Firemen were "smoke eaters" and athletes were "jocks." Buffalo's audience ate him up!

Those three anchors: Weinstein, Azar and Jolls, took off like a rocket. That trio remained together for 24 years and for most all that time they held the number one rating in the market.

That longevity for an entire news team remains today an American television record.

Some years after I left the Buffalo market, Weinstein wrote me a note thanking me for not changing his name, and reminded me of an anecdote that circulated around town for quite a long time. It was that the NCCJ (the *National Conference of Christians and Jews*) had chosen me for their annual award for the furtherance of human relations...just by putting Irv Weinstein on the air and not changing his name.

The Weather Outside, which originated at WKBW-TV, and later showed up on a number of local stations, produced many memorable moments. The camera was always positioned in such a way as to provide a view of the street on which cars and pedestrians were passing by. We wanted the viewers to know, for certain, that their weather was really being reported from "outside." We did this every day, in all conceivable types of conditions.

One day a car, moving very slowly down the street, timed its drive to arrive at the exact moment the red light on the camera came on. On the passenger side, a guy stuck his bare rear end out of the window, and the live audience got a full force view. Tom Jolls got a quirky grin on his face and said, "I was going to tell you at the end of this weathercast about the full moon we might get tonight!"

In the mid-60's, Capital Cities began to grow. Radio and TV acquisitions were followed by a move into the publishing business with the purchase of Fairchild Publications (*Women's Wear Daily*) and then daily newspapers, like the *Kansas City Star* and the *Ft.*

Worth Star Telegram. In 1969, I was named to head the television division, reporting to one of the industry's nicest guys ever on the planet, Joe Dougherty, President of the broadcast division. Joe and I remained a team for 8 years until corporate bosses Tom Murphy and Dan Burke asked me to concentrate on matters relating to Washington, D.C., as they might affect all aspects of our company...broadcasting, publishing and cable.

For a number of years it was my responsibility to handle the annual Cap Cities Management Meeting...to choose locations, schedule the sessions, plan the meeting agenda and to make provisions for the general happiness of our management personnel in all divisions of the company.

We always began with a Sunday evening cocktail reception and gave everyone the opportunity to go to dinner wherever they wished. We did the same on Mondays and Tuesdays. The only "formal" evening affair was on Wednesday night.

One of Capital Cities newcomers was a veteran publishing executive out of Texas - Jim Hale - a "good ol' boy" who really knew his newspapering. Within the first 20 or 25 minutes of Jim's first dinner with us, several of us noted that he was missing. We had some distinguished guests with us that evening...former President Gerald Ford, ex-Texas Governor John Connolly, our colleague, Lowel Thomas...and we all wanted Jim present for the evening.

I found him at the bar, sipping on a bourbon. "Jim, is something the matter?" I asked. 'No," he said. "After the shrimp cocktail and the salad, they brought me a sherbet. I figured that was dessert, and where I come from, dessert means dinner is over!"

I ran for the *National Association of Broadcasting* Television Board, and became the TV Board Chairman in my rookie year. I spent a lot of time in Washington over a four year period and learned something about life "inside the Beltway." I also learned something about

a disease still prevalent there called "Potomac Fever," and was greatly relieved when that phase of my life drew to a close. I had really
missed operating management at the station level.

A chance meeting led to my decision to leave Capital Cities
after 21 very happy years. A "middle man" in the station representative business brought me to the attention of Tribune Broadcasting,
and in 1982, I left for Chicago to become President and General
Manager of WGN-TV. Independent television was a missing ingredi-
ent in my field of experience and I thought it'd be great fun to return
to station management at that hugely successful property.

I arrived in the Windy City full of hope and anticipation that I
could make a difference at WGN. My boss, Jim Dowdle, talked at
length during our interview process about the need to introduce some
"fresh air" into the troops at Channel 9. As President of the broadcast
division, I believe Jim was the first "outsider" to be brought into the
upper management ranks at Tribune in many, many years. I followed,
as the first "outsider" to manage the station in the 34 years since the
station signed on the air in April of 1948.

Over the years, when a department head at WGN was replaced,
he was generally moved down the hall, given an office and some kind
of title, and just stayed around, drawing a salary. Or, he became a
"consultant" to the company. Change and progress, I thought, were
going to be very difficult to come by.

Almost immediately upon my arrival, we launched a reorgani-
zation plan. There were a number of executive positions which con-
tained a hyphenated title...Promotion Director of Radio & TV...Public
Affairs Director of Radio & TV, and so on. I observed that they were
not very effective in either endeavor and the stations suffered from
this overlap. My counterpart, the General Manager of WGN radio,
Wayne Vriesman, agreed, and we set out to separate the two stations
entirely.

We launched a "zero-based" budget plan. We eliminated 105 positions and without a dollar in additional sales, put $2,500,000 on the bottom line. In some circles, I wasn't the most popular guy on the block! But I was very proud that progress had begun. And, I had begun to re-staff the station with some very bright new people.

The famous and legendary Harry Carey had been hired the year before I arrived, but was beginning his premiere year on WGN in the spring of '82. I hired Steve Stone, a former Cy Young Award pitcher, as Harry's sidekick in the Chicago Cubs' broadcast booth. I was lucky enough to find Dennis FitzSimons working in New York and was successful in enticing him to come to WGN-TV as our Sales Director. Over the next dozen or more years, FitzSimons flourished in the broadcast division and later, throughout the company. He became the CEO and Chairman of the entire Tribune company in the summer of 2003.

WGN was the "Superstation," being carried by satellite literally throughout the world. We began to structure our rate card to reflect this vast additional coverage to our national clients. Every day brought a new kind of problem and every day was exciting.

But...gnawing at me almost from the start was the "style" of executive management. I had grown spoiled by the Capital Cities culture...hands off...decisions are made in the field by Station Managers and editors...not back at headquarters. Here at WGN, one might get a call from the Tribune Tower corporate headquarters on Michigan Avenue about what I thought were somewhat trivial matters that belonged with the station and not at the corporate level. But...true, I had been tutored in a different type of management style.

I believe I knew that my hope for a long ride in Chicago was doomed during my first summer at WGN. It was 1982.

The infamous *Tylenol* scare hit Illinois in a big way. Some deranged person had mixed poison into some capsules before they were purchased by some innocent consumer. Nobody could be sure how many capsules were similarly tainted. The state Attorney General was Ty Fahner and he was knee-deep in the midst of this matteer. Law suits were likely against the product manufacturer, Johnson & Johnson. Radio and television and print coverage was relentless, and the sound bites were plentiful. People were downright scared. News coverage was minute-by-minute over this mystery.

It also happened to be an election year for Ty Fahner. He was running for re-election in November and his opponent was Mike Madigan, the man endorsed by the *Chicago Tribune* for this very important statewide office.

I received several calls from the 'Tower' questioning whether our news department was being "balanced and fair" in our coverage of these two candidates. I patiently explained that reporting about *Tylenol* was serious and meaningful news coverage of a potentially catastrophic event, in which the Attorney General was a key player. I said I felt sure that our coverage of election matters was balanced. Our News Director, Paul Davis, actually counted words and lines devoted to each candidate...on each individual newscast...and delineated those which were about the election and those which were about *Tylenol*.

It was clear that the folks at the 'Tower' were not pleased with the "extra" coverage being given to Fahner by virtue of this tragedy. They made their feelings quite clear to those of us at WGN. I thought it was meddling...that it was about politics and power...and I didn't like it.

My stay at WGN-TV was much more brief than I would have liked...but being spoiled is being spoiled!

I left WGN in the spring of 1983...after only about a year on the job. I felt that with a few shares of Capital Cities stock and a fairly decent reputation in the industry, I could successfully compete as an

independent "consultant." Indeed, that portion of my next career lasted another very pleasant ten years more.

Fridays With Art

"Go figure that."

...Art Greenfield

Total Recall
by Lew Blumberg*

HOW DOES IT FEEL TO BE A TELEVISION PIONEER?

How did I get involved? Is it in the genes or family history or both? You figure It out after reading this.

My Dad, Nathan (Nate), in 1910 at age 16, was working as an assistant stage manager in a Burlesque/Vaudeville theater in Milwaukee. Show Biz! Luckily he was fired. A few days later, in a saloon, he met with his friend, Harold Fitzgerald (Fitz), all of 18 years, who had become shipper for a film exchange. Nate had followed Fitzgerald into his theater job. Now Fitz offered Nate a new job as his shipping clerk.

A few years later, Nate went on to become a film salesman for

---

* (Editor's note: Lew Blumberg did not wish his chapter to be edited. It is reproduced here in the form in which it was submitted.)

Famous-Players, Lasky in Minneapolis and managed to amass a few bucks; enough to become a theater owner, in Milwaukee. It was a flop. Salvaging some money and finding a money partner in Racine, they purchased a theater which became a success. Afterwards, a series of positions in theater companies led to his being involved in the creation of the RKO theater company. The "O" was for the Orpheum chain which was the dominant vaudeville theater company in the U.S. RKO was a combination of David Sarnoff of RCA, a media pioneer in his own right, and a Boston financier, Joe Kennedy, who had merged the Keith, Albee and Orpheum circuits into an important national chain.

By late 1935, Dad had become VP and General Manager of RKO theaters. In January, 1938, Nate was hired by Universal as President to get the company out of business and financial troubles. The controlling group was called Standard Capital. Standard had bought the stock of the Laemmle estate. The Chairman of Standard and Universal was J. Cheever Cowdin, an investment banker.

Nate brought in his own crew of executives who had theater and distribution experience, but no entertainment production experience except for vaudeville, some of which became producers. One of these new execs was Dad's young brother-in-law, Matty Fox. My uncle Matty had come to New York from Milwaukee at age 19. He found a job at Skouras Theaters, a chain of some 60 theaters in New York and New Jersey. By age 26 he had become assistant head buyer.

As for myself, I had theater jobs as gofer, usher, and for two summer months as an Assistant Manager beginning when I was 12-16 years old. What a learning experience learning Greek and Jewish business concepts.

Now in L.A., I worked summers at Universal Studio as a gofer again, as an apprentice, then assistant film editor, primarily working on trailers by myself. In autumn 1941 I began two years at UCLA and then came WW II in which I became a navigator/bombardier in heavy bombers in Europe. I was discharged as a First Lieutenant. I tried returning to UCLA, but I needed to simmer down. Work would help. So I became an apprentice booker at the Universal branch sales office in Los Angeles. After several months I became an apprentice salesman.

In early 1947 I was asked to go to New York to be a gofer again, but this was now "big time." Universal was acquiring International Pictures and beginning negotiations with the J. Arthur Rank Organization. Dad and Matty were conducting the negotiations in New York and London. These two deals brought Universal into an industry level unanticipated eight years before. Rank had over 1,000 theaters in Canada, the UK, Europe, East and South Africa, and India. Rank also had the two best production studios in England and the Universal distribution franchise for England. Concurrently, Universal acquired International Productions which created Universal-International. I loved the redundancy of that name. By this time I could have written a book on how to be a gofer/apprentice.

The U-I sales staff was loaded with its own product. Out of Rank's studios, Gaumont and Pinewood, seven or eight could be sold to the general American audience. There were some seven to eight films that would well qualify for the "art theater" market.

The problem for Universal was to find competent sales executives and daring salesmen to sell English films which were considered as foreign. While gofering this deal I was introduced to some attorneys at a prestigious film industry N.Y. firm. They had a client, Ilya Lopert, who owned rights to some French and Italian films. Lopert wanted to buy some more foreign films and some existing art theaters around the US. These lawyers included Robert Benjamin and Arthur Krim who would put some of their personal money in the deal.

They had heard that I was being considered the Assistant Sales Manager of the Rank "art film" group. Lopert had been with Metro-Goldwyn-Mayer (MGM) and was very knowledgeable about European film makers. If I was going to be selling Rank's art films, this man Lopert could be a fountainhead of information. He knew 'art theater' operations.

I met with Lopert. He suggested I invest in his company. This needed an okay from U-I. So, I went to see uncle Matty Fox who was in charge of organizing the Rank units at U-I. I pointed out that I could be in a position of placing some of the Rank "art films" in Lopert theaters. He said okay, but clear it with McGinley, the recently appointed sales head of the Rank "art film" group which had been given the name of Prestige Pictures. I was to be his assistant. All was okay.

Selling English pictures was a very difficult task. Almost every one of the "Big Eight" production/distribution firms had tried and for the most part failed. To work in a sales operation that would only have the Rank films was a great challenge. My Lopert Films (Lopert) relationship was now about to bear fruit. Lopert was now acquiring, subject to financing, several films and seven theaters. The package would need $200,000 cash. We investors had planned only a total of $50,000. I went to Nate for any thoughts on where we could find a loan for the venture. "Try Bankers Trust." U-I had just left Bankers Trust for First of Boston. "Bankers Trust may have an interest. They may want to keep a possible foot in the door for some of Universal's business."

A few days later, I and Seymour Peyser, a young attorney in the law firm where Benjamin and Krim were partners, left the Bankers Trust Wall Street office with a commitment for $125,000 if we increased our equity to $75,000. We celebrated our victory with martinis at the *King Cole Bar* at the *St. Regis Hotel.*

In ninety days the financing, theater leases and purchase agreements were signed. I learned how fast and well attorneys can work when they have a vested interest. Lopert himself became an ever flowing and somewhat arcane fountain of art theater information. The people and some of their business practices were quite different from the more traditional motion picture milieu. That's saying a lot, as the movie business itself was quite different from the norms of American business itself.

The Prestige target was to have 100 art theater clients in two years. A theater owner would have to be in trouble to make the change from US films to European. Most exhibitors agreed with Churchill's comment that the US and England were separated by a common language. What was our targeted market? Based on the existing experience, art film goers were most typically from the intellectual and psuedo-intellectual population; often found near universities; *New Yorker* magazine readers. Letters went out to the 32 U-I domestic branches: "Are there any small theaters near universities in trouble in your district?" Successful art films had long runs in small theaters, another lesson. So, an availability of several artsy films per year was an important factor to assure sufficient programming to warrant such a theater owner to change its policy.

We also needed to start with a bang. We guessed that David Lean's *Brief Encounter* would be the one. Lopert concurred. Now to find the theater to launch our project. Lopert advised us that the *Little Carnegie* theater, between *Carnegie Hall* and the *Russian Tea Room* was the art film equivalent to the RKO *Radio City Music Hall*. The *Little Carnegie* owner looked, he liked. The *Brief Encounter* was a long term success: sixty weeks, record ticket sales for an art film. Its star, Trevor Howard, became an international favorite. David Lean became one of the most celebrated directors with films like *Bridge on the River Kwai, Lawrence of Arabia*, et al.

About three months later I received a call from Nate. I was to call Sam Rintzler, of Frisch & Rintzler theaters, who owned about 40-50 theaters in the greater New York area. He had an ailing theater about a mile east of the *Little Carnegie* abutting the rich, snooty Sutton Place area. Sam said of course, no percentage. I said no flat rental. He then had his district manager, Clem Perry, look at our next projected release, *I Know Where I'm Going*. We consulted with the manager of U-I's New York branch, Dave Levy. He advised us that that theater was having big problems. Too much competition from Loew's and RKO in the area. We enlisted Levy's help. After all, one of our goals was to eventually involve the entire U-I sales force in the sales of all the Rank product.

In the course of the negotiations we found out what Perry's operating costs were. I proposed a "four wall" deal. U-I had a recent success with *The Killers*, the film that made Burt Lancaster a star, with a "four wall" deal at the *Winter Garden* theater in Time's Square. This 400 seat theater caused a meeting at the highest level of U-I: Nate, Matty, and Scully. It pencilled out if we grossed half of what the 300 seat Little Carnegie grossed. We were on fairly solid ground. Perry agreed, provided the rent period was for two months minimum. The first month we out-grossed *Brief Encounter*; but it didn't have the legs...it lasted only seven months.

My next assignment was to spread the good tidings to the U-I sales force. In five weeks I covered the 32 U-I branches. The highlight was going to Milwaukee. There I met with "Uncle" Harold Fitzgerald, now managing partner with 20th Century Fox Theaters for Wisconsin and Minnesota. Remember, this was my Dad's mentor. He had a problem theater, the *Milwaukee Downer*, the first theater Dad owned. "Fitz" would try almost anything to get the '*Downer*' theater to break even. The change of marketing was a success; the Downer was now making money. Fitz bought all the Prestige product and Lopert's as well. This was the first conversion from a traditional to an art theater.

There being few secrets in the theater business, other theater owners around the US began calling either the local U-I Sales office or the Prestige office in NY. The two year timetable for the 100 art theaters was met. Surprisingly, we earned more money for some of the Rank films than was earned in England. Dad would proudly say that his son made a go in a location where he failed. Never a greater praise from a father.

Among the more memorable experiences at that time was a call I had from the new U-I branch manager in New Haven, Art Greenfield. We had met a couple of years earlier at West Coast sales meetings of U-I. "Lukie, there's a small theater near the Yale campus not doing well, a possible candidate for 'art films.'" The following week he had the World Premiere of *Winchester '73* starring James Stewart, New Haven being the factory headquarters of Winchester. "Come up for the opening. The next day we'll go sell Rank Pictures." We made the sale. This was the first sale made by a branch office. Art would never forget one of the pictures in this first package, *The Tawny Pippit*. He didn't care too much for the film, but he loved the name.

I had a big scare in another learning experience. While I was on a road trip, Bill Scully, U-I's General Sales Manager left a message with my secretary..."problems with my expense account; see him immediately on my return!" For the next three days I was in a sweat. I had kept every receipt. I didn't charge my laundry as an expense. Unless I ate with a client I did not go to the expensive restaurants. What could be the problem? The morning I returned I called Scully's secretary for an appointment. Come upstairs immediately. It was winter but I was in a sweat. Scully was a big, imposing man, usually with a smile. As I walked in he wore a frown, gestured for me to sit down.

Gruffly he spoke. "Luke, your expenses accounts are causing considerable embarrassment for me." I shiver. I thought I was on the up and
up. I did go to one expensive restaurant in Cincinnati for lunch. I was
caught. Suddenly he stands up and lets out a big laugh. "Luke you're
not spending enough. It's making it tough on our managers from top
to bottom. You are hereby instructed to increase your accounts by a
minimum of 25%. And that will still leave you short of the rest of us."
With a big slap on the back and another laugh he sent me unpacking.

The general condition of the "Big Five" film companies (Fox,
Loew's/MGM, Paramount, RKO, and Warners) was now in near
chaos. To settle an anti-trust suit, practices by those production companies which owned theaters, the parent companies entered into a settlement agreement with the Department of Justice wherein the theater
companies were split off from the production/distribution operations.
With its Rank relationship, U-I had preferred access to theaters in the
foreign markets where US anti-trust laws did not prevail. Nate had
foreseen this coming.

U-I was breaking another sector of new ground. In examining
possible new revenue sources at minimal costs, Matty had chosen the
educational, home and institutional market for 16mm films. U-I had
a small operation in this area, as did most of the major companies, for
their own features, cartoons and shorts. Matty was empowered to set
up a new growth subsidiary, United World Films, with he as its
Chairman, while still retaining his position as Executive V.P. of U-I.

The first purchase was the largest 16mm library, especially
educational, Castle Films. The next largest 16mm library was Bell &
Howell's (B&H). They operated their film division to provide a sales
packaging tool for their equipment sales. This would have been an
easy deal except that a young B&H attorney, Charles Percy, wanted
to make a name for himself. With us his name was _____!!! Yet, several years later he became U.S. Senator for Illinois.

It was now toward the end of the second year of the Rank operation. Matty told me that he was also green lighted to start a television operation dubbed United World. U-I had to be completely out of the picture as they were very afraid that the exhibitors would raise the roof at U-I's support of this new competitive medium. No U-I studio product, past, present, or future, were available for TV. He had already hired a production head, Steve Alexander, director of the *Theater Guild's* Westport summer theater operation. The intent was to produce new TV shows in New York. About two months later, Matty called, let's talk. Alexander is only a creative guy. As to business and sales, he's a problem. He was taking me out of Prestige to head the entire TV activity. I was to be made a VP of United World. I told him to hold on the VP. I hadn't as yet earned it, at least in my mind enough to overcome my concern that nepotism would be raised. Matty countered with the good job I'd done at Prestige. We made a deal. If I'm still around after one year the title is okay.

A new learning curve was involved. The most important factor, quickly learned, was that nobody had any more knowledge in TV than me. The advertising agencies, Madison Avenue, controlled most of radio programming. They were deathly afraid of competition from the movie companies. The film firms had control of a goodly portion of the actors who were working in radio. The film studios paid performers more for one film than they could make in radio in a year. But the ad agencies controlled the advertising clients; and so a stand-off. How to break that up?

Alexander and I went to Universal's ad agency. As a rule, the movie firms had better creative artists and better copywriters working in their studio advertising departments than the ad agencies could find. The primary functions of the typical film company's ad agency was to place ads and buy spot time. But U-I's ad agency did offer one piece of advice..."make shows in New York with lesser names than the studios required." Maybe some has-beens out of the legitimate theater and movies. Did we have any films which might be used for filler? Better yet, a series of some sort. We now had clues with which we could go back to the drawing board.

What did we have to work with? The U-I newsreel operations, headquartered in New York, were completely divorced from the studio. They had a news library of millions of feet accumulated over twenty years. They produced two ten minute newsreels every week and some ten to twenty one and two reel short subjects per year. There was also a lot of unused footage. Some of their newsreel commentators were known to the public. A goodly portion of the Castle and B&H libraries were perfect programming for the nascent TV stations.

U-I Newsreel, headquartered in NYC, had produced a number of short subject series such as: *Stranger Than Fiction, Variety Views, Big Band Musicals*, etc. Not great product but they were better than most of TV. We had our filler programming. What did we have for kids? U-I had black and white cartoons going back to the period before sound. The producers included, most notably, Walter Lantz. Though produced in L.A., they were not at the Studio; so we had an out. Matty successfully pleaded our cause before the Board.

Alexander came to the front. He knew the Broadway crowd, most of whom were hungry to work. Let's do a quiz show using news and celebrity, etc., clips. Show the clip, the panelists have to identify the person, place, or whatever. Conrad Nagel, as the MC, was the hungriest. Kitty Carlisle was available as a regular. A few rotating guest contestants filled the casting. The show went on the air. It was well produced and received. Steve delivered. We had money coming in. The ad agencies were selling time on it. Now we, the camel, had gotten our nose under the ad agency tent. A year later our coup, Dennis James as MC. Nagel went from MC to a regular panel member.

At that time a most fortuitous happening. Into my office entered Mr. Saul Reiss, a radio time salesman. He wanted to switch from his firm to UW-TV. His firm was moving too slowly into TV. He'd never sold TV programming before but he was well acquainted with the agencies. He did not like their rife anti-Semitism. But a buck is a buck. He had a no-nonsense, brusk, no bullshit manner. He'll take a salary cut if he gets a percentage. No percentage, but if he produces in 90 days, he goes to regular salary. If he's with us after one year, a ten percent increase. Done.

"Saul, what's the best way to approach the stations at the local level with our films?"

"Get a major station to buy it first. The first deal is the toughest. Lew, you make it. You know the product best. You represent a major film company, which your father heads. They understand power."

"Saul, make a list of the five top stations in your opinion and the top man." There were only fifty stations opened nationally at that time. Further, there was very little hook-up between cities.

The next day Saul hands me his list. Included was WCAU, Philadelphia. Walter Annenberg! Dad knows him from Milwaukee. "Dad, I need your help. How good is your relationship with Walter Annenberg?"

"Lew, we talk about once a month. Why?"

I lay out the plan.

"Lukie, call him yourself. Send him my regards. Go see him."

The next day I call. I go to Philadelphia two days later. After a few minutes on catching up on family relationships, Mr. Annenberg calls in his Program Director and I present my spiel. After about twenty minutes of questions and answers, he asks his Program Manager if he has any problems with my proposal. No problems.

Then draw up an agreement. Now I'm suspicious. This has gone too easily. The contract must be a zinger. Three days later the contract arrives and I take it the U-I legal department. Time is of the essence. They may change their mind. A few small changes agreed to by U-I's attorney and WCAU's. It's signed! I don't believe it! Two years for $30,000!

Saul is more impressed than I - that's saying a lot. Saul now goes to the station reps. A few weeks pass and no deals from Saul. "Lew, I was wrong. The second deal is the toughest." As we talk, he gets a phone call. He hangs up with a yell. "The whole package. To one of the top five!" We now plan a tour for him to make to the hustings. There were only about fifty stations in some twenty cities at that time. Saul does not like to be on the road: he's a good family man. He wants a few more weeks in NY with the reps. A couple more deals come in but only for portions of our library.

Saul comes in one day in a possible disturbed demeanor. "Lew, I haven't been as diligent as I should have been." Oh, oh, I think. "Are you sure that we can't do anything with the Studio?" he asks. "What about producing commercials? I think I might have a major agency with a major client. The idea of having commercials produced at a major studio has got them dreaming. The agency's client is a leader in their industry. No more chintzy animation in NY. They want people, the excitement only a major Hollywood studio can give."

"Saul, I'll go see Matty."

The next day I met with Saul. We're cleared, but only deals with a minimum 30% profit for the studio. Our sales costs and profits are to be added on. The usually phlegmatic Saul jumped in the air and let out a shriek. He then asked "can they meet some starlets?"

"Forget it. They couldn't afford the markup."

Within six months the volume of commercial business was so extensive, the assistant studio manager, Morrie Weiner, was appointed to head a special commercial unit. Within the first year the billings were over $1 million. Saul did not go on the road, he was so busy selling commercials. Now I had to handle syndication sales for awhile. In two months I covered almost every station in the country. In its first full year the TV operation had achieved the top return on sales of any division of U-I and UW, $250,000 in the first full year. I became a Vice President.

Road experience was fine but I could spend my time better in NY. Good fortune came via Milwaukee again, but indirectly through Joseph Seidelman, U-I's Foreign Sales Manager. Joe was also an ex-Milwaukeean. He was looking for a place for his son, Bob. Bob was also a fellow skier. He couldn't be too bad. So Bob now went on the road. We are now in early 1950.

The Lopert films are doing fine. I asked Lopert if he knew of any product in Europe that could be used for TV. U-I, like the rest of the film industry, had 90% of their foreign income blocked for indefinite time periods by the various countries. The economic effects of WWII caused big shortages of US dollars by European nations. The movie companies could use their local money only for film production or acquisition in that country. His advice - go there yourself. He gave me some names.

I called Joe Seidelman to get our inventory of money and more names of film product sources. U-I's offices were alerted to make their screening rooms and expense money available. He was excited at the prospect of getting rid of a lot of frozen Deutschmarks, Francs, Lira, etc. U-I had no trouble getting their money out of England because of the Rank deal.

The highlight of the trip occurred as I spent April, 1950 in Paris where I had a five day schedule, six to eight hours a day of screenings. On the fourth day, a very slim older man, late forties perhaps, and two plain slim younger men, my age, showed up with ten or so reels of underwater wrecks off the coast near Marseille. It's great stuff. I asked Mr. Jaques Cousteau how much footage he had altogether, 150,000 feet or so. I asked if we could send a few of the reels of what I'd seen to New York for a few weeks. On my return to New York I screened those reels with Tom Mead, the head of the newsreel/short subject department in NY. He was excited enough for U-I to buy Cousteau's footage. From Cousteau's footage, Tom Mead produced a two reel short which won an *Academy Award* two years later, by which time I would be far gone from the US and TV.

More TV stations were now receiving licenses. In Miami, two stations had been approved. One station was owned by one of the largest Florida theater chains, Wometco, Wolfson and Meyers. They were regular but difficult buyers of U-I's product. They knew Nate from his theater years. I went to see them in late April. The prices they offered were 50% of our target. No negotiations. So, I saw the other approved station as well. They would agree to all of our general terms and pricing but wanted to review the contract. No committment until all was accepted.

On returning to NY I had our attorney began to draft the contract with station 2. A day or two later I get a call from Nate. "Luke, I just made a TV deal for us in Miami with Mitch Wolfson."

"Dad, I just made a deal with their competitor." I went through the story of my Miami dealings.

"But Luke, I gave my word to Mitch."

"Dad, I know how much your word means to you. Also consider that you've always told me my word was to be as inviolable as yours. Let me call you back shortly. I need to think."

I went to his office later. "Dad, there is only one solution. Neither of us has to break his word. If one of us is no longer with U-I, then only the remaining party's word is at issue. The party staying with U-I will have to explain to the two Miami stations as to the sit-

348

uation. Obviously, you, the President of the parent company, U-I, cannot be expected to leave. I will have my resignation to you within the hour." Within the hour I presented Dad with my resignation. He thanked me for my work and especially this last assignment. We hugged and cried and made dinner plans together for the next night.

By the time I returned to my office there was a call from Matty. "Please come down the hall. I've already heard from Nate." I quickly go. "Luke, maybe its for the best. I'd like you to go to Indonesia and be the Treasurer for my operations there." For the past four years Matty had been financing the Indonesian Revolution against the Dutch. The Dutch, only a few weeks earlier, had agreed to settlement terms with the Indonesians.

I left for Indonesia six weeks later after several injections for tropical diseases, some of which I'd never heard of. Our first project was to build an assembly plant for Dodge and Willys autos and trucks. We also represented RCA Communications Equipment, Westinghouse for power generators, Remington Rand office equipment, Indian motorcycles, Baldwin-Lima railroad engines; from England, the Rootes Group autos; and from Germany, the Talbot Wagonwerks of Aachen railroad cars. One of my bombing raid targets had been Talbot. Our only entertainment business...subtitling American films into Bahasa Indonesian (the local language). Our first client, naturally, was U-I.

TWO YEARS LATER

June, 1952 - I'm surprised. Dad sends a letter; he always calls. Mom is the family correspondent. He is to be honored as Motion Picture Pioneer of the Year in New York in November. Can I come? Among the three prior recipients were Barney Balaban, Chairman of Paramount, and Nick Schenk, Chairman of Loew's. Of course I'll be there. Also, Dad has a TV film syndication possibility for me. Nat

Kramer, a former sales manager for U-I in England has come to the States with a package of about 50 English and Australian films to distribute. On my return I met with Nat and struck a deal. He kept the worldwide theatrical rights. I got the similar rights for TV.

Matty called, come home in a month. He was closing a deal with Eliot Hyman to acquire the Allied Artist/Monogram library for TV syndication and closing a deal to acquire United Artists. I had loaned Matty some money to tie up both these projects. I returned in about six weeks.

Matty thanked me for the job in Indonesia. Our first year sales were $20 million, second year $35 million. He's happy and the Indonesians are happy. He fills me in on the UA deal. Matty has brought into UA the key personnel: Bob Benjamin, Chairman; Arthur Krim, President; Bill Heinemann, U-I's head of sales for the Rank division; Max Youngstein, Production Coordinator; and Arnold Picker from Columbia for advertising and promotion. I got 1/10th of his share. Because of possible conflict-of-interest issues, he had just resigned as Executive VP of U-I.

Matty asked if I'd like to work at his new TV distribution company, MPTV, Motion Pictures For Television. Besides the buyout of Eliot Hyman's library, he has made a purchase of the Goldwyn and Selznick libraries. I ask Matty if he had won them in a gin rummy game. They loved to play gin with Matty even when they were losing, which was often. Both Goldwyn and Selznick were often short of funds. He smiled. He got the TV rights, they kept theatrical.

Matty wanted me to head the TV production for MPTV. I then explained two conflicts: the deal about the English/Australian films. He said "take a few months to make some sales." The second problem I expressed was that I wanted to get into the TV station business. We then discussed a plan I had conceived when at United World for U-I to build a TV network. We agreed that it was still a good idea.

A few days after my return Bob Benjamin called, excited about UA and our Lopert Film venture. We had an offer to buy 50% of the company for seven times our investment. The buyer, Robert Dowling, also gets a three year option for our remaining 50%. Dowling, a major New York real estate investor who had recently been acquiring several Broadway legitimate theaters, is interested in "art theaters and art film."

I was able to obtain a goodly number of sales for my TV feature package with phone calls. Matty and I now agree that he takes over my feature library and I get stock in MPTV. If sales go over a benchmark, I'll receive part of the additional income in cash. I became head of new production and can have time to organize the television stations I'd proposed...Bakersfield, CA and Spokane, WA. Any more after that will be subject to discussion.

I advised Nat Kramer that I've transferred my TV rights of the British/Australian films to MPTV. Also, I tell him of the sales I'd made. He made an offer to buy the rights from MPTV. Matty and I can both use the cash. So, in about three months, current and future cash flow are exceeding plans.

I then spent a couple of weeks in Los Angeles at Mom and Dad's home. After a couple of barbecue dinners at their home with their show biz friends, I now had an investment group for the station project consisting of Jack Benny, Jesse Block, Danny Kaye and Bill Goetz. Goetz is L.B. Mayer's (of MGM) son-in-law, co-founder of Twentieth Century Pictures that merged with Fox, and co-founder of International Pictures that merged with Universal in 1946. The FCC wanted new applicants to show that they had show biz or media people involved as well as local participation.

The first city for our venture was Bakersfield. The local participation began with a UCLA friend and classmate, Morrie Harrison, now in retail clothing. He brought in a doctor and the daughter of one of the biggest cattlemen and feedlot operators in California's San Joaquin Valley, Eleanor Rudnick. Her father, the Yiddishe Cowboy, had ten children. He gave each of them $1 million on their 21st birthday. Eleanor, an able pilot in her own right, purchased a small airport for crop dusters, charters, etc., and for smuggling old US Army Air Corps fighter planes to Israel. That was against the law and she almost went to jail for it. She was really made of "the right stuff." Our Washington attorney knew a woman, retired in Bakersfield, Pearl Lemeirt, who had been Allen Dumont's assistant for the many years he was developing the cathode ray tube for TV and other TV equipment. Dumont had been purchased by Paramount Pictures and became the base for their three TV stations already on the air.

A few weeks after we filed our FCC application for the only VHF channel, 10, a local radio station filed for the same channel. That station was owned and operated by Gene deYoung, of a prominent, wealthy San Francisco family. Our Washington attorney and deYoung's attorney recommend the merger of our two groups. A contested hearing process would be a long, costly and uncertain process. So we elect to merge. Half a loaf is better than none. Each group puts up half the money and gets 50% of the ownership. I became VP and manager of programming excluding local and network, obviously film.

Concurrently, our investor group prepared to file for a VHF channel in Spokane. We associated with some local businessmen organized by Eric Johnson, then President of the *Motion Picture Association*. Before that position Johnson was a prominent businessman in Spokane and Chairman of the *U.S. Chamber of Commerce*. Obviously this contact was through Nate. As the FCC application was being drafted by our attorneys, Eric decided to pull out. Questions had been raised by some persons in the motion picture industry as to his having a conflict of interest. Though he attempted to keep the rest of his Spokane group together without his involvement, there were not sufficient local monies available. So we dropped the project.

To warm up for my VP position in Bakersfield, I decided to see where I might get a crash course in operating a smaller city TV station. Through friends I met Julie Kaufman, Station Manager of the ABC affiliate in Phoenix. Phoenix was not the metropolitan area as we now know it. I learned a great lesson from the 60 days in Phoenix. Julie was one hellava Station Manager. I was now able to assist deYoung in organizing our Bakersfield TV operation.

MPTV was growing rapidly. In addition to the small, but strong sales force of Sy Weintraub in NY and Dave Wolper in LA, such newcomers as Dalton Danon, Erwin Ezzes, and Dick Feiner, a cousin, were hired. The new production program was being planned. For Hollywood production we started with Ella Raines, a Universal star, as the lead in *Janet Dean, Registered Nurse*. That was followed by *Duffy's Tavern*, a highly successful radio comedy show with creator, writer, and star Ed Gardner.

The inevitable personality tribulations arose with our two Hollywood projects. Curing them required trips to LA which gave me the opportunity to maintain good contact with Bakersfield.

We concurrently organized two series to be produced in France: *Paris Precinct*, a Paris *Dragnet* starring Louis Jourdan and Claude Dauphin. The producer was Andre Hakim, who had recently married Suzie Zanuck, daughter of Darryl Zanuck, head of Twentieth Century Fox Studio. I arrived in Paris in April, 1954. Production was to begin in mid-May. Andre had only four or five scripts at or near completion. He had no one to write more. He was too busy keeping Suzie happy.

Another recent marriage was to get us out of trouble, at least for a short time. Before leaving NY I attended a wedding of a friend, TV writer Paul Monash, and his bride, Karen. They had planned a European honeymoon which had fizzled out as an expected writing

353

contract fell though. I called Paul. "Your European honeymoon is back on track if you can finish four scripts here in Paris before driving around Europe." He was hungry and his price was right. In three days, Paul and Karen are in Paris. But Karen didn't want Paul to work too hard on their honeymoon. Four teleplays before touring were too much. A new deal. He can leave if he gets the first two finished in ten days, subject to the work being acceptable. If not, he must do any needed rewrites first. Another condition: he writes three more, not the two more when they return.

I called Matty to tell him of the predicament and the progress. I still need more writers. Matty is to contact Max Wilk, a mutual writer friend, who has done some TV shows. Paul had told me that a Broadway show Max wrote had recently been delayed indefinitely. Max is on his flight to Paris in ten days.

We had planned to shoot an episode per week. But not under French union practices. Shooting starts at noon, work seven hours without a break. Overtime work is allowed only at the discretion of the union steward on the set. Built into the budget was an allocation for tips; the steward is the prime recipient. Our big problem was that the crews typically consumed a large French lunch before work, which in local custom, requires a consumption of an appropriate amount of wine, a truly heady problem. As a result, the American director requires more time to shoot an episode. Another call to Matty, find us a director. Does U-I have any B director that might be available? Matty is now pissed at his buddy, Andre. A couple of days pass, Matty calls. Chuck Haas, a director, has just finished a picture. He is also a back-up writer.

Matty then informs me that the lady he has been dating is going to be his wife, Yolanda Betbeze, Miss America of 1948. The wedding will be at our family home in Sherman Oaks. He'd love to have Nilda and me there, but I have to stay in Paris. So, he is sending Nilda to

Paris. The budgets are being increased to allow for her travel and getting a better apartment for us.

Our other Paris production was *Sherlock Holmes*! The producer was Sheldon Reynolds who had shortly before finshed three years of production of the successful *Foreign Intrigue*, starring Jerome Thorpe. Shelly was not only a producer, director, writer, but he had a very good production manager, his girl friend, Countess (for real) Nicole Millinaire. She had proved her capability by handling production matters for the last two years of *Foreign Intrigue*.

One morning Shelly and Nicole's door bell rang. The police have a summons for Shelly. He is accused of being the father of a child their maid is carrying. Nicole roared with laughter as she relates the events and explains the niceties of French justice. Old feudal law, still in effect, states that any child conceived out of wedlock by a nonmarried female residing in a household is deemed to be sired by the head of the house, in this case, Shelly. Shelly did not get the humor, which made Nicole laugh even more. She helped to settle the matter with the court by testifying that after taking care of her, Shelly is incapable of servicing the maid. With such testimony from such a reliable source, French justice acquitted Shelly. Only a few production days were lost. He could have been jailed. C'est la vie.

The recap of Paris. Paul Monash came back to Paris for his second round of script writing. Paul turned out some good scripts; good enough for me to have him write a couple of scripts for feature films for me a few years later. Paul then went on to write the pilot script for the very successful *Untouchables* TV series and became the chief writer for that series. Following that he became the producer/writer for the *Peyton Place* series and picked up an Emmy on the way.

Max Wilk got his Broadway show produced and continued to write some TV shows. Now that he has TV directing and writing credits added to his resume, Chuck Haas's career is more active.

Countess Nicole leaves Shelly a few years later. She moves up on the nobility scale by marrying the Duke of Bedford and so adds Duchess to her titles.

After seven months in Paris I returned to New York. Matty has an idea for a new syndication show. He had been working with Drew Pearson, probably the then most respected political journalist, to film a weekly half hour news commentary in Washington, D.C. Pearson demanded that it be shot there. My challenge is to find, in DC, film crews, laboratories, editors, and to secure a director. We set Friday night shipment for thirty prints of the episodes to the TV stations for the latest arrival to be for Sunday AM air time. At that time there was only minimal cable or microwave transmisssion available between some cities.

Universal's newsreel operation in NY had some Washington connections as they covered news stories there. With Tom Mead's advice we are able to find our missing pieces. We set a Thursday night shoot. The local lab processed the film so that we can edit in the negative, a dangerous but necessary risk. This was before jet air planes. Flight times were not as fast or reliable as now. The show is a sales and logistic success.

A few months into the series Drew called. He has a coup. Igor Guzenko, one of the first of the Russian defectors, is under a witness protection program in Canada. Igor had been the code officer at the Russian Embassy in Ottawa. He had been secretly and fully interrogated by the Royal Canadian Mounted Police and other Canadian intelligence units. Drew will now get Igor's first public interview.

We have to use a Canadian film crew so that the RCMP can more readily perform their security needs. Gouzenko will have his head covered by a black hood; a white hood might raise some questions. The studio is to be a special farm house used by the Mounties who will drive us to the location in cars with blacked out windows.

Again, Tom Mead to the rescue. He puts me in touch with his prime Canadian "stringer" who gave us the needed room size and acoustic requirements to pass on to the RCMP. Pearson, the director, Matty's attorney, Basil Estrich, and I are met at the Toronto airport by plain clothes Mounties and Gouzenko's agent. Igor is learning capitalism quickly. They already have the film crew in another car. We did not even get the opportunity to meet with the crew before going to the "farm studio." Gouzenko had been separately delivered to the location.

For space and security reasons, only Pearson, the director, and camera/sound crew are allowed to be in the farm house. After three and a half hours of shivering in a car, in the bitter cold of a Canadian winter night, the shoot is over. It's after midnight. Basil pays half of Igor's fee to his agent. The RCMP took the film to the lab for immediate processing.

On our way back to the hotel the RCMP officer advised that there were a "few security edits." We screened the footage by noon. It was great: enough for two shows. Igor got his final payment and we are to go home with the negative and a print. Basil paid up, to the agent of course. Igor is so ecstatic that he invites us to dine with him, as his guests, at the most exclusive private club in Toronto. In Russian fashion he makes so many toasts that he is soon swacked. The ever-present Mounties are so fearful of his blowing his cover that they rush him from the premises.

The response to the Pearson shows was so good that Matty decides to make a biography film about Igor. It could go theatrical, which it did in a few theaters. It was fine for TV, the lowest budget possible.

The next part of the Matty/MPTV saga came to surface a few months later, in the Spring of 1954. Matty had heard that the RKO Studio, distribution, and film library were for sale. The price was millions of $s which he didn't have. But with those assets something might be done. He asked me to evaluate the package in light of his primary goal, to acquire the film library. In a few weeks I presented my analysis. The deal can make sense if the studio can be sold for about $6 million. That leaves about the same amount for the library. Who might buy the studio? How can the balance be financed?

During Matty's one year stint with the WWII War Production Board he met one of the General Tire Company VPs, Tom O'Neill, son of the Chairman. Tom had expressed an interest in getting into the entertainment business. Matty had kept their cordial relationship active in the post-war years. A phone call to O'Neill brought a positive interest. How to finance the library? If he brought in an investor he could lose control. But what bank would lend him enough at an affordable rate?

Serge Semenenko of the First National Bank of Boston was approached. In the late 1940's, under Matty's direction, U-I became the first film industry borrower from that bank. By 1954, the bank was aggressive in building a substantial film clientele. But TV was a new, untested business. After reviewing our projections Serge offered to put up 100% of the library cost if Matty can get a high grade corporate guarantee. How could the corporate guarantees be arranged? Could the library be sold quickly enough to sufficient stations before closing the purchase. The sales staff said, no. No syndicator ever had such a large quality package before. Could we get part cash and part station ad time? If we got time, how many advertisers would be needed?

A few days later Matty makes his first pitch. The Chairman of Playtex Bras was one of the regulars at Matty's nightly gin rummy games. Playtex was thinking of expanding its TV advertising. If Matty could deliver several million dollars in spots, in good time slots, and at good discounts over two or three years, it's a deal. For a deal of this size and complexity, it was one of the fastest okays I'd ever seen. The next morning Matty assigned me to work with Erwin Ezzes to develop a series of schedules for submission to Playtex and to Serge. Ez was to be the sales manager for this special "barter" operation. There had been no barter activity in TV on a scale such as this. Ez starts putting out feelers to some stations. He reports "doable" but not easy if maximizing the return is needed. It was quickly realized that at least one more deal like Playtex was needed.

One of Serge's bank's clients, Shell Oil, might be a possibility. Matty made the Shell sale. The deal is barely enough for funding the loan. MPTV started a major new trend in large TV barter sales. As the sales effort was beginning in early 1955, Dad had a second congestive heart failure attack. He was at home in Sherman Oaks. So my wife and three month old son go to LA.

Dad's recovery is slow. So we stay there for a couple of months. I returned to NY for a few weeks. Matty had a new project to be analyzed, Skiatron. Skiatron had a patent for a Pay TV system and had developed a good level of technology. What a market for the MPTV libraries. Another financial evaluation for me. Skiatron had something else. Its stock was publicly owned, traded over-the-counter at a sizeable discount from its original offering. The management lacked capable marketing tools: they were mostly engineering types. The big problem was the imposing opposition from theater owners, and, to lesser extent, from some TV stations. Matty's deal was to buy management's controlling interest. It looked good enough for me to take my fee in stock. The per share price was at a discount from the market.

Matty determined that selling his United Artists stock was his only source of funds to buy Skiatron control. UA stock, being controlled by management, meant management could dictate the price. Arthur Krim was the negotiator. Aware of Matty's predicament, Krim squeezed. My shares had to be included. We made a profit, but it was 50% of what Matty or anyone else had estimated. Years later, two of the UA management group which bought Matty's stock told me they were ashamed of the way Krim had screwed Matty. They had raised only minor opposition; they were afraid of retaliation. Matty had made them millionaires.

Matty then approached Sylvester "Pat" Weaver, President of NBC, to take over the presidency of Skiatron. Matty was aware of Pat's having some problems with the NBC board. Weaver's entry into Skiatron gave the stock a boost.

At this same time I had a call from Lopert to inform me that Dowling was exercising his option to buy the other 50% of the company. It was a week before his option was to expire.

The payment was to be forthcoming in a few days. My last obligations in NY were over. I was now free to consider Dad's wishes for me to relocate to LA. His medical condition required less travel on his part.

While still in NY, Bob Benjamin, UA's Chairman, called. He would like to discuss my producing a couple of films for UA financing and release. He had heard that I'd bought a book by a noted syndicated columnist. The mystery was set in exotic Cuba. I was to work out the terms with their production head, Max Youngstein. I'd met Max before. We concluded a two picture deal. I then called Paul Monash, whose TV credits had been expanding, but he had yet to write a movie. He jumped at the chance.

Now for casting and a director. Dad suggests Errol Flynn. U-I had just released a Flynn film: it's doing good business in spite of his recently being arrested on a marijuana charge. For the director, U-I had available on a loan-out, Dick Wilson, who had been part of Orson Welles' original *Mercury Theater Group*. In the early 1950's he joined U-I's stable of young producers, directors, and writers. He had just finished directing Robert Mitchum in a western. The package is approved by Flynn's agent, subject to okay of the final script. Wilson and I were troubled with Monash's draft.

While in NY, I met a film writer, Joe Eisenger, who had begun his writing careeer as a newspaper police reporter, perfect for a mystery. Joe's credits included *Gilda* which made a star of Rita Hayworth. Flynn's agent is excited with Wilson as director and Eisenger's script. Max at UA is elated. The balance of the casting included American/Mexican star Pedro Armendariz (great for the Latin American market). My production manager, Hank Spitz, and I go to Havana to plan production details including government relations. The Universal Havana Sales Manager makes sure we meet with the right officials, in this case an assistant to President Batista. We also find that it's necessary to process our film and post-production in Mexico City. Fortunately, Spitz has been production manager of several westerns shot in Mexico.

A new cloud appears. A Cuban revolutionary with about a hundred supporters has landed in the southeast part of the island. Fidel Castro and Che are shooting up a couple of rural police stations. A call to our Havana police captain informed me that this is only a nuisance a few hundred miles east. The US Embassy confirms this evaluation. They say that after all, Sam Goldwyn, Jr. is midway through his production, *Shark Fighter*, with Victor Mature. And Hemingway's *Old Man and the Sea* is still on schedule to start before we finish our shooting. Yet, for such a mild "incident," the security at the airport several weeks later was most stringent.

Errol called me from London, collect of course; he liked the revised script and is looking forward to possibly meeting with Castro. He felt it would be good publicity for the film

We finished shooting only a few days over schedule in spite of Errol's being drunk on many an afternoon. Now we badly need Errol in Mexico to dub over his garbled moments. He would like to stay in Havana for a week with his new found chum, wealthy Cuban play-boy, Pepe Rodriguez. That's okay. We'll need to have a rough cut ready before his arrival.

Flynn doesn't show up on the date set. I called our Havana police chaperone to find out what he knows of Flynn's whereabouts. The captain calls back in a humbled tone of voice. Flynn and "chum" Pepe have gone off to have a few drinks at Castro's East Cuba hide-away. I asked "where is this hideaway." If he knew, there could be a battle, as Castro is now more than a nuisance. Besides, they had a couple of women with them. This SOB could get himself killed and me with his work unfinished. Does production insurance include rebellions as a "war exclusion?"

About a week later the captain calls. Flynn returned to Havana. He has been under military intelligence grilling to find out what he knew about Castro's location. Flynn hasn't talked, but being such a celebrity, they couldn't be too tough on their talk inducement proce-dures. Errol arrives the next morning full of "war stories," and, yes, a lot of publicity. He's too tired to work the first day. So, he, director Wilson, Spitz, a local security guard and I take Errol to dinner. It's a large, fun restaurant; music, dancing, etc.

At a table next to us is the Mexican heroine, bullfighter Conchita Citron. The MC is excited about having two such high level celebrities in one evening. The MC asked Errol to say a few words and help him introduce Conchita, who Errol had met while in Spain acting in *The Sun Also Rises*. Through an alcoholic mist he slurs out some general remarks. He then introduced "his dear friend, Conchita Cabrona." (Cabrona is a female cuckold.) The audience leaps to its feet, screaming at Flynn for defaming their heroine and started to make a charge at him. The guard hustled us out before Errol was too badly bruised. It helped that he was feeling no pain. After a couple of days of recovery Errol is able to perform the required dubbing.

For the past year I'd been thinking about returning to UCLA to complete my war-interrupted program in Business. Business finance is becoming more professional throughout the economy. I asked Dad and Matty for their thoughts. Dad had finished only seventh grade of elementary school. Matty had only two years of high school. Yet, they both were avid readers and working in theaters where Shakespeare and other plays were performed, and where concert music played. They were cultured men. And extremely successful in business. They loved the idea. I would be the first college graduate in the Blumberg and Fox families.

Being an independent producer gave me freedom to plan my time. UCLA offered special programs to returning veterans who worked and went to classes: reduced work units per semester, priority in class availability, etc. My military classess in navigation, math, etc. counted toward University requirements. Not realizing it at the time, I began my segue from entertainment to economics, finance and real estate. I completed my two picture deal with UA by co-producing a WWII film with Aubrey Schenck, nephew of Nick Schenck. He had a screenplay but needed some money and a star. I provided Tony Curtis who began his career at Universal. UA okayed it.

In the Spring of 1960, Dad concluded merger negotiations for Universal/Decca with MCA. The management "troika" for the merged entity was Jules Stein, Chairman, Nate Blumberg, Vice Chairman, and Lew Wasserman, President. These three were not new to each other. In Chicago, Dad, as head buyer and booker for the Orpheum Circuit, played Jules Stein's clients. Lew Wasserman had worked for RKO Theaters as manager of RKO's Ohio theaters before joining MCA. Almost immediately after signing the merger papers, the Department of Justice filed an anti-trust action. It eventually took nearly three years to consummate the merger. Dad did not live to see that occur. He died ninety days after the signing.

During this period, Matty asked if I could help "Pat" Weaver on a Skiatron problem. They were having difficulty in obtaining California regulatory approval for operating a Pay-TV system. Theater owners were up in arms at this expanded form of TV and actively lobbied against Pay-TV. I met with Pat and he showed me his plan to base his lobbying around the great entertainment and educational attributes Skiatron would bring. I countered with "Pat, this is not a network client. It's pure politics. I have a top lawyer, Paul Ziffren who is very active politically and wants to break into the entertainment business. He is optimistic about Skiatron's chances." But Pat made clear his preference for his approach. So I reported to Matty. He wanted Pat to run his own show. I replied, "Matty, you have the first shot to buy my Skiatron stock." He's upset but understands. The next day I sold my Skiatron stock and bowed out of TV.

UA asked if I could find another project. A screenwriter who had done several films for U-I, Don Rose, had an option for a magazine story, *Bad Day at Black Rock*. He asked if I'd join him in working with him on the screenplay and fund the option extension. It had a controversial subject, the community murder of a Japanese born farmer in Arizona. UA liked it. But it was difficult to get a star. So we sold it to MGM for a tidy profit. They cast one of their contract actors, Spencer Tracy, for the leading role, and Robert Ryan as co-star for good measure. My film career ended.

A few years later I got a call from Art Greenfield. He's moved to LA, he's in TV now, working for the Alexander brothers in feature syndication, "Let's have lunch." We often lunched at *Musso & Frank's*, a mutual favorite. He left Universal as Seattle branch manager and has been in TV distribution for several years. He told me a story about his ongoing education in sales. There was a Seattle theater owner who had monopoly theater positions in some small towns. Art could not make a sale to him even though the U-I production list was full of westerns, good for small towns.

In conversations with this theater owner, Art discovered that the man had been buying a new Cadillac every year in spite of vowing he doesn't need a new car. Art found out the name of the Cadillac dealer. Maybe he has something on the theater man? He met with the dealer who explained his ploy. He knew the theater man was crazy for colors. Each year he went to discuss repainting to another color. Out came the color chart. After determining the color, the theater man calculated the cost and inconvenience of a paint job and bought a new car.

Art again met with his theater man and pitched only Technicolor pictures. He made his first sale. The story is finished with a typical Art euphemism, "go figure that."

Fridays With Art

Art Goes Back to School
by Herb Farmer
(Professor Emeritus, Cinema Department, University of Southern California)

Although I have only recently become a sometimes member of Art Greenfield's *Friday Lunch Bunch*, I am pleased and honored to have been asked to add a footnote to the collected thoughts of many of the long time members. The simple fact is that by an act of fate, I probably made Art's acquaintance before any of the other members and was present when he made his way into the motion picture industry.

A little background. It was 1938 when a friend of mine and I left Buffalo and enrolled in the University of Southern California's recently established Department of Cinema. When we checked into our room at the University dorm we met another expatriot from Niagara Falls, and the three of us transplants, all interested in the world of Cinema, became close friends.

Soon we all became deeply involved with the *Trojan Newsreel*, a volunteer student activity, which actually had nothing to do with the fledgling Department of Cinema, at that time operating out of one small classroom/studio with very little hand-me-down equipment, and housed in the basement of Old College.

I think I first became acquainted with Art when we featured him in a short newsreel sequence about Doheny Library. In particular it spoke to the problems of a 300 pound student with his typewriter, books and papers trying to work in one of the small cubicles assigned to a graduate student.

At the time, we had no sound recording equipment and our newsreels were accompanied with live narration and "non-sync" music and sound effects from dual turntables. Art frequently served as our narrator. He never used a script, just some notes, and the rest was ad-lib. We both frequently recalled the time that did get us into a bit of trouble. It was the day that both the Chancellor and the Academic Vice President of the University were standing in the rear of the auditorium. When a shot with a long focus (telephoto) showed two rather well endowed coeds running toward the camera, the 'visual effect' was quite interesting but the effect was greatly enhanced when the narrator remarked, "And here they come, four abreast."

The "with-it" young people in the audience loved this irreverent observation.

Art took classes in 1939-1940, and since he was a graduate student and we were still "lower division" students working on the pre-major requirements, we were not taking the same classes. Our paths did cross many times, however, especially when Art began working as a student in the Cinema office.

To put the situation in perspective, the standard pay scale for student workers was 40 cents per hour for undergraduates and 50 cents for graduates. (At the time the cost of tuition was about $14 per unit.) Among his other duties, Art's job called for him to answer the telephone.

One day a call came in asking that a message be put on the bulletin board requesting applicants for an opening at the Universal Film Exchange over near 20th Street and Vermont Avenue, perhaps a mile away. As Art told the story many times, without hesitation he folded the note, put it in his pocket and took off on foot for Universal. I suspect he made his way back to school to tell us what happened, that he had a job, but I am not sure of that. As I remember it, this was the contact he wanted to make and he dropped out of school to accept it.

In the fall of 1941, our senior year, World War II was at its height in Europe and on December 7, 1941, the war in the Pacific started. We (Dan, Dave and I) were all physically able and were contemplating military service after graduation. Even though he had already left school, I don't think Art had to worry about this because of his weight.

As things worked out, about April 1, 1942, Warren Scott, Head of the Department of Cinema at the time, and also a Captain in the Army Engineers, was called to active duty and since I had become quite involved in the business management of the Cinema Department, I was asked to become acting head as well as finish teaching his classes for the semester. My buddies and I all graduated on schedule in May, 1942. Soon thereafter, all three of us entered various branches of the armed services.

I joined the Navy as a junior photo officer and after the war ended I returned for duty in Pensacola, Florida where I met a Navy nurse whom I married. Then USC offered me a teaching position starting in the summer of 1946.

When we got back to Los Angeles my work at USC Cinema started right away. My classes from 1946 to 1966 were the usual basic technology and production subjects in our academic curriculum at the time. About the early 1960's, my administrative USC responsibilities shifted from primarily the academic program of Cinema to the business and management problems of our department in the university systems. This included starting an official instructional technology service operation for the whole University, and installing a 35mm projection facility in Bovard Auditorium where we ran feature films for the students on the weekend since most of the neighborhood theaters in the area had closed during the war.

Shortly after World War II ended, USC became involved with many government contracts and Cinema had its share. I was able to arrange a special training program with the Navy in motion pictures, for both Navy and Marine officers and enlisted personnel, which ran for almost twenty years. The training experiences and the development of greatly improved equipment and materials during the war and in the years following caused marked growth in the 16mm non-theatrical field. This opened the door for many educational institutions to start programs that involved production as well as utilization.

My responsibilities included what might be called the business management of these projects working through the University's Business Offices and Contracts and Grants system. At various times this enabled us to bring back former students and others who had gained experience, including in the military, as our basic instructors. These individuals were well qualified to see that the core factors were covered in the various classes, and all were encouraged to bring guests from related sections of the industry to add contemporary information. Typical were courses such as Motion Picture Laboratory Practices, taught for years by Sidney Solow, President of Consolidated Film Industries, and Makeup for Motion Pictures, by William Tuttle, head of the makeup department at MGM

It was also during this period that we fully realized the importance and contribution of guest lecturers from the industry. The fact is that the present School started with a lecture series in 1929, presented by the University in cooperation with the *Academy of Motion Picture Arts and Sciences*. A list of the speakers who have visited classes over the years is like a *Who's Who* of the industry.

In 1966, while all of my activities kept me more than busy, I developed a course on Film Business Procedures and Distribution. At the start, I told my classes that I was assuming they should accept that all the steps of production - the writing, directing, shooting, editing, etc. (arts), are all creative processes but that the results are entirely dependent on the technology, equipment, processes and materials (sciences), and that we must take the position that an equally, if not more, important factor is business and finances. Either you must have an angel willing to finance your project regardless of its income potential, or a business plan which works. The comparison has frequently been made to a three legged stool. If even one leg collapses, so does the stool.

My plan was to have guests for at least half of the sessions during the semester, covering many of the different ways of doing business theatrical, educational, industrial, sponsored, and markets which have unique problems. I also tried to have one or two guests on legal, contract, copyright, releases, etc.

When it came to theatrical, Art was at the top of the list. He could cover the early days from first hand experience, BC (before computers), and from film exchanges in most major cities to just a few regional offices to serve the whole country. Art also usually brought an associate or guests who were members of his Friday lunch group, and the sessions were fun as well as very informative. His later experiences as an independent TV distributor rounded out the picture.

The input that Art Greenfield and the guests that he brought to the class helped a great deal in my effort to get the students to really

371

accept that business decisions are really the key factor in our industry.

Dick Who?
by Arthur Gardner

I left Marinette, Wisconsin the day after I graduated from high school in 1927 and headed for Hollywood, full of confidence I could get a job as a movie actor. In retrospect, I guess my confidence was at least equal to my talent. First things first. I saw an ad in the (old) *Los Angeles Examiner* under "rooms to let" and managed to rent a little room in the back of a house for $11 a month. Then the next day I commenced making the rounds of the studios, heading first for MGM, the most famous of them at that time. Being just another 18-year old kid, I couldn't get past the friendly security guard at the gate, but while chatting with him, who do I see walking out of the studio but Lionel Barrymore! I knew all about actors of course, having read every fan magazine I could get my hands on. I said, "Hello, Mr. Barrymore." He answered, "Hi, son." I couldn't wait to get back to my room and write my father I had just said 'hi' to Mr. Barrymore.

I knew that Universal Studios was owned by Carl Laemmle, and from all my reading about the motion picture business, I knew that before he went into the motion picture business he owned a furniture store in Oshkosh, Wisconsin which is about 50 miles away from my hometown. So I thought, what the hell, I'll write a letter to Carl Laemmle. I don't remember what I said, but I think it was something like this: "Dear Mr. Laemmle. My name is Arthur Goldberg, I'm 18 years old. I'm from Marinette and I know you once owned a furniture store in Oshkosh. Mr. Laemmle, I'm a great actor and all I need is a chance. I'm just asking you for the opportunity to come out and meet you and convince you that I'm a great actor." It was some corny stuff like that. I mailed it to Universal. The next day I went around to visit RKO and Paramount and Fox, and when I came home my landlady said, "Arthur, Universal Studios called you! They want you out there tomorrow morning to see Mr. Laemmle!"

I didn't sleep much that night. I was at the studio at seven o'clock in the morning. The front door didn't open until eight. At nine, they ushered me into the studio. A woman came out to greet me. Her name was one I'll never forget: Lillian Russell. She was Carl Laemmle's secretary, a very nice woman.

She said, "Arthur, this is the first letter that Mr. Laemmle has ever responded to of all the letters he gets, and he gets thousands of them. But I opened it and I said, 'Why don't you see this young man?'" She was telling me this as we were walking down the hall to Carl Laemmle's office. She opened the door and it was a huge office. Sitting behind a big desk was this little man, maybe about 5 feet 2 inches tall, with a bald head. In a very pronounced Jewish accent, as I came up to him he said, "Nice to meet you son, sit down." So I sat down and went into my pitch about what a great actor I was, thanking him for giving me a chance, so on and so forth. He said, "Arthur, I want you to meet my son, Carl Laemmle, Jr. It was nice meeting you. My secretary will take you down to Jr.'s office."

Carl Laemmle, Jr. at that time was only 21 years old and he was running the studio. So I went down to his office. His secretary told me to have a seat. I sat there all day. He never saw me. She told me to come back the following morning. I came back and again sat there all day but he never saw me.

Finally at the end of the day the secretary said, "I want you to meet the casting director because Mr. Laemmle is too busy to see you. So she took me down to see Fred Datig. He was nice to me and the next day I got a call from the studio to work as an extra. I got $3 a day plus a box lunch. Soon I was working two or three days a week on Universal's huge back lot where they were shooting low budget silent Westerns. I remember one interior scene was in a tent and in order to save money, each extra had a dummy sitting on either side of him. All the dummies had hats on so you couldn't see their faces very well, and when the director yelled "*Action!*" everybody shook their dummies. It was corny beyond belief.

Universal had dabbled in sound films and one of the first was a series of short comedies titled *The Collegians* in which both future superstars Loretta Young and Clark Gable started their careers.

In those days people would actually stop and pick up a hitch-hiker and that was how I got back and forth from Hollywood to the studio. One day I was standing in front of Universal trying for a ride when a Jewish looking man with glasses stopped his two-seater car and offered me a lift. His name was George Cukor, later to become a very famous director, but at that time he was the dialog director of a movie in pre-production called *All Quiet On The Western Front*. He not only gave me a lift, but arranged for me to be hired on that film as an extra at the fee of $75 per week. I was assigned to play a German soldier in this World War I drama, and all of us were given several days of intense drilling and teaching on how to be a German soldier by a German who had actually been a non-commissioned soldier in that conflict. This man was a tyrant. He was one of the first Nazis, I'm sure.

After about 4 days of drilling and training I made some kind of wisecrack, and this sergeant said to me, "Listen Goldberg, you goddam Jew, I warned you a dozen times not to kid around. You're fired!" I left the back lot and went up to the office and saw George Cukor. I told him I knew I had been out of line with my humor, but he had no right to call me a goddamn Jew. They called him up to the office and fired him. I stayed on the picture and behaved myself. And I decided that the only way I could become a movie star was to change my name, so I picked "Gardner."

I don't remember how I got the lead in an independent picture called *Assassin of Youth*, one of the first pictures made about the evils of marijuana. I was paid the grand total of $150 for starring in the film. *Assassin of Youth*, together with *Reefer Madness*, has become a cult movie through the years. It's on sale at most video stores.

In 1935, during the depression years, the federal government established a theater project and when they sent out a call for young actors I signed on for the fee of $96 per month. We put on plays all over town and a casting director from Warner Bros. saw me in some and cast me as the juvenile lead in a film called *Waterfront*, for which I was paid $50 a day.

Then I got a strange job offer where I was given the choice of playing the lead in a film and working only six days for $150, or working two weeks on the same film as the assistant director at $75 per week. I quickly chose the assistant director job, and was allowed to become a member of the *Director's Guild* as an A.D. I nominated a friend of mine to replace me as the lead: Alan Ladd. So he picked up the $150 fee for his work in *Paper Bullets*.

Gradually I became more and more involved in production.

Then, like most men in the early 1940's, I entered the Armed Forces during World War II, which is where and when I met my future business partners, Jules Levy and Arnold Laven. All of us were then involved in making training films for the Air Force, so it was natural for us, when the war was over, to continue with our roles as producers, and we did so, making many theatrical motion pictures.

In 1958, the team of Levy-Gardner-Laven decided to take a crack at television, and we decided our first effort would be a half-hour Western series.

We were already employing a young writer named Sam Peckinpah to adapt a book we owned into a feature film screenplay. It was his first film job and we had hired him on the recommendation of a friend.

Sam had a pecular writing habit. Our offices were at Hal Roach Studios at the time. Jules, Arnold, our secretary and I would all leave the office at 5:30 or 6:00 p.m.. We had rented a little office for Sam. He'd come in around 7 or 8 in the evening, lie down on the couch with a tape recorder on his chest, and dictate through the night. He'd leave the tape for our secretary to transcribe the following morning.

This procedure resulted in the pilot script for *The Rifleman*.

I can't remember what we paid him, but it was very little, being a first time writer.

Our agents, the William Morris office, gave *The Rifleman* script to Dick Powell to read. Powell was actively running Four Star Productions. He loved the script and we made a 50-50 deal. He was anxious to get started and suggested a half dozen actors for the lead, none of whom we liked.

One Sunday afternoon my wife and our two boys and I went to the *Fox Wilshire Theater* to see a Disney-produced Western movie. A scene unfolded before us involving a six foot six cowboy and a little boy. My jaw dropped. This was *The Rifleman* incarnate!

The actor was Chuck Connors, an actor we had turned down for one of our feature films. I couldn't wait to talk to my partners. They saw the film that night and were as enthusiastic as I was.

Back on the lot the next morning, as we were preparing to call Connor's agent, Meyer Mishkin, we spotted Chuck walking down the studio street with Charles Bronson. They were headed for the commisary.

Arnold ran down the stairs to find that Bronson was still there, but Connors had already gone into the restaurant, so he asked Bronson to give Connors the script. Thirty minutes later Connors was pounding on our office door. "This is me! I'm the *Rifleman*!"

We had a hell of a time convincing Meyer Mishkin to let Connors take the role. Mishkin was convinced Chuck was headed for feature film stardom because of his success in *The Big Country*, but Connors finally convinced him.

Tom McDermott, who headed Four Star after Dick Powell died, introduced us to Lou Edelman, who had a deal with Barbara Stanwyck to do a western series titled *The Big Valley*, but the pilot script he had was bad. So Tom convinced Lou that we should do the show. We liked the idea but wanted a new script, so we hired Christopher Knopf who had written '*Rifleman*' scripts for us.

Chris's script was terrific, ABC loved it, and we proceeded to hire the supporting cast: Richard Long, Peter Breck, Linda Evans, Lee Majors and Charles Briles.

The series ran for four years and won many awards. And working with Barbara Stanwyck was a dream. But there was one small incident.

We hadn't yet gone on the air but were already shooting our fifth or sixth episode. It was around 6 o'clock in the evening and I was in my office with my wife, waiting for the company to finish for the day when my phone rang. It was the assistant director. There was a problem on the set and he asked me to come down.

I jumped on my bike and pedaled to the back lot. Paul Henreid, the former Warner Bros. star, was our director (and a nicer man never existed) and he was wringing his hands. There was one shot remaining to be filmed, the sun was going down, and Lee Majors, a young actor in his first show, was insisting on doing something in the script that Barbara objected to.

I tried to reason with Lee, but he wouldn't give in. So I fired him off the show. Paul went on with the shot and I went back, had dinner across the street from the studio with my wife, then drove home.

When I arrived home the phone was ringing off the hook -- it was Lee's agent, explaining that Lee wanted to apologize, he was a young inexperienced man who thought he was doing the right thing. I told the agent the only way I'd let him back was for him to apologize to Barbara, the cast and the entire crew. The following morning Lee did just that and in the ensuing years became a very good friend of mine.

In 1960, Robert Taylor and his agency, the William Morris office, decided he should do a television series and we agreed to produce it. It was called *The Detectives*. Bob didn't want to work every day of the week so we devised a formula wherein we'd shoot all his scenes in the script in one day, and on every fourth show he'd work the full schedule. It worked out well, and a finer man than Bob Taylor didn't exist. I never met a movie star with less ego that he. Barbara Stanwyck and he, once married to each other, remained good friends.

Our partnership was, of course, producing theatrical films at the same time as the TV series, but because there were three of us, we managed to spread the work. We did another TV series called *Law of the Plainsman*, starring Michael Ansara, but it only ran a year.

When Tom McDermott died, Four Star was rudderless, so we

made a deal to exchange our interest in *The Big Valley, The Detectives* and *The Plainsman* for a good cash settlement and 100% ownership of *The Rifleman*, which we own to this day.

We made a distribution deal with some guy named Dick Colbert, whom we met in a decrepit saloon in Chinatown. I'm sure no one reading these pages has ever heard of him.

INDEX

INDEX A

INDEX A-B

INDEX B

INDEX C

INDEX C-D

INDEX D-E-F

INDEX F-G

INDEX G-H

INDEX H-I

INDEX I-J-K

INDEX K

INDEX K-L

INDEX L-M

INDEX M

INDEX M-N-O

INDEX O-P

INDEX P-Q-R

INDEX R-S

INDEX S

INDEX S-T

INDEX T-U-V-W

INDEX W

INDEX W-X-Y-Z

(*Editor's note:* I'm sure there are some errors and omissions among the nearly 5,000 entries in this index, so I will apologize in advance. The author submitting the longest list of such slights will be awarded a free pass for one adult for a day at *Legoland*. Transportation not included. Offer void in 47 states and the protectorates.)

ADDENDUM

(Dalton Danon has requested the inclusion of the following:)

In addition to those stellar individuals previously mentioned in my chapter, I would like to pay homage to many of those who contributed profoundly to my rewarding experience in this great industry over a 39 year period. In alphabetical order:

Merv Adelson	Leon Drew	Seymour Horowitz
Babe Alexander	Joe Drilling	Ray Hubbard
Charles Alsup	Loring d'Usseau	Ward Ingram
Carlo Anneke	Doug Ellison	Don Joannes
Walt Baker	Irving Feld	Bruce Johansen
Nancy Baltimore	Jean Findlater	Dick Jolliffe
Bob Bennett	Len Firestone	Julie Kaufman
Jay Berkson	Al Flanagan	Bob Kelly
Dick Block	Bill Flynn	Dave Kenin
Susan L. Boettner	Frank Fouce	Pat Kenny
Norman Boggs	Kevin Francis	Mal Klein
Cal Bollwinkle	Sandy Frank	Mark Lipsky
Tom Breen	Hank Gillespie	Terry Lee
John Brophy	Chuck Gingold	Al P. Lefton, Jr.
Jack Brown	Bob Glaser	Bob Levi
Bruce Campbell	Alan Gleitsman	Jerry Marcus
Gene Cless	Hal Golden	Jack Matranga
Sid Cohen	Bob Greenberg	Tom McDermott
Dick Colbert	Art Greenfield	Jim McGowan
Marty Colby	Marvin Grieve	Bill Michaels
Shelly Cooper	Art Gross	Stan Moger
Russ Coughlin	Bob Guy	Art Mortenson
Don Dahlman	Ed Hewitt	Ed Murray
Tom Dargan	Jackson Hill	Greg Nathanson
Henry Davis	Neil Hoffman	Bob Newgard
Phil Donahue	Norman Horowitz	Bob O'Connor

ADDENDUM

Frank O'Driscoll
Bill Pabst
Ken Page
Jack Petrik
John Proffitt
Ward Quall
Bob Quinlan
Verla Rammel
Manny Reiner
Lee Rich
John Reynolds

Dick Robertson
Mort Rosenman
Marty Ross
Jerry Sacks
Bill Sawyers
Lionel Schaen
Cecil Seavey
Selig Seligman
Tom Shannon
Lloyd Sigmon
Mary Silverman

Skip Steloff
Art Swift
Dick Thiriot
Fred Thrower
Barry Thurston
John Walden
Jerry Weisfeldt
Bill White
Dick Woollen
Leon Wray
Derk Zimmerman